IOWA
PRIDE

IOWA

DUANE

PRIDE

A. SCHMIDT

Iowa State University Press / Ames

Other books by Duane Schmidt

The Late J.C.

Three Steps to the Million Dollar Practice

Earn More/Work Less

Hands On: Dental Computers Made Easy

Schmidt's Anatomy of a Successful Dental Practice

© 1996 Duane A. Schmidt

∞ Printed on acid-free paper in the United States of America

First edition, 1996

Cover illustration by LeaAnn Randall

Library of Congress Cataloging-in-Publication Data

Schmidt, Duane A.
    Iowa pride / Duane A. Schmidt.—1st ed.
      p. cm.
    Includes bibliographical references.
    ISBN 0-8138-2844-9
    1. Iowa—Biography. 2. Iowa—History. I. Title.
    CT234.S35   1996
    977.7—dc20
                                                   96-21318

Last digit is the print number: 9 8 7 6 5 4 3 2 1

TO DIANNE, *the beautiful Iowan I love dearly*

C ONTENTS

Foreword *by Loren N. Horton, xi*
Introduction, *xiii*
Iowa Corn Song, *xxi*

IOWANS WHO MADE IT HERE

NOEL M. ANDERSON, *invented the frostproof hydrant,* **3**
DAVID A. ARMBRUSTER, *invented the butterfly swim stroke,* **5**
JOHN VINCENT ATANASOFF, *invented the digital computer,* **7**
CLIFFORD BERRY, *co-invented the digital computer,* **12**
WILLIAM P. BETTENDORF, *invented the power-lift plow,* **14**
SAMUEL O. BLANC, *invented the Roto-Rooter®,* **16**
AMELIA JENKS BLOOMER, *pioneer suffragist, editor, and reformer,* **19**
ROY CARVER, *created the finest tire retread,* **21**
CARRIE LANE CHAPMAN CATT, *championed women's right to vote,* **23**
ARTHUR A. COLLINS, *communications pioneer,* **27**
MARVIN CONE, *renowned artist,* **30**
JAY NORWOOD "Ding" DARLING, *cartoonist and conservationist,* **32**
PAUL ENGLE, *built the Iowa Writers' Workshop,* **38**
WILLIAM FISHER, *invented a new water-pressure control,* **40**
JOHN FROELICH, *invented the gasoline-powered tractor,* **42**
DAN GABLE, *kingpin of wrestling,* **46**
GEORGE GALLUP, *developed sampling methods to predict human behavior,* **49**
BURT GRAY, *invented (?) the hamburger,* **52**
BEULAH GUNDLING, *invented aquatic art,* **55**
JESSE HIATT, *discovered the Delicious apple,* **58**
CORA BUSSEY HILLIS, *child welfare advocate, founded the first Child Welfare Research Station,* **61**
ARTHUR L. HUBBARD, *refined the mechanical cotton picker,* **63**
W.A. JENNINGS, *invented a portable concrete form,* **66**

MACKINLAY KANTOR, *novelist specializing in the Civil War,* **68**

KARL L. KING, *world-renowned band music composer,* **70**

NILE KINNICK, *Heisman trophy winner,* **72**

MAURICIO LASANSKY, *world-renowned printmaker,* **75**

DAVE LENNOX, *invented the sheet metal furnace,* **78**

MONSIGNOR LUIGI LIGUTTI, *founded the National Catholic Rural Life Conference,* **81**

E.F. LINDQUIST, *created the Iowa Tests of Basic Skills,* **83**

LESTER MARTIN, *invented direct mail advertising,* **86**

FRED L. MAYTAG, *developed the agitator washing machine,* **88**

JAMES ALAN MCPHERSON, *Pulitzer Prize-winning author, Guggenheim Fellow and MacArthur Fellow,* **91**

E.T. MEREDITH, *created national magazines,* **93**

VIOLA BABCOCK MILLER, *founded the Iowa Highway Patrol,* **96**

CLARK R. MOLLENHOFF, *nationally known investigative reporter,* **98**

THOMAS D. MURPHY, *founded the art calendar industry,* **101**

JOHN L. NAUGHTON, *invented sit-down dentistry,* **104**

CHRISTIAN K. NELSON, *invented the Eskimo Pie®,* **108**

DAVID C. NICHOLAS, *speeded up the fax,* **111**

GEORGE P. NISSEN, *invented the trampoline,* **114**

AUSTIN N. PALMER, *invented the Palmer Method of writing,* **117**

D.D. PALMER, *discovered the science of chiropractic,* **120**

WILLIAM D. "SHORTY" PAUL, *developed Bufferin® and Rolaids®,* **124**

CARL EMIL SEASHORE, *invented speech pathology and audiology,* **126**

JESSIE FIELD SHAMBAUGH, *founded 4-H Clubs International,* **129**

WALTER A. SHEAFFER, *invented the first practical self-filling fountain pen,* **131**

JANE SMILEY, *Pulitzer Prize-winning author,* **134**

CLOID H. SMITH, *built the world's largest pop corn business,* **136**

FRANK H. SPEDDING, *co-invented the production process of pure uranium,* **139**

CONTENTS

PHIL STONG, *wrote* State Fair, **141**

ORLAND R. SWEENEY, *created useful products from agricultural waste,* **143**

WILLIAM P. SWITZER, *created the vaccine for atrophic rhinitis in swine,* **146**

JOHN J. TOKHEIM, *invented the gasoline pump,* **149**

RAY TOWNSEND, *invented new ways to process meat,* **152**

JAMES VAN ALLEN, *astrophysicist, discovered earth-encircling radiation belts,* **155**

GARY J. VERMEER, *agri-industrialist, invented the large round hay bale,* **158**

HENRY A. WALLACE, *Vice President of the United States, pioneered hybrid seed corn,* **161**

HARLEY A. WILHELM, *co-invented the pure uranium production process,* **164**

ANNIE WITTENMYER, *founded diet kitchen management,* **167**

F.A. WITTERN, *invented the change-giving vending machine,* **170**

GRANT WOOD, *America's painter laureate,* **173**

IOWANS WHO MADE IT ELSEWHERE

BESS STREETER ALDRICH, *widely-read author,* **179**

BIX BEIDERBECKE, *renowned cornet jazz stylist,* **181**

MILDRED WIRT BENSON, *prolific and acclaimed author,* **183**

NORMAN BORLAUG, *Nobel laureate,* **185**

JOHNNY CARSON, *noted talk show host,* **187**

GEORGE WASHINGTON CARVER, *acclaimed botanist and humanitarian,* **189**

WILLIAM F. CODY, *"Buffalo Bill," frontier plainsman,* **191**

LEE DEFOREST, *father of the wireless, commercial radio, and talking pictures,* **193**

WYATT EARP, *frontier marshal,* **195**

MAMIE DOUD EISENHOWER, *First Lady,* **197**

SIMON ESTES, *renowned bass-baritone,* **199**

BOB FELLER, *Hall of Fame baseball player,* **201**

ESTHER P. AND PAULINE E. FRIEDMAN, *the world's most-read women,* **203**

HAMLIN GARLAND, *dean of American letters,* **205**
HERBERT HOOVER, *President of the United States,* **207**
LAURENCE C. JONES, *established the Piney Woods Country Life School,* **209**
CLORIS LEACHMAN, *Oscar-winning actress,* **211**
JOHN L. LEWIS, *foremost union organizer,* **213**
GLENN MILLER, *invented the big band sound,* **215**
JOHN R. MOTT, *Nobel laureate,* **217**
ROBERT N. NOYCE, *invented the computer chip,* **219**
DONNA REED, *Academy Award-winning actress,* **221**
BEARDSLEY RUML, *developed the pay-as-you-go tax plan,* **223**
WILLIAM L. SHIRER, *renowned journalist, historian,* **225**
MONA VAN DUYN, *Pulitzer Prize-winning poet,* **227**
JOHN WAYNE, *Academy Award-winning actor,* **229**
MEREDITH WILLSON, *"The Music Man,"* **231**

IOWA FIRSTS

First Agricultural Experimental Station, **237**
First Appendicitis Operation, **237**
First Baby Contest, **238**
First Band Law, **239**
First Basketball Game (Intercollegiate), **239**
First Can of Beer, **240**
First Cast Gold Dental Crown, **241**
First Chartered Land-Grant College, **241**
First Continuing Education Course for Herdsmen, **242**
First County Cooperative Extension Program, **242**
First Dance Critic, **242**
First Dance-Fitness Franchise, **243**
First Educational Television, **244**
First Educationally Owned Television Station, **244**
First Electronic Newsroom, **245**
First Experimental Kitchen, **245**
First Extension Services, **245**
First Fast-Food Franchise, **246**
First Food Additive and More, **246**
First Home Microwave Oven, **247**
First Mosque and First Muslim Cemetery in North America, **248**
First State-Supported School of Religion, **249**

CONTENTS

First Statistical Laboratory, **249**
First Woman Chair of the Republican Party, **250**
First Woman Dentist, **250**
First Woman Electoral College Board President, **251**
First Woman Engineering Teacher, **251**
First Woman Notary, **252**
First Woman Professor of Journalism, **252**
First Woman Professor of Physical Education, **253**
First Woman School Superintendent, **254**
First Women Lawyers, **254**
First Women to Enter College as Equals to Men, **254**
First Women's Army Corps Training Center, **255**

CONCLUSION: The Level Prairies of Iowa, **257**

References, *263*
Bibliography, *269*
Acknowledgments, *275*

FOREWORD

Iowa is a land of variety. Not only is the geography composed of several different landforms, the population consists of many ethnic groups. At first each identifiable group manifested certain unique characteristics, but as generations succeeded each other they blended together.

Although the people who came to live in Iowa had many differences, we must not overemphasize this aspect. They had many similarities too. Common to all settlers was the need for food, for clothing, for shelter, and for jobs. The majority of people who came to Iowa had a strong interest in religion, in education, and in a framework of law. Very few aspects of life had to be reinvented when settlers arrived in Iowa, regardless of whether they came here from Europe or from eastern and southern states of this country. They brought with them a certain amount of intellectual baggage, and the material culture—the things of everyday life—with which they were familiar. What was not needed was discarded, what was not known before was improvised, and as these people reacted to their environment, so they acted upon it.

Just as people carried their customs with them when they arrived in Iowa, so they reacted to the geography in different ways. Some immigrants preferred to live in places that resembled their homelands. Others chose what they considered to be the prime farmlands. Still others purchased whatever was available or cheap.

Iowa changed very little with the occupation of the Native Americans. But after 1833, with the coming of the white settlers, much change occurred. The prairies were plowed; the timber was cut for housing, fencing, and fuel; minerals were extracted from the ground; rivers and streams were dammed for gristmills and sawmills; and roads took the place of simple trails. Attitudes accounted for part of this changing landscape, but numbers of people was probably the more influential factor. Iowa's population grew very rapidly, from only 43,000 in 1840 (the first federal census) to 2,231,853 in 1900. So many people required a vast amount of housing, transportation systems, places of work, and public buildings. Naturally this altered the landscape, until by the end of the twentieth century there are only fragmentary remnants of the natural history as it was prior to 1833.

The people who settled Iowa were a varied lot, not only because of ethnicity and places of origin, but also because as individuals they had courage, imagination, and ambition. Because of these qualities, Iowans changed the tools, implements, and machines with which they worked; increased the varieties of food, clothing, and furnishings with which they surrounded themselves; and generally were a very ingenious group.

This book highlights some of those Iowans who were not satisfied with the status quo, those Iowans who thought of better ways of doing things, or better things to be made, of life in the future that was better than they found it in the present. They are presented in bewildering varieties, a true kaleidoscope of personalities. Some made changes that we all recognize, some made changes that were so subtle that we rarely notice them. Still others made changes that were so logical and full of common sense that we wonder why no one thought of such a change before. That is the true measure of change, when it seems so ordinary that we are amazed that it took so long to come to such a sensible conclusion.

Iowa history is a fascinating subject. No one who truly tries to understand it can be bored by it. Join with me now in Duane Schmidt's fascinating *Iowa Pride,* a new adventure in Iowa history, a journey with the women and men who made things different, and better, for all of us.

LOREN N. HORTON
Iowa historian

INTRODUCTION

"You must visit Santes!" Marielle commanded. Our two-week plan was to visit her 200-year-old chateau in southern France to soak up things French—food, wine, language, culture, and customs. She called her little plot of soil *La Ferme*. It was as much like an Iowa farm as a liter of wine is like a quart of milk.

"*Pourquoi*? (Why)" we asked.

"Because it is the birthplace of a famous French doctor," she said.

Notable French scientists, such as Marc Dax (right brain/left brain), Louis Pasteur (germs), and Marie Curie (radioactivity) have revolutionized medical science. My daughter Catherine, a dental hygienist, and I, a dentist, at once went on alert. Things medical trip our trigger.

Who was this famous doctor? we asked.

"Doctor *Gee'yo-teehn*," she said. Like all French speakers, she spoke mostly through her nose. Catherine and I cocked our heads in silence for a moment. Suddenly the real name struck us both.

"Doctor ... Guillotine?" we asked.

"*Oui, naturellement* (Yes, naturally)," she answered.

Marielle explained that during the French Revolution Dr. G. noticed that getting rid of royalty was not as easy as you'd think. We admitted we sure hadn't thought about that. The neck is thick, she explained. ... We nodded numbly, waving her away from the crimson details.

Dr. Guillotine's invention speedily caused heaps of uncrowned and a few French crowned heads to roll. Which caused the proletariat to cheer, sack the treasury, eat cake, and honor this heady contribution by naming it the "guillotine."

The French are fiercely proud people, bragging about every grape that we tourists gulp down or gargoyle we gape at. If the French can claim bragging rights over an invention to decapitate their fellow citizens, what would they do with some of the awesome facts we Iowans can claim?

They'd brag their ... er ... heads off. Just like we Iowans should.

If you've ever been ashamed to admit you are an Iowan; if you've ever felt uncomfortable under the barbs and digs of a Minnesotan, Missourian, or Illinoisan; or if you've ever agreed that potatoes grow in Iowa, rather than correct an errant Easterner who thinks we're Idaho, then *Iowa Pride* should restore your justifiable belief that Iowa is just about the best place in the world to live and Iowans are just about the best people to have as friends and neighbors.

When is an Iowan an Iowan?

TV talk show host Johnny Carson, actor John Wayne, bandleader Glenn Miller, first ladies Mamie Eisenhower and Lou Henry Hoover, and President Herbert Hoover were all born in Iowa. But after several months, or a few years at most, these Iowa babies were trundled away, never to return. Does being born in Iowa stamp one an Iowan forever?

Frontier plainsman Buffalo Bill, operatic bass-baritone Simon Estes, and union leader John L. Lewis all were born and raised in Iowa before they left to rewrite history in the Old West, western Europe, and the nation's coal mines. So were Nobel Laureate Norman Borlaug and "Music Man" Meredith Willson, who went on to raise wheat or musical batons in other places. Is that enough to qualify them as bona fide Iowans, even though they were educated and thrived away from Iowa's plains?

On the other hand, Carl Seashore saw first light of day in Sweden and, though he was raised in Iowa, was educated at Yale

University, before he founded speech pathology in Iowa. Furnace inventor Dave Lennox (from Detroit, Michigan) and Roto-Rooter® inventor Sam Blanc (from Menominee Falls, Wisconsin) immigrated to Iowa where they claimed fame. John Vincent Atanasoff, John Tokheim, and William Switzer also immigrated to Iowa, first to study, then invent the digital computer, the gasoline pump and swine vaccine, in that order. Can Iowans rightfully claim them?

Neither Carrie Lane Chapman Catt, D.D. Palmer, nor Dave Armbruster were born in Iowa. They were raised and educated here and then made important marks from within Iowa boundaries. Carrie, the ultimate suffragist, spearheaded the drive for passage of the Nineteenth Amendment to the U.S. Constitution. D.D. founded the science of chiropractic. Dave invented the butterfly swim stroke. Are we to claim them as Iowans, too?

Of course Iowa Writers' Workshop leader Paul Engle, 4-H founder Jessie Field Shambaugh, washing machine magnate Fred Maytag, trampoline inventor George Nissen, astrophysicist James Van Allen, and America's painter laureate Grant Wood earned their Iowa stripes the hard way. They were born, raised, and educated here, and so lived here virtually all their lives. We, who claim to be Iowans, may sing their praises from Iowa shore to muddy shore.

Important Iowans come dressed in both genders, splashed in black or white, and with relationships to Iowa soil as versatile as ours who hold these pages. Whether you arrived in Iowa early or late in life, whether you learned your Iowa lore from a brook or a book, whether you shook the world or just your neighbor's hand, it's OK to be proud of your Iowa heritage. Iowans who have made a difference: We claim them all.

Who's In? Who's Out?

The decision to include—it's more fair to say the decision to exclude—was the toughest cut of all. So many excelling Iowans have done so many excellent things. Many sensitive and perceptive Iowans helped establish the measures of whose lives should be extolled.

INTRODUCTION ─────────────────────

Some places and some things were left out. This is the story of Iowa people, not of the Effigy Mounds, Loess Hills, Little Brown Church, a Frank Lloyd Wright home (Cedar Rock at Quasqueton), or of wonderful Iowa lakes, parks, clocks (Bily at Spillville), sites (Grotto of the Redemption at West Bend), or settlements (Amana Colonies).

Iowa superlative claims ending in -est were excluded. Not that those claims aren't interesting. They are. Every Iowan should know where to enjoy them. But again, this isn't the story of the biggest statue (Albert the Bull in Audubon), smallest chapel (St. Anthony of Padua, near Festina), widest main street (Onawa's), and crookedest street (Burlington's Snake Alley). We cherish these Iowa treasures, but they aren't our focus.

Time played a role in our choices. This book is written for contemporary Iowans, who may feel out of touch with Iowans of yesteryear. Connecting the past to the present would make a valuable contribution to Iowa lore, but not all notables of bygone times could be included here.

For example, most Iowans, outside of residents of Humboldt, would have difficulty recalling the 1880s wrestling exploits of the internationally famous Frank Gotch. Humboldt named a park in his honor. The same faded fame would be true of Iowan Billy Sunday, a turn-of-the-century professional baseball player-turned-evangelist.

Had *Iowa Pride* been written years ago, surely Bill Hoag would have been included, for in 1872 this inventive Monticello native dreamed up the feather duster. Bill then produced millions of his quilled devices to tidy up a dusty world, even importing tons of exotic ostrich feathers for pricey designer dusters. Today's sad news is the factory has been torn down, the workers are long gone, the industry and the era both vanished.

Iowan Keith Vawter would have been included in that earlier book. In 1903 this 31-year-old Cedar Rapidian got the idea of shipping Chautauqua shows around the country, erecting tents, and bringing cultural entertainment to small-town America.

Before then the shows were seen only in a relatively few permanent pavilions.

How important was Chautauqua? President Theodore Roosevelt called it "the most important American thing in America." Culture and promise came alive on Chautauqua stages bringing hope and happiness to lives searching for both. But when radio dials glowed bright in American homes, Chautauquans struck their tents, swept up the sawdust, and tucked the era away in their scrapbooks.

In an earlier day we might have included Iowan James Weaver, successively nominated by the Greenback and the Populist Party for President of the United States, or Iowa Senator James Harlan, President Lincoln's Secretary of the Interior. Certainly, they were important Iowans playing leading roles in crucial times. It's not a slight to leave them out; it's only perspective.

Many Iowa "firsts" are included, but not all. Being first at anything important is a record that cannot be broken and often is worth calling attention to, but not always. Jesse James pulled off history's first train robbery in Iowa. Want to brag about it?

In McGregor, John Ringling, the circus entrepreneur, headlined his first show for his performing brothers. That night John had Iowans in stitches and the greasepaint got in his veins. But it was a fleeting instance of doubtful impact. The archivist of the circus museum in Baraboo, Wisconsin, discounts the importance of the moment.

Early in the history of aviation, Grinnell's Billy Wilder flew airmail from Des Moines to Chicago. Certainly Billy's flight—in terms of equipment and navigational aids of the day—demonstrated an intrepid Iowan's courage and skill. But Billy was the *second* pilot of an airmail flight, not the first. Sorry, Billy.

Some brief Iowa encounters by notable people were skipped. For example, John Brown, the fiery abolitionist, hung around Iowa for a few months before he got himself hung around Harper's Ferry. Are cantankerous Old Brown and his Iowa sojourn worth claiming bragging rights to?

Antonín Dvořák, one of the finest composers in history, summered in Iowa and wrote a tune or two here. But Iowa historians agree that it's stretching the point to feast on the refrain of his brief Iowa melody.

World-class wildlife artist John J. Audubon painted some Iowa birds and certainly a town and a county were both named for him. But Audubon's Iowa stay was abbreviated, for J.J. migrated south with his birds.

Orville and Wilbur Wright lived a few of their childhood dreams in Cedar Rapids. In their autobiography they claimed to have received a toy autogiro from an uncle while living in Iowa. The Wrights vowed that toy prompted their later interest in flying.

Little House on the Prairie author Laura Ingalls Wilder apparently lived in Iowa for a few months. Her father was said to have worked in a hotel near Decorah during the time in question. However, even if she lived here, her Iowa visit doesn't appear to have influenced anything she wrote.

Ann-Margret, singer-dancer-actress, got her first show business breakthrough in Des Moines.

Some notables simply schooled here and went on to varying kinds of glory. For example: Kurt Vonnegut and Tennessee Williams, Iowa Writers' Workshop teachers and best-selling authors; S.D. Stookey, Coe College graduate who invented Pyroceram®; Bruce Jenner of Graceland College, Olympic Gold Medalist in the decathlon; and Marv Levy, Coe College graduate, coach, then NFL Buffalo Bills coach and four-time Super Bowl coach. Actor Gary Cooper attended Grinnell College for a couple of years.

But with files full of Iowans whose roots are firm in Iowa soil, isn't it stretching the point to include fly-by or drop-in "Iowans" too?

We ached to include some unproven historical gems. For example, the Republican Party may have seen dawn's early light in Crawfordsville, a tiny town about 40 miles south of Iowa City. Historians, however, believe that the Republican Party probably sprang up at various places in the United States at about the same time. Crawfordsville was one of them.

Who was first? Hard to tell. So hard that I won't try to second-guess the experts. Republican headquarters staff in Washington, D.C., fail to confirm that Iowa gave birth to the GOP. Personally, I want to believe the Crawfordsville version, but beliefs are poor substitutes for facts.

For some the Iowa tie was not relevant to the way they made their mark. Earlier in this century, Alexander Lippisch, born and raised in Germany, invented the delta wing, making supersonic flight a reality. Just prior to World War II, he made major contributions to the design of both the British Spitfire aircraft and the German Messerschmitt. After the war, Arthur Collins brought Lippisch to work in Collins avionics in Cedar Rapids, where for over two decades he was to continue inventing air and watercraft of somewhat lesser significance than the delta wing. Lippisch's feats require a book of their own, but his most significant work was accomplished before he came to Iowa.

Wealth was not one of the yardsticks used. Simply having made a lot of money—nice as that prospect might appear—doesn't qualify a candidate. For example, Iowa pianist Roger Williams, actress Chloris Leachman, and singer Andy Williams all have found unusually talented ways to tap the treasury. But making money isn't what this book is about. Leachman qualifies on peer review and on worth other than net. Perhaps the others will too in a future book.

The creative trick was to decide when an Iowan's impact upon his or her field—like a nuclear reaction—reached critical mass, when that person's inclusion shouldn't be stopped. After offering all these demurrers, here are some qualifiers we leaned on in selecting the Iowans to portray.

- worldwide recognition
- tangible notability
- a patent of overwhelming significance

- development of an industry
- a Hall of Fame selection
- a world prize, such as the Nobel
- a national award, such as an Oscar, Emmy, Tony, Heisman, or Pulitzer Prize

These then are our own, Iowans who have made a difference. Some accomplished their feat with their own feet firmly planted on Iowa soil. Others paused with us for varying periods of time—to be born, grow up or get an education—before conquering their dragons in other places. That measure seemed like a method of dividing our winners into two groups. Even so, not all qualified Iowans could be included. The list of those whose stories we do not tell in this book, but who honor us by being our fellow Iowans, already fills files that, who knows, may become *Iowa Pride, II.*

As the years have whizzed by in the preparation of this book, my esteem for Iowa has soared. I hope your appreciation of this beautiful land and its people grows apace as you reflect on the remarkable Iowans whose lives we honor.

Just for easier reading, the initials UI refer to the University of Iowa, at Iowa City. We will ignore the fact that until 1955 or so it was known as SUI (State University of Iowa). The initials ISU refer to Iowa State University, at Ames. ISU was formerly named Iowa State College; however, only the newer name is used, even though an event being reported took place under the dated name. The initials UNI refer to the University of Northern Iowa, which was first known as Iowa State Teachers College. All cities listed are in Iowa, unless otherwise noted

Oh Yes—About the Cartoons

They were a happy afterthought. "Don't we have something to fill the blank spots?" the publisher asked. "How about a cartoon?" I responded. "Sort of a fastfood version of *Iowa Pride.*" They agreed, I drew, and here they are, scattered throughout. I hope you enjoy them.

IOWA CORN SONG*

Let's sing of grand old I O W A Y,
  Yo-ho; yo-ho; yo-ho.
Our love is stronger ev'ry day,
  Yo-ho; yo-ho; yo-ho.
So come along and join the throng,
Sev'ral hundred thousand strong,
As you come, just sing this song:
  Yo-ho; yo-ho; yo-ho.
          Chorus:
We're from Ioway, Ioway;
  State of all the land,
  Joy on every hand;
We're from Ioway, Ioway.
That's where the tall corn grows.

Our land is full of ripening corn,
  Yo-ho; yo-ho; yo-ho.
We've watched it grow by night and morn,
  Yo-ho; yo-ho; yo-ho.
But now we rest, we've stood the test;
All that's good, we have the best;
Ioway has reached the crest;
  Yo-ho; yo-ho; yo-ho.
          Chorus.

Nobody loves a parade like a Shriner. One of their slogans announces "We parade so children can walk!" Another (from the German philosopher Goethe) says "No man stands so straight as he who stoops to help a child." To prove it, Shriners pay for three burns hospitals and nineteen orthopedics hospitals around the United States where they provide millions of

---

*By John T. Beeston and George E. Hamilton ©1928, John T. Beeston. Reprinted by permission of Bob Beeston.

dollars' worth of free medical care to suffering children.

But in 1912, at a Shriner Conclave in Los Angeles, Iowa Shriners got their feelings stepped on. Other delegates, from seemingly far less important states, paraded out songs extolling their states' surely inadequate virtues. Iowa Shriners returned home bent on commissioning a musical score to even the score.

One of the delegates, George Hamilton, got the bandwagon rolling by putting words to the chorus of an old song, "Traveling." A couple of years later, Iowan John Beeston, an immigrant pipe-organ builder from England, scored the song for the Shrine band. That year, the "Iowa Corn Song" was the hit of the Georgia Conclave.

Today, honky-tonk piano players from Heidelberg to Hong Kong inspire loyal Iowans to reach their arms in the air and cheer the chorus line, "That's where the tall corn grows."

Now, to tell you the truth, Iowa has two state songs. At the turn of the twentieth century, Iowan S.H.M. Byers, who had languished in a Civil War prison, vowed he would take the Rebel tune his captors had tormented him with and improve it with loyal Iowa words. The Rebel song "Maryland, My Maryland"—taken from the German "O Tannenbaum"—became Unionized into "The Song of Iowa."

A historical footnote: A higher percentage of Iowans volunteered for service in the Civil War than volunteered from any other state. Isn't that just like Iowans for you?

Iowans
who
made
it
here

Noel M.

ANDERSON (1916–)

Invented the frostproof hydrant

Noel M. Anderson.
Photo courtesy of Noel M.
Anderson.

On his folks' Iowa farm, Noel was Dr. Fixit. He spent his youth learning to diagnose trouble and nurse machines back to life to work the soil, harvest crops, and nurture livestock. When something went haywire on the farm, Noel was always on call.

Despite his interest in machinery, after high school Noel went to Des Moines to learn bookkeeping. While in school he took a job selling water controls. But Noel quickly found a serious problem in the product he was hired to sell—the water controls occasionally froze solid in the winter. The best farmer in the world can't water livestock through a frozen valve.

Noel went to his shop and worked on a sample solution. When the next winter blew into Iowa, Noel found his new hydrant invention worked. It didn't freeze as other hydrants did. After obtaining patents on it, he mortgaged his house and car and set up his manufacturing plant ... in his garage.

One Friday, after Noel had called on many prospects and made but few sales, he demonstrated his hydrant to the people at Leighton (plumbing) Supply in Ft. Dodge. Leighton company managers liked what they saw and offered to sell the hydrant if Noel could deliver a half-dozen cutaway samples by the following Monday.

Iowa Pride _____

Noel worked feverishly that weekend, cutting through the tough steel of six sample hydrants. By 8 A.M. on Monday, the samples were in the salesmen's hands and by noon the postmaster delivered incredibly good news—an order for 100 valves, resulting from a prior sales call. On Friday, Leighton Supply capped the most important week of Noel's life with an order for 400 valves.

Within a few years, one million of Noel's hydrants protected water flow all over the world from freezing. He then looked for other water control problems to solve, and soon created the Merrill pitless adapter, to help well owners prevent dangerous chemicals from leaching into their wells from the surrounding soil, and a flotation device to separate air and water in pressure tanks.

By this time Merrill Manufacturing accepted an invitation from Storm Lake to be a part of that city's growth. A large facility was built and has been expanded constantly as Noel's patents—and those of his son Stephen—brought a flow of new products to the water well industry and well-earned success to an inventive Iowan who could fix things very well.

FOUNDED THE MERRILL MANUFACTURING COMPANY. Holds many patents on specialty pump products, including the pitless adapter and a float-type air volume control for domestic water systems.

Born: April 12, 1916, on a farm near Cylinder, Iowa. *Educated:* Capital City Commercial College, Des Moines. *Family:* Mary, wife; Merrill, Stephen, sons. *Iowa Connection:* born, raised, educated, invented and manufactured in Iowa.

Honors: Iowa Inventors Hall of Fame. During World War II, as a pilot flying 181 combat missions, he received the Air Medal four times and the Distinguished Flying Cross twice.

David A.
ARMBRUSTER (1890–1985)
Invented the butterfly swim stroke

A landlocked Iowan is probably the last person you would expect to invent a water sport. But Dave Armbruster didn't know that.

Dave invented a new swim stroke, which might amaze those with the notion that all swimming strokes have been known since man first supposedly dripped dry coming out of the primordial soup.

In 1935, working with Jack Seig, one of his swimming students at the University of Iowa, Dave perfected the technique for a new way to manipulate a body through water. He liked the name he gave it best: the *dolphin fishtail butterfly swimming stroke*. The name *butterfly* stuck, however, and for the next few decades Dave splashed through some stormy waters getting the swimming world to accept his new stroke.

Coaches around the country with excellent breast stroke swimmers on their teams were against changing swimming rules to allow competition in the new event. But Dave stroked on, and soon, with the help of European swimmers and coaches, the reefs parted. In 1956, the butterfly was finally added to the list of Olympic events.

The time frame of Dave's 42 years as coach of the UI swimmers and divers was a particularly prolific period for other creative Iowans. One of Dave's UI All-American divers, George Nissen, went on to invent the trampoline and the sport of trampolining. See the story on Iowan George Nissen.

Another cohort of Dave's, Beulah Gundling (see story), was

Iowa Pride

the first woman to present a program in the Dolphins annual swimming fraternity show at UI, and was the Iowan who invented swimming as an aquatic art.

Iowan Dave Armbruster made quite a splash in everyone's pool.

PERFECTED FLIP TURNS for speed swimming. Designed underwater observation windows to improve swimming technique. Authored: *Basic Skills in Sports* (eight editions published) and *Swimming and Diving*. Coached 75 All-American swimmers and divers. Coached two Olympic medalist swimmers.

Born: August 18, 1890, Spencerville, Ohio. *Educated:* Iowa Wesleyan three years; B.A. and M.A. at UI. *Family:* Edna, wife; Merlin and David, sons; Betty and Dorothy, daughters. *Iowa Connection:* educated, taught, invented and lived in Iowa.

Honor: International Swimming Hall of Fame.

John Vincent
A TANASOFF (1903–1995)
Invented the digital computer

J.V. Atanasoff at the blackboard, ISU 1930s. Photo courtesy of Iowa State University, Office of University Relations.

John Vincent Atanasoff did something most nine-year-olds don't. He figured out how to use his father's slide rule.

Then he quickly went through his mother's college algebra book. When he graduated from the University of Florida with a nearly perfect grade point average in electrical engineering, he accepted a teaching post at ISU.

While at ISU, he earned a master's degree in mathematics and taught, and thought. A great many of his thoughts dealt with how to compute a series of problems more rapidly than by hand. For months he struggled to find a way to solve the problem of speeding up mathematical solutions.

Late on a cold winter afternoon in 1938, JVA got in his car and started driving, an exercise he found cleared his mind. As he drove he mused on his mathematical problem, feeling that a solution was nearby, just eluding his mental grasp.

The Atanasoff-Berry Computer (the ABC). Photo provided by Iowa State University.

John Vincent Atanasoff. Photo provided by Iowa State University.

He drove east of Ames on Highway 30, then south to Highway 6, through Belle Plaine and Marengo, and east again to the Mississippi river and across into Illinois. It was night now and the lights of a tavern beckoned. He went in, hung up his heavy coat and took a table in the corner where he ordered a drink, lost in his thoughts.

An hour or two went by and gradually the haze that covered his problem parted and the young professor saw, for the first time, the elements he needed. He decided to

1. Use electronics for speed;
2. Defy the decimal (base-ten) custom and use the binary (base-two) system;
3. Use condensers for memory and use a regenerative or "jogging" process to avoid lapses caused by a leakage of power; and
4. Compute by direct logical action, and not by enumeration as in analog calculating devices.

JVA requested funds to hire an assistant and build a prototype of his computer. The school gave him a small grant which he used to hire Iowan Clifford Berry, a brilliant young graduate student. Over the next months the two mathematical geniuses labored together, each synergistically complementing the other's thoughts, creating a crude device that worked well enough to prove them right. Atanasoff named their device the ABC, the Atanasoff-Berry Computer.

As World War II began, both Atanasoff and Berry were called into military support services. Neither had the time nor was in a position to ensure that patent applications were properly pursued. To their everlasting regret, the college failed to apply for patents that eventually would have yielded billions of dollars in royalties both to ISU and to the inventors.

There was another problem. A fellow scientist, John Mauchly, a physicist at Ursinus College, just north of Philadelphia, had been a guest in JVA's home, and JVA had naively revealed to him detailed drawings, plans, theories, and the working model of this first computer.

Mauchly quietly prepared his own version of the ABC, then fashioned a deal with the U.S. Army to build his Electronic Numerical Integrator and Computer, the ENIAC, for use in computing ballistics trajectories. Since the ENIAC was considered top secret, JVA could not gain access to either the device or the patents for which Mauchly was quick to file.

Iowa Pride_____

Years later, when Mauchly had become known as the father of the computer (due to ENIAC), other large computer companies contested the patents that Mauchly had sold to the Sperry Rand Corporation. Their motive was purely economic, as Sperry Rand planned to charge exorbitant fees for their use.

The trial was one of the longest and costliest in history, with more than $5 million spent by Sperry Rand and $3 million by the Honeywell Company, not counting court costs for a seven-year trial that yielded to over 20,000 pages of trial transcripts.

When the trial was over, Judge Earl Larson unequivocally found that Mauchly's ENIAC was "derived from Atanasoff and that the invention claimed in the Mauchly patent was derived from Atanasoff." Larson ruled that Mauchly's computer patent was invalid and Atanasoff clearly emerged the winner.

The coming century has been called the age of information. No device in history has allowed humankind a better tool to fashion and use vast amounts of information in the service of humanity than has the digital computer.

Dr. John Vincent Atanasoff simply reinvented civilization.

_____

HELD 32 PATENTS in such diverse fields as agriculture, mathematics and information science.

Born: October 4, 1903, Hamilton, New York. *Educated:* B.S., electrical engineering, Univ. of Florida, 1925; M.S., mathematics, Iowa State University, 1926; Ph.D., theoretical physics, Univ. of Wisconsin, 1930. *Family:* Wife: Lura Meeks Atanasoff, married 1926; Elsie and Joanne, daughters; John, son. Wife, Alice Crosby Atanasoff (Webster City, Iowa), married 1949. *Iowa Connection:* studied, taught and invented at Iowa State College (now Iowa State University) from 1926–42.

Honors: DSA, Distinguished Service Award, U.S. Navy, 1945. Honorary Dr. of Science, Univ. of Florida, 1974. Presidential Medallion, Univ. of Florida, 1974. Iowa Inventors Hall of Fame, 1978. Honorary Dr. of Science, Moravian College, 1981. Film of the birth of the computer titled: " ... *from one John Vincent Atanasoff,"* Iowa State University, 1981. Distinguished Achievement Citation, Iowa State University Alumni Assoc., 1983. Honorary Dr. of Letters, Western Maryland College, 1984. "Computer Pioneer" recognition from the Institute of Electrical & Electronic Engineers, for having designed the first electronic computer with serial memory, 1984. Nominated for the Nobel Prize, 1984. Iowa

Governor's Science Medal, 1985. Order of Bulgaria, First Class, 1985. Computing Appreciation Award, by EDUCOM, 1985. Holley Medal, American Soc. of Mechanical Engineers, 1985. The first Coors American Ingenuity Award, 1986. Dr. John Vincent Atanasoff Day, state of Colorado, 1986. Honorary Dr. of Science, Univ. of Wisconsin, 1987. Electrical Engineering Milestone, IEEE, 1990. Honorary LL.D., Mount St. Mary's College, 1990. USA National Medal of Technology "For his invention of the electronic digital computer, and for contributions toward the development of a technically-trained U.S. workforce." Medal presented at the White House by President George Bush, 1990.

Clifford

BERRY (1918–1963)

Co-invented the digital computer

Clifford Berry, Iowa's forgotten computer genius. Photo provided by Iowa State University.

The night they pinned on his brand-new Eagle Scout badge, Clifford Berry was the proudest Boy Scout in Gladbrook.

But nobody in the room would have thought that within a few years this bright Iowa Boy Scout would co-invent the ABC and change the course of civilization.

For his remarkable co-invention would revolutionize the world's information storage and retrieval, communications systems, scientific exploration and the conduct of businesses and governments. Ultimately, the product of this Iowan's mind would deeply affect every human life on this planet.

So profound would be the influence of the ABC on humanity that its creation would be likened to the discovery of fire or the invention of the wheel.

At age 21, Clifford, in the ISU graduate school, noticed a call for a lab assistant. The job would be to work with ISU mathematics wizard John Vincent Atanasoff (JVA). Professor Atanasoff had developed concepts he wanted to prove or disprove. Clifford leaped at the chance and won the coveted job.

JVA, with a small grant from ISU, sought someone to match his genius and help him build an unusual device: a machine that would add 2 plus 2 and get 4 every time.

Soon after these two joined forces, the world's first digital computer amazingly added 2 + 2 and got 4. It also solved a problem that dealt with variables. For example, in the problem 3X = 12 there is a single variable, represented by X. The ABC solved problems with as many as 29 variables. It worked exactly as Atanasoff had planned and precisely the way Atanasoff and Berry constructed it.

Even though Atanasoff had conceived the concepts that developed the computer, he gave a full measure of credit to his youthful assistant. He expressed his thanks to Berry for Clifford's important design contributions by naming the machine the ABC machine, the **Atanasoff-Berry** Computer.

Iowan Clifford Berry, although he died at age 45 in New York—too young to have seen the fruits of his awesome invention—is worthy of every accolade a world of happy hackers can modem his way.

ASSISTED J.V. Atanasoff in building the prototype of the digital computer.

Born: April 19, 1918, Gladbrook, Iowa. *Educated:* B.S., M.S. electrical engineering, ISU. *Family:* Jean, wife. *Iowa Connection:* born, raised, educated, and invented in Iowa.

Honor: Eagle Scout.

William P.
BETTENDORF (1857–1910)
Invented the power-lift plow

Can you imagine being so important that your friends and neighbors rename the
town in your honor?

That happened at least once in Iowa and
there was plenty of good reason. In 1902, when W.P. Bettendorf
was 45 years old, the townsfolk decided to rename their town of
Gilbert after him.

W.P. employed 800 men of the community. He treated them
fairly, paid them well, even provided steam heat in his factory for
their comfort. At the turn of the century there weren't a lot of
warm factories in America. Those were plenty of reasons to love
the beneficent mogul of the Bettendorf Axle Company.

Bill Bettendorf was a creative genius. When he was only 21
he obtained his first patent, inventing a power-lift sulky plow—
sulky meaning it rolled on two wheels. The item was so good 80
percent of the plowing manufacturers adopted it at once, giving
Bill his first stake, and first real taste of success.

But the road he traveled to his 21st birthday was not an easy
path. At age 13 he left school to become a messenger boy, in a
small town in Kansas. He then became a clerk in a store for two
years, after which he became a machinist's apprentice in a plow
company. While there, he invented his power-lift plow.

His next invention was the Bettendorf metal wheel for farm
equipment. To make it easy to produce the wheel, he invented a
dozen machines to manufacture it. But there was a problem.
Company officials said they would put up the money for one of

his manufacturing machines, but not all 12. Their response prompted Bill to go shopping. He soon discovered a man in Gilbert, Iowa, who was willing to take a chance on Bill Bettendorf.

It was a good gamble. Bill brought in his brother and started the Bettendorf Metal Wheel Company. Invention followed invention and soon his company took shape.

When he was 45 the town renamed itself in his honor. At age 53, W.P. Bettendorf succumbed to the ravages of cancer, dying during an operation being performed in his living room by two doctors whom he brought to Bettendorf in a special train expressly for the operation.

W.P. Bettendorf's two children died in infancy, but his other legacies, his ingenious inventions, live on, serving not only the town that renamed itself in his honor, but the world as well.

INVENTED the Bettendorf metal wheel used on agricultural equipment. Obtained over 90 patents in machinery and equipment. Invented a running gear. Invented a hydraulic hoist for a farm plow. Invented a self-oiling, hollow steel axle. Invented a bolster and stakes for farm wagons. Invented a side frame for railway car trucks. Invented two dozen machines to produce his other inventions. Formed several major manufacturing companies.

Born: July 1, 1857, Mendota, Illinois. *Educated:* Indian Mission grade schools only. *Family:* Mary, wife; Elizabeth, wife; Etta, daughter; Henry, son. *Iowa Connection:* worked, invented and lived in Bettendorf.

Honor: 1990, Iowa Inventors Hall of Fame.

Samuel O. _____
BLANC (1883–1964)

Invented the Roto-Rooter®

Sam Blanc sent troubles down the drain. Photo courtesy of Eric G. Peterson.

When Milt Blanc's wife wanted to get rid of potato peelings, she just flushed them down the toilet. She didn't get a good grade for that.

For a time she got by with her little peelings caper until one day, flushed with success, the drain failed to live up to its name. The drain was chock-full of peelings, so Milt called his dad, Sam Blanc, over to help solve the problem.

Seven years earlier Sam had tried unsuccessfully to sell hand augers made by a firm in Chicago. The devices were known as "snakes" and one still hung in Sam's garage. Milton had remembered that and so he and Sam labored an afternoon augering the potato peelings out of Milton's sewer line.

Job done, Sam went home and told his wife Lettie, "There's got to be a better way." Sam was the resolute kind of man to take correspondence courses in electrical and mechanical engineering. He wasn't easily dissuaded from whatever he set his mind to achieve.

For months Sam labored on the sewer problem he sought to solve. Finally, in 1934, Sam hooked up Lettie's Maytag washing machine motor to a spiraled cable armed with cutting augers on one end, and mounted on wheels from a child's wagon. Sam was now ready to root out the cause of clogged sewers, well ahead of the rest of the world.

Lettie liked Sam's idea so much she volunteered one of the most popular names of all times to label the invention. "Call it a Roto-Rooter, Sam," she advised. Sam was smart enough to perceive the wisdom of her perfect choice of words.

The mid-thirties were the toughest of depression times. Sam advertised he could not merely open drains, but clean them like never before. His ads claimed,

No digging, no lawn damage, no street cutting,
Samuel O. Blanc's 'Roto-Rooter®' cuts roots out of
sewer lines in an inexpensive, guaranteed way.

It wasn't long before people came to Sam saying they'd like to use his machine in their cities. Sam obliged. Soon, Roto-Rooter businesses sprang up across the land, many electing to be on call 24 hours daily. Sam's licensees were one of the forerunners of what became the franchise industry.

In the early 1950s Captain Stubby and the Buccaneers, at WLS in Chicago, recorded what was to become the most memorable ad jingle of all time. The song went,

Call Roto-Rooter®,
That's the name,
And away go troubles
Down the drain.

The nation adopted the song so well that it achieved greater recognition than the national anthem; 96 percent of those asked know the name RotoRooter® and appreciate the greatest ad campaign ever created.

Between 1935 and 1945, Sam obtained three additional patents on a variety of sewer cleaning machines. One industrial machine was as large as an auto.

An additional ad campaign of recent years has added another dimension to consumer recognition for Roto-Rooter. It came about during a company brainstorming session. Executives hit upon the idea of sponsoring a Monster Root Contest among Roto-Rooter franchisees. Within just a few months Johnny Carson wove the idea into a comedy routine he used to open his

17

evening show.

Today, every city over 50,000 people in the United States has Roto-Rooter service, making the company by far the biggest American drain cleaner. Recently Roto-Rooter became the largest plumbing repair firm as well, expanding internationally into Japanese markets. An incredible one in seven service calls, both for clogged drains and for sewer repairs, rings into a Roto-Rooter phone line somewhere. And not an ad slogan, logo, or jingle in the world is more familiar than the Roto-Rooter campaign.

Although the Roto-Rooter® patents expired in 1955, allowing competitors to enter the field with similar devices, the growth and service of America's Number One Trademark continue unabated. And Iowa-based Roto-Rooter just keeps on singing ... all the way to the bank.

ESTABLISHED the Roto-Rooter company and franchise system.

Born: February 13, 1883, Menomonee Falls, Wisconsin. *Education:* Wisconsin to the fifth grade, correspondence courses in mechanical and electrical engineering. *Family:* Lettie, wife; Violet, Lorraine, Norma, daughters; Milton, son. *Iowa Connection:* worked, invented, lived in Iowa.

Amelia Jenks

BLOOMER (1818–1894)

Pioneer suffragist, editor, and reformer

When Amelia Jenks married Dexter Bloomer, she had the word "obey" struck from her wedding vows. The action today may not seem unusual, but in 1840 only a rebellious woman would require such a restriction. If nothing else, Amelia Jenks Bloomer was perfectly at ease making bold statements.

Dexter Bloomer edited a newspaper and he, better than many, understood his 22-year-old bride's determination. After all, editorials denouncing slavery were his stock-in-trade. If anyone could appreciate the reasoning behind Amelia's stand, certainly an antislavery editor would.

A few years after they were married, Amelia became the editor of *Lily,* a nationally circulated newspaper. Its masthead was no less bold than its editor, stating that it would fight for the "Emancipation of Women from Intemperance, Injustice and Bigotry."

In *Lily,* Amelia championed dress reform, advocating Turkish-style "pantaloons." For many years, she wore a costume consisting of a jacket, a shirt, and the garment that came to bear her name, "bloomers." Actually, the original design of the *bloomer suit* appears to have been made by another American, Elizabeth Smith Miller. However, as one reference notes, it is difficult to imagine bloomers being called "millers."

By the late 1800s bloomers became the preferred dress of woman bicyclists, but feminists moved away from them, believing that the costume turned attention away from more important issues.

Iowa Pride_____

In 1855 Amelia and her husband moved to Council Bluffs, where she continued to edit *Lily* and lecture on temperance, unjust marriage laws, and women's rights. During the Civil War she organized the Soldiers' Aid Society of Council Bluffs, and by 1865 she coordinated statewide contributions to the U.S. Sanitary Commission, working hand in glove with another famous Iowa woman, Annie Wittenmyer.

The Iowa Woman Suffrage Society captured her interest after the war and she became its president in 1871. Until her death in 1894, the woman who lent her name to one of the most famous items of apparel continued a defense of her ideals both in print and on the lecture platform. Truly Amelia Jenks Bloomer wore her name well.

REFORMER, women's rights editor, temperance advocate, and suffragist. Founded (1849–1864) feminist paper *Lily.* Championed women's rights to wear trousers.

Born: May 27, 1818, in Homer, New York. Moved to Council Bluffs, Iowa, in 1855. *Education:* instruction at home from her mother and some rudimentary training in a district school. Permitted to teach at age seventeen. *Family:* Dexter Chamberlain Bloomer, husband; adopted one daughter and one son. *Iowa Connection:* edited the *Lily* newspaper and lectured in Iowa.

Honors: Became president of the newly formed Iowa Woman Suffrage Society in 1871. Represented Iowa at meeting of American Equal Rights Association in New York City in 1869. Inducted into Iowa Women's Hall of Fame in 1975.

Roy
CARVER (1909–1981)
Created the finest tire retread

Roy Carver was never content. He wasn't content with the languages he knew. He died learning Italian, to add to the English, French, Spanish and German fluency he possessed. He wasn't content with his philanthropy. He died trying to figure out how he could give away more of his fortune than anyone guessed possible, having already surpassed the gifts of mundane millionaires.

He wasn't content with his incredible business success. He died with new businesses budding in far-off lands. He wasn't content with his flying skills. He died planning new trips to wherever. He wasn't content with the toys he had accumulated. He died with more in the works. And he died planning his next party.

Roy James Carver was a man whose only content was his discontent.

Roy's trek to fiscal stardom began in the Depression years when he put together a better pump than his competitors. Being a born salesman, Roy took his pump to the government, who suggested he talk with England, then at war with Germany. England bought Carver pumps and this success fired his lifelong discontents.

A few months later, when America entered the war, Roy assembled a pump factory to meet a burgeoning demand for Carver quality. Roy's first million was well on its way to the bank.

Since automobile gasoline was rationed and airplane fuel not, Roy took up flying and continued to fuel his factory with orders for Carver pumps from his flying sales trips.

On a postwar trip to Germany, Roy saw a distinctive tire tread that piqued his interest. Obtaining the world rights to it, he brought the process home and worked for six years to perfect it, first creating a new buffing unit that allowed the tires to be prepared in an inflated position; then personally devising an ingenious flexible rubber envelope to permit the retreading of a tire of any size or shape; finally, supporting associate Ed Brodie in the creation of a superior bonding cement.

With all the elements in place, Bandag® —a cold retreading process that lasted far longer than conventional retreads—was ready for marketing through franchise dealers. The rest of the story is pure gold, as money from satisfied users filled the Bandag coffers.

Roy Carver's discontent with the status quo revolutionized the auto tire retreading industry. In the process, he was able to finance many of his other discontents, always with an eye toward leaving either someone or something better off than when he found them.

Roy James Carver, who weathered the seasons of his discontents in Muscatine, was one special kind of Iowan.

CREATED AND FOUNDED the Carver Pump Company. Founded the Carver Foundry Products. Conducted enormous philanthropies.

Born: December 15, 1909, Preemption, Illinois. *Educated:* University of Illinois, electrical engineering. *Family:* Irene, wife; Charlotte, daughter; Lucille, wife; Roy Jr., John, Clayton and Martin, sons. *Iowa Connection:* lived, invented, created, founded and conducted numerous philanthropies in Iowa.

Honors: 1968 Presidential "E" Award for excellence in exporting. 1972 UI Distinguished Service Award. 1974 B'Nai B'rith Man of the Year Award. 1976 Horatio Alger Award. Industry Leadership Award, American Retreaders Association.

Carrie Lane Chapman ⸻
C ATT (1859–1947)

Championed women's right to vote

Carrie Chapman Catt, the ultimate suffragist. Photo courtesy of Iowa State University/University Archives.

C arrie took one word out of the United States Constitution. It only took her one lifetime to get the job done.

Today, millions of people will testify that that single word stained America's soil. For the word banned freedom to over half the U.S. population.

Carrie's word was "male." And when it was stricken from the U.S. Constitution, women could vote. The issue: suffrage. The time: the turn of the 20th century. The place: rooted in Iowa and spreading over the country. The leader: Carrie Lane Chapman Catt.

Growing up on a farm near Charles City, Carrie asked her father why he voted and her mother couldn't. She didn't understand his response and he felt uncomfortable trying to answer her question. Through later years, hearing the complacent statement, "Women's place is in the home," she always asked, "Are women people, too?"

Women's rights were ripe in Iowa, the state with the first woman dentist (1865), where women were allowed to enter college equal to men (1856), where the first woman notary (1866), school superintendent (1874) and lawyers (1869, 1875) found welcome acceptance. Iowa was the first state to make women eligible to be Recorder of Deeds, and the Iowa legislature was first

23

to make women eligible to serve on most state boards and commissions.

The Republican Party (possibly founded in Iowa) was first to allow women to become campaign speakers. Iowa women had always believed they were the equal of men and Iowa men agreed. Carrie set out to prove that women were smart enough to vote as well.

After finishing high school she obtained a teacher's certificate and was hired to teach in the summer months. When winter came, traditionally a man took over, but Carrie had so impressed the school board they hired her to teach all year.

After a year of teaching she enrolled at Iowa State University. Carrie was the only woman in her class. Her classmates also remembered her as their valedictorian. Forty years later she returned to become the first female commencement speaker at ISU.

After graduation Carrie became superintendent of schools in Mason City, taking charge on her first day on the job. Wielding a two-foot strap of harness leather, she visited the schools where troublemaker students disrupted class, jerked them out in the hallway and impressed upon them who was boss. They never forgot.

Carrie soon met Leo Chapman, a talented journalist, married him and helped him on his local newspaper. It was there that she polished communicative skills that stood her in good stead throughout her career. Her newspaper column entitled "Women's World" was far ahead of other feminist banners.

At this time the Iowa legislature was considering a bill for municipal suffrage for women. Carrie gathered a petition with the signatures of virtually every woman in town. She broke the city into wards and assigned leaders to get the precinct jobs done. Her successful format she later called her "Winning Plan." It was the same technique which Carrie used to carry the day for women's suffrage in the national arena.

After two years, she and Leo moved to San Francisco, but Leo contracted typhoid fever and died, and Carrie returned to Iowa. She renewed a friendship with George Catt and soon they married. Before the ceremony, they both agreed that Carrie would work two months in both the spring and the fall for woman's suffrage.

Carrie quickly founded the Iowa Woman Suffrage Association, then organized the National American Woman Suffrage Association (NAWSA) and in a few years was handed the national presidency of NAWSA by another outstanding feminist advocate, Susan B. Anthony. During these years she tirelessly toured the country, organizing NAWSA's two million members.

In 1920, with final ratification of the Nineteenth Amendment, people thought Carrie's jobs were over. But Carrie immediately organized the League of Women Voters, to teach women how to use their vote. To best appreciate the scope of this pioneer woman's life, look to her own words:

"To get that word 'male' out of the Constitution cost the women of this country 52 years of pauseless campaign, 56 state referendum campaigns, 480 legislative campaigns to get state suffrage amendments submitted, 47 state constitutional convention campaigns, 277 state party convention campaigns, 30 national party convention campaigns to get suffrage planks in party platforms, 19 campaigns with 19 successive Congresses to get the federal amendment submitted, and the final ratification campaign."

VALEDICTORIAN of her ISU graduating class. County Superintendent of the Mason City Schools. Led the battle for passage of the Nineteenth Amendment. Organized the National American Woman Suffrage Association (NAWSA), 1892. Elected Chair of NAWSA, 1895; National President of NAWSA, 1915–1938. Founder and President of the International Women's Suffrage Alliance, 1902; Honorary President 1923–1938. Cofounded Women's Peace Party with Jane Addams. Founded the League of Women Voters, 1920; Honorary President 1920–1938. First woman commencement speaker at ISU, 1921. Coauthored *Women's Suffrage in Politics,* 1923. Founded the "Committee on Cause and Cure of War," 1925. Worked toward establishment of the United Nations.

Born: January 9, 1859, Ripon, Wisconsin. *Educated:* Charles City, Iowa; B.S., ISU, 1880. *Family:* Leo Chapman, husband; George W. Catt, husband.

Iowa Connection: raised, educated, and worked for women's rights and world peace in Iowa.

Honors: Appointed to the first Women's Committee on National Defense by President Woodrow Wilson. 1920 Honorary LL.D. degrees from the University of Wyoming and Iowa State College (ISU). 1922 Honorary LL.D. from Smith College for Women. 1926 *Time* magazine cover picture. 1930 Annual $5,000 Achievement Award from *Pictorial Review* as "The American woman who has contributed most to the nation's life in letters, art, science, philanthropy or social welfare." 1931 Elected one of America's 12 Greatest Women. 1933 American Hebrew Medal. 1940 National Social Sciences Institute Award. Gold Medal Pioneer Award from the General Federation of Women's Clubs. Conference Honoree, Women's Centennial Exposition. Woman of the Year, American Women's Association. 1941 Honorary Degree, Moravian College for Women. Chi Omega Gold Medal Award presented at the White House by First Lady Eleanor Roosevelt. Gold Medal, National Institute of Science. 1942 White Rose Order from the government of Finland. 1975 One of the first four Inductees into the Iowa Women's Hall of Fame. 1992 The Iowa Award.

Arthur A. ————————
C OLLINS (1909–1987)

Communications pioneer

*Arthur Collins, ham operator
9CXX. Photo courtesy of Collins
Avionics of Rockwell
International.*

Art Collins made his first radio from a Quaker Oats® box, a spark coil from a Model T Ford, and some telephone parts.

It wasn't that much of a big deal, unless you know that Art was nine years old at the time and this was one of the first radios in Iowa. While a teen he attended a two-day course in radio at ISU and soon obtained ham radio call letters (9CXX). Art promptly began corresponding with radio operators around the country.

One of his ham friends was John Reinartz, who had developed the new idea that short wave lengths could be skipped on an ionized layer encircling the earth. Reinartz proposed to bounce a 20-meter signal from his radio set in Massachusetts to 15-year-old Collins in Cedar Rapids, who would then bounce it on to California.

The transmission was perfect and just in time, for Reinartz

had accepted a radio operator's job with Arctic explorer Capt. Donald MacMillan's journey to Greenland. He arranged to report daily the expedition's progress to Collins on the 20-meter wave lengths which they had already proven worked over long distances.

Each day, at the appointed hour, Collins received the message, then pedaled to the Western Union office to relay to a breathless world the only news from the explorers.

Collins soon assembled a radio that was superior to others, and because of the quality of his product, and perhaps due to his new-found fame, he began selling all the fine radios he and his crew could produce. As the product line grew, police departments and the military soon employed Collins' radios.

In 1933, CBS radio decided to broadcast from Rear Admiral Richard E. Byrd's second expedition to the Antarctic. It was a huge gamble, for if the broadcast failed, the reputations of Admiral Byrd, CBS and now Collins Radio stood to suffer. The then 24-year-old Collins laid his reputation on the line and provided the equipment for flawless broadcasts from the South Pole.

Soon Collins and his team of engineers came up with an instrument they called the Autotune®. With this device, pilots could easily switch from one radio band to another. When World War II broke out, Collins radio gear was credited with a major role in the Allied victory in the air.

Allied pilots, using Collins radios, could switch station frequencies rapidly, in flight, with the pilot not losing sight of his quarry. Enemy radio jammers were not as agile and their disruptive effect on radio communications was minimized.

In a few years, the Collins product line grew to over 500 radio-related products. Included was a flight director system for instrument landings which over 80 percent of all commercial airlines adopted.

Other products were airline antennas, a weather radar system, an autopilot, a radio sextant, and a transponder. A Dallas television station bought one of the radar weather detectors and became the first TV station in the world to present weather radar to its viewers.

During the Cold War the Voice of America network went out

over Collins' equipment. Transhorizon communications techniques were developed under Arthur's leadership, as was the first commercially built cyclotron for the Atomic Energy Commission.

The first television transmission signals bounced off from the moon when astronaut Neil Armstrong said, "That's one small step for man ... one giant leap for mankind" on Collins' radios.

Iowan Arthur Collins took his small step for man when he wired that first little radio inside that Quaker Oats® box. And mankind took a giant step with him.

AS A 15-YEAR-OLD BOY he participated in the first transcontinental sending of 20-meter short wave radio signals. Created the Autotune®, with his engineering team. Collins Radio Company became a world leader in quality aviation and space electronic equipment. His company was the principal developer of practical single sideband radio. Brought together the team and worked with them to develop many radio firsts.

Born: September 9, 1909, Kingfisher, Oklahoma. *Educated:* As a teenager, a two-day short course on radio at ISU; short periods of radio and electronic education at Coe College, UI, and Amherst College, Massachusetts. *Family:* Margaret Van Dyke, wife; Mary Margaret Meis, wife; four children. *Iowa Connection:* raised, educated, worked in Iowa.

Honors: 1954, Honorary Doctor of Science, Coe College. 1962, Distinguished Public Service Award Citation, Secretary of the Navy. 1966, Distinguished Service Award, Iowa Broadcasters' Association. 1968, National Academy of Engineering, elected to membership. 1968, Honorary Doctorate, Polytechnic Institute of Brooklyn. 1970, Honorary Doctor of Engineering, Southern Methodist University. 1974, Honorary Doctor of Science, Mount Mercy College, Cedar Rapids. 1979, David Sarnoff Award, Armed Forces Communications and Electronics Association. 1980, Medal of Honor, Electronics Industries Association.

Marvin

CONE (1892–1965)

Renowned artist

Marvin Cone teaching charcoal sketching at Coe College. Photo courtesy of George T. Henry, Cedar Rapids.

The paintings of Marvin Cone have a directness and honesty characteristic of the artist himself. ... It is the full-bodied art of a man who loves the simplest qualities that meet the eye and depicts them with clarity and sound craftsmanship. ... It is the mature work of a distinguished artist.

—GRANT WOOD

Marvin Cone claimed Cedar Rapids as his place of birth and surely Iowa was where he made his mark, but his educational pursuits led him to Chicago, France, and Mexico. After his graduation from Coe College in 1910 with a degree in French, Cone studied at the Art Institute of Chicago. From there he joined the AEF in World War I and served in France as an interpreter.

Returning to Cedar Rapids, he was engaged by Coe College to teach French, and to start an art department on the side. In the summer of 1920, Cone and his painter pal, Grant Wood, shipped over to France to paint and try to become impressionists. They failed and decided that regionalistic was what they both were and regionalism was what they both would paint.

On the return trip to America, Cone met a lovely Canadian, Winifred Swift. The shipboard romance blossomed into a lifetime marriage.

Cone continued to head the art department at Coe until 1960, putting in a half-century of devotion to his students, the college, to his canvases, and to his brand of Iowa regionalism.

After viewing a traveling exhibit of the art works of Cone and Wood, Susan Freudenheim, art critic for the *San Diego Tribune,* wrote, "Both Cone and Wood were sophisticated painters. ... The portraits here are mostly straightforward, demonstrating the hard-edged puritanism we tend to associate with Iowans."

Today, Cone's work has been exhibited in museums throughout the world and hangs in many of their permanent collections. The Cedar Rapids Museum of Art showcases several hundred of his works in a special room dedicated to this Iowa artist.

LED, with Grant Wood, a "paint Iowa" movement.

Born: October 21, 1891, Cedar Rapids, Iowa. *Education:* graduated magna cum laude with a Bachelor of Science degree from Coe College, Cedar Rapids, Iowa, 1914; majored in French. Studied at the Art Institute of Chicago School from 1914 to 1917. *Family:* Winifred Swift, wife; Doris, daughter. *Iowa Connection:* born, raised, educated, taught, and painted in Iowa.

Honors: Paintings have been exhibited by the Metropolitan Museum, the National Academy of Design, and the Audubon Artists, all in New York; the Art Institute of Chicago; Carnegie Institute, Pittsburgh; Walker Art Center, Minneapolis; Joslyn Art Museum, Omaha; Pennsylvania Academy, Philadelphia; Butler Museum, Youngstown, Ohio; the Mid-American Exhibit, Kansas City, Missouri; the Denver Museum; the American Federation of Arts traveling shows, and smaller galleries throughout the country. Work is in the permanent collections of art museums in Minneapolis, West Palm Beach, New York, Topeka, Omaha, Davenport, Des Moines and Cedar Rapids.

Jay Norwood D'ing×_____

DARLING (1876–1962)

Cartoonist and conservationist

Ding Darling at work, 1942. Photo by Herbert Schwartz; courtesy of the J.N."Ding" Darling Foundation.

He started as a reporter, but he soon learned that his drawing pen was mightier than his writing sword.

The son of a preacher, Jay grew up in Sioux City, the town that drew him back after his college days at Yankton College in South Dakota and Beloit College in Wisconsin. In college Jay signed his drawings *D'ing*—a contraction of his last name *Darling,* deleting the *arl*—a signature that within a decade would be known to millions of newspaper readers across the nation.

In Sioux City Jay took a job as cub reporter on the *Journal.* One assignment required a photograph of a lawyer who angrily refused to have his picture taken. Jay drew a cartoon of the lawyer and in the process began a cartooning career that quickly eclipsed his prose.

A cartoon of a school board president in Sioux City drew

Ding's ouster from the *Journal* and he promptly accepted a job with the Des Moines *Register and Leader.* His new assignment was to provide a cartoon for the newspaper's front page each day. Ding was now officially a cartoonist and during the following five years his skills grew as he learned to master the metaphor of

IN GOOD OLD U. S. A.

AN ORPHAN AT 8 IS NOW ONE OF THE WORLD'S GREATEST MINING ENGINEERS AND ECONOMISTS WHOSE AMBITION IS TO ELIMINATE THE CYCLE OF DEPRESSION AND UNEMPLOYMENT

THE SON OF A PLASTERER IS NOW THE WORLD'S GREATEST NEUROLOGIST AND HIS HOBBY IS GOOD HEALTH FOR POOR CHILDREN

A PRINTER'S APPRENTICE IS NOW CHIEF EXECUTIVE OF THE UNITED STATES

BUT THEY DIDN'T GET THERE BY HANGING AROUND THE CORNER DRUG STORE

The 1923 cartoon that won Ding his first Pulitzer Prize. Courtesy of the J.N."Ding" Darling Foundation.

cartoon commentary. Fellow cartoonist Rube Goldberg said that Ding " ... developed the art of gentle ridicule better than anyone in the world."

A call from the *Globe* in New York City took Ding and his family to New York to reach a larger market and syndicate his cartoons to 130 other newspapers around the nation. For the next two years, Ding hobnobbed with the movers and shakers in America, Edna Ferber, Henry Ford, Teddy Roosevelt and others. The thrill of the city began to pale as Ding perceived metropolitan insincerity and he longed to return to his old paper in Des Moines.

Ding said, "The people of Iowa think more to the square inch than the people of New York think to the square mile."

At this time a creeping atrophy of his right arm, due to a fall from a horse as a youth, caused him to wonder if his drawing career might be at an end. To forestall that possibility, Ding taught himself to draw left-handed, an incredibly difficult task for a person considered to be one of the world's premier cartoonists.

Back at the *Register and Leader,* Ding was enticed by other newspapers to join them and eventually accepted syndication by the New York *Herald-Tribune.* A conservation thread had worked its way into his drawings, rooted in his love of the outdoors. Ding wrote, "Wild ducks and geese and teeter-assed shore birds are only the delicate indicators of the prognosis for human existence just as sure as God made little green apples."

Ding's new syndication deal required his attendance more and more in New York until, once more, he moved to New York City with his family and stuck it out for a year before he returned to Des Moines. This time he wrote to a friend, "As the Bard of Avon was wont to say, I would rather live in a tent in Iowa than to be a door keeper in (New York City) houses of wickedness forever at three times the salary."

In 1919 Ding drew what was probably his best-known and most-reproduced drawing titled "The Long, Long Trail." It was a quickly drawn sketch of his friend Teddy Roosevelt who had died that day. He rushed it into print in the *Register and Leader,* planning to refine the drawing later for syndication. But the cartoon worked and he never changed it.

During the next years, as Ding deepened his interest in conservation, he became embroiled in Republican Party politics and battled bouts of serious, asthmatic illness. Another fellow Iowan, neurologist Dr. Frederick Peterson, gave new life to Ding's drawing arm by designing and performing an operation that virtually cured his ailment.

In 1924 Ding immortalized Dr. Peterson, and Presidents Warren G. Harding and Herbert Hoover, in a single cartoon that won for him the second cartoonist's Pulitzer Prize ever awarded. Ding's future was firmly planted in Iowa soil, from which it towered over America.

When President Franklin D. Roosevelt was swept into office, Ding's friend Henry A. Wallace became Secretary of Agriculture and weighed upon Ding to accept the position of Head of the Bureau of Biological Survey, forerunner of the U.S. Fish and Wildlife Service. Ding always joked that President Roosevelt kept him busy with wildlife management so he would not have time to draw anti–New Deal drawings.

For nearly two stormy years, Ding upset the federal applecart, fighting large dam projects, steering the Survey to acquire wilderness lands for game replenishment, and taming the wanton massacre of wildlife by commercial interests. During these years Ding designed the first Duck Stamp and the flying goose logo of the National Wildlife Refuge System, creating not only the logo but the system the logo stands for.

Returning to Des Moines, he again cartooned his way to a Pulitzer Prize with a depiction of bureaucratic waste titled "What a Place for a Waste Paper Salvage Campaign." As the clock ticked down on an aging and feisty Ding—a man who believed with all his heart that conservation of our natural resources was crucial to the survival of humanity—Ding drew his final cartoon.

On February 12, 1962, an obituary of Ding Darling appeared in *The Des Moines Tribune*. The following day, a front-page cartoon appeared in *The Des Moines Register.* Ding's cartoon was titled "Bye Now—It's Been Wonderful Knowing You." As the millions of acres of wildlife refuge and the enormous return of wildlife that was nearing extinction attest, it's been wonderful knowing you, too, our Iowan friend Ding Darling.

Iowa Pride

Ding's design for the first federal Duck Stamp. Courtesy of the J.N."Ding" Darling Foundation.

FOUNDED the National Wildlife Refuge Program and designed its logo. Designed the first federal Duck Stamp. Responsible for establishing the Sanibel National Wildlife Refuge. Instrumental in founding the Cooperative Wildlife Research Program in cooperation with ISU, the American Wildlife Institute, the American Wildlife Federation, which became the National Wildlife Federation, the North American Wildlife Conference, and the General Wildlife Federation. Founded National Wildlife Week.

Born: October 21, 1876, Norwood, Michigan. *Education:* B.A., Beloit College, Wisconsin. *Family:* Genevieve, wife; John, son; Mary, daughter. *Iowa Connection:* raised, worked, created, and philanthropized in Iowa.

Honors: 1924, 1942, Pulitzer Prizes. Doctor of Letters, Beloit College. Doctor of Laws, Drake University. Roosevelt Medal for conservation, 1942. J.N. "Ding" Darling Wildlife Refuge in Sanibel, Florida, named for him. Distinguished Service Award presented by the Ding Darling women's chapter of the Iowa Izaak Walton League. DSA for Conservation from the trustees of Public Reservations. American Forestry Association life membership. Award of Merit from the National Physicians' Committee. Honorary membership in the Society of Professional Journalists, Sigma Delta Chi. U.S. Postal Service created a 20-cent stamp depicting his conservation efforts. Honored by the Bison Society of America and the National Wildlife Association. The Register and

Tribune building in Des Moines was designated a historical site due to his having drawn there. Darling Lake on Honey Creek named for him. *Nature* magazine denoted him "one of a handful of changemakers in the world of natural resources management and preservation." Jay Darling crabapple tree in Des Moines' Denman Park named for him. Izaak Walton League of America Hall of Fame. Audubon Medal for service to conservation. Florence K. Hutchinson Award from the Garden Club of America. Honorary member of Teddy Roosevelt's Boone and Crockett Club. Ding Island in Lower Souris Refuge, in Canada, was named for him. Co-chairman (with Walt Disney) of National Wildlife Week in 1962. J.N. "Ding" Darling Children's Forest in Des Moines was named for him. The Iowa Award.

Paul
ENGLE (1908–1991)

Built the Iowa Writers' Workshop

Paul Engle. Photo courtesy of International Writing Program, University of Iowa.

Are published writers born to greatness?

Until about the 1930s, English professors believed that a Poe or Pound, a Sandburg or Stevenson, and even a Twain, had some peculiar combination of genes, brains and environment that produced a great writer. The prevailing thought was that one could no more be taught to be a writer than be taught to be two inches taller.

But some professors at UI thought writing was, if not a skill that could be taught, at least a skill that could be encouraged. A UI Writers' Workshop brochure notes, "In 1922, Carl Seashore, dean of the Graduate College, set a national precedent by announcing that creative work would be acceptable as a thesis for advanced degrees."

Norman Foerster, director of the School of Letters, began to offer courses in writing in which promising pupils were given counsel by seasoned writers. In 1936, Professor Wilbur Schramm offered a series of conferences for verse writers. On Schramm's death, the poetic genius of Paul Engle stepped in to nurse fame for what was now to be the Iowa Writers' Workshop.

After attending Coe College, Engle took graduate work at UI and in an Ivy League college, then won the Yale Series of Younger Poets Prize with his first manuscript, which became his thesis for a UI Master of Fine Arts degree.

When he had established the prominence of the Workshop, Engle founded the UI Translation Workshop and then, with his wife, Chinese novelist Hua-ling Nieh, founded the International Writing Program. In 1976 the Engles were nominated for the Nobel Peace Prize for their pioneering work with writers of many cultures.

Clark Blaise, a graduate of the Writers' Workshop who later directed the International Program, describes Engle as "the most influential writer of this century, not for what he wrote, but for what he did for other writers."

Among the many prominent writers who have studied or taught at the Writers' Workshop are Robert Frost, Stephen Vincent Benet, Flannery O'Connor, Kurt Vonnegut, John Irving, John Cheever, Gail Godwin, Philip Roth, T.C. Boyle, U.S. poet laureate Mark Strand, Tracy Kidder, and John Casey.

A talented Iowa boy named Paul Engle plowed new literary soil, sowed seeds of greatness, and reaped a harvest of great credit to his state and justifiably for himself.

IOWA'S POET LAUREATE. Cofounded the International Writing Program. Founded the Translation Workshop. Wrote and edited 20 books.

Born: October 12, 1908, Cedar Rapids, Iowa. *Educated:* B.A. Coe College; M.A. UI; graduate work, Columbia University; B.A. Oxford. *Family:* Mary Nissen, wife; Mary and Sara, daughters; Hua-ling Nieh, wife; Lan-Lan Wang, Wei-Wei Wang, stepdaughters. *Iowa Connection:* born, raised, educated and wrote in Iowa.

Honors: Paul and his wife, Hua-Ling Nieh, were nominated for the Nobel Peace Prize for their lifetime achievements. At the time of his death, Engle was in O'Hare International Airport, en route to Europe to receive the Order of Merit from the Polish government. Three Guggenheim Fellowships. The Friends of American Writers Award. The Lamont Award of the Academy of American Poets. 1990, Engle was voted the Award for Distinguished Service to the Arts by the American Academy and Institute of Arts and Letters. Novelist James Michener has funded Writers' Workshop scholarships in Engle's honor.

William _____

F ISHER (1856–1906)

Invented a new
water-pressure control

Will Fisher called it the worst night of his life.

That night began with tongues of flames bouncing from wooden building to wooden building, leaving behind smoldering piles of rubble and ashes. The folks in Marshalltown called it a debacle. Will's exhaustion came from handthrottling the steam-driven water pumps to fight the fire.

Months later, this 24-year-old engineer immigrant from England assembled the world's first constant pressure pump governor. And the Fisher Governor Company was founded. For the first few years, the going was tough and Will sold cameras and bicycles to finance his dream. In a few years the world began to learn of his pump governors and he could devote all his energies to the company.

Will Fisher died when he was only 50, but his wife and other family members continued company growth. In 1944, Will's 30-year-old grandson, J.W. "Bill" Fisher, took control of the company. Under his leadership, sales volume of Fisher Governor grew from $3.5 million to $65 million until Fisher Governor became the undisputed leader in the control industry.

Bill's career was marked by notable philanthropies. He spent considerable time, talent and money overseeing extensive charitable activities in Marshalltown, in Iowa and across the nation. He was perhaps better known for his patronage of the arts, especially of opera.

The New York Times once called Bill Fisher "a major force in opera in the United States." A member of the board of directors of the Metropolitan Opera Company in New York City, he mounted—that is, financed—operas, musical and theatrical performances throughout the world.

And it all began when a 24-year-old immigrant from England gave of himself to fight the Marshalltown fire of 1880.

INVENTED the constant pressure pump governor. Founded the Fisher Governor Company.

Born: 1856, England. *Educated:* England. *Family:* Martha, wife; Jasper, son. *Iowa Connection:* invented, lived, worked in Iowa.

John
FROELICH (1849–1933)

Invented the gasoline-powered tractor

John Froelich, the tractor man. Photo courtesy of the Froelich Foundation.

> It could be operated in your parlor without driving you outdoors for a breath or spoiling your carpet or curtains.
> —BROCHURE FROM THE WATERLOO GASOLINE
> TRACTION ENGINE COMPANY, 1894

The hyperbole of this ad copy for the first gasoline-powered traction engine possibly overstated the case a bit. Investors in John Froelich's **trac**tion motor, or trac**tor**, as it was to be known, knew it was a winner. The problem was how to get farmers to keep their horses in the barn and use the many horses in the tractor instead. But farmers were skeptical. Gasoline engines frightened not only horses but their owners, too.

John Froelich ran a grain elevator in Froelich, Iowa, a tiny town in Clayton county named for his father. Each summer he toured Iowa and the Dakotas with 16 hired hands, threshing wheat for farmers, using a J.I. Case steam engine for power.

One summer in 1890, John bought a Van Duzen gasoline engine to power his elevator. The minute it was installed he had a brilliant idea. What if he would take one of these new gasoline engines and put it on a steam engine base?

Steam power was costly, slow to generate, required an engineer to produce, was inconvenient, and often ignited the prairie when stray sparks from the boiler lit on dry wheat. Sometimes the engines exploded, and steam engines were cumbersome to move from field to field.

The people in Froelich snickered at John's tractor. But, on the day of its first trial, they were honest enough to cheer when John drove off at the incredible speed of 3 miles an hour, roughly the pace of a brisk stroll. For people who had never seen a machine move, it was an unforgettable sight.

John immediately tested his tractor on a neighbor's farm and it worked perfectly. John loaded his tractor onto a train and took it to the wheat fields of South Dakota. During the first two months they threshed over a thousand bushels of wheat a day, using only 26 gallons of gasoline and without starting a single prairie fire.

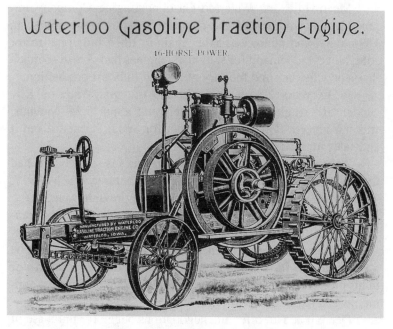

The Waterloo Gasoline Traction Engine. Photo courtesy of the Froelich Foundation.

Iowa Pride

Flushed with threshing success, John found eight men willing to put up $50,000 to build and sell tractors. In 1894, the Waterloo Gasoline Traction Engine Company was incorporated and patents were applied for. Four prototype tractors were built, two of which were sold, both of which were returned.

Hard times were at hand both for the nation and for the company. To keep the company alive, the group turned their interest to stationary engines, selling one of their first ones to the *Waterloo Courier* newspaper pressroom. The company's efforts in stationary engines weren't particularly promising, so the group sold out to another group, who then formed the Waterloo Gasoline Engine Company.

During the period of the financial bust, John Froelich lost most of his savings and property. He sold his interest in the company and moved to Dubuque, where he worked as an engineer in the Novelty Iron Works, a company that manufactured gasoline engines. Later he moved to St. Paul and became an investment counselor.

Meanwhile, the Waterloo Gasoline Engine Company improved their tractor and the company's stationary engines. In 1896, only one tractor was sold. Again in 1897, only one tractor sold; however, demand for stationary engines had grown so much that a new factory and foundry were built to boost production.

In 15 years 20 tractors sold and the first Waterloo Boy Model "R" singlespeed tractor, weighing about 5,240 pounds, was introduced. It sold to the farmer for $985. Farmers liked it and sales jumped to 118.

Across the Mississippi, John Deere and his son Charles had their watchful eyes on the Waterloo manufacturer, for, by 1917, 4,558 tractors were sold, up from 2,762 the previous year.

At that time, Deere and Company was a heavyweight manufacturer of the popular self-cleansing plows John Deere had invented and other farm implements. John Deere realized that to be a well-rounded farm manufacturer he had to have a good tractor in his product line. The Waterloo Boy, being one of the most popular, was a natural acquisition target.

Deere made an offer and negotiations began for purchase of the Waterloo plant by Deere and Company. On March 14, 1918,

Deere paid $2,350,000 for the Waterloo Gasoline Engine Company.

Iowa-born inventor John Froelich's magic machine transformed the prairie sod and changed world food production as no other invention had done.

GRANTED 14 patents for various improvements to the combustion engine and numerous other farm-related devices.

Born: November 24, 1849, Giard, Iowa. *Family:* Kathryn Bickel, wife; C.H. and Benjamin, sons; Jenetie and Anna, daughters. *Iowa Connection:* born, raised, worked and invented in Iowa.

Dan

G ABLE (1948–)

Kingpin of wrestling

Dan Gable, the handbook of wrestling. Photo courtesy of Iowa State University Photo Service.

He is the handbook of wrestling.

—UI STUDENT WRESTLER

Most slight high school students wouldn't dream of becoming a world-class athlete, an Olympic gold medalist, and a living legend of a sport they dominated. Most high school students aren't Waterloo's Dan Gable.

Sports always seemed to come easy for Dan. In grade school Dan was a pretty fair Little League baseball player. In junior high he quarterbacked an undefeated football team; then he won a state swimming championship. Yet, upon entering high school, he faced the same decision every athletic youngster encounters. The question is simple: Which sports shall I concentrate on?

Dan's answer was cerebral; it was to be wrestling. He knew that it's tough for a small man to compete in many sports, but wrestling is weighted by class. He knew in wrestling he would always compete against men his size.

With the choice made, Dan entered training in earnest on the new barbell set his dad had given him for his 13th birthday. The race was on. After three decades of training, Dan has never quit. He can't. He doesn't know how. He says the reason is clear, "I don't have the words 'quit' and 'give up' in my vocabulary!"

The record bears out this singleness of purpose. Winning 364 wrestling matches, the vast majority being pins, against two defeats is a record difficult to imagine. On his way to the Olympic Gold Medal, Dan didn't surrender a single point.

After the Olympics Dan joined the UI wrestling program, becoming head coach four years later. The program has never been the same, for Dan has done with his team what he did for himself—and that is amass an unequaled array of wins.

Whether one considers his record in the NCAA Championships, the Big Ten Championships, the number of All-Americans, number of Olympic qualifiers, or number of Olympic wrestling champions, Dan's records surpass an armchair athlete's understanding.

Dan's enthusiasm goes to the core of his being. At the Munich Olympics he was so fired up that officials administered several drug tests, just to "see if his spunk was real"!

OLYMPIC wrestler and distinguished coach.

Born: October 25, 1948, Waterloo, Iowa. *Educated:* B.S., ISU, 1971. *Family:* Kathy, wife; Jennifer, Annie, Molly and Mackenzie, daughters. *Iowa Connection:* born, raised, educated, wrestled and coached in Iowa.

Honors: Olympic Gold Medal, wrestling, 1972 Summer Olympics, without surrendering a single point to his opponents. Through high school and college a wrestling record of 182-1. Undefeated in 64 prep matches. College record was 118-1: won his first 117 matches in college, an NCAA record. Three state titles at Waterloo West. Two NCAA titles at ISU. Three-time All-American. Three-time Big Eight champion. Postcollegiate titles at the Pan-American Games, Tbilisi Tournament and the World Championships. Won an unprece-

Iowa Pride

dented six Midlands Open championships: was voted the meet's outstanding wrestler five times. 1985, U.S. Olympic Hall of Fame. 1980, U.S.A. Wrestling Hall of Fame. 1977, NCAA Rookie Wrestling Coach of the Year. 1970, Named the nation's outstanding wrestler by the AAU. 1971, Named the nation's outstanding wrestler by the U.S. Wrestling Federation. 1970, *Amateur Wrestling News* Man of the Year. 1978, 1983, 1991, NCAA Coach of the Year.

George

GALLUP (1901–1984)

*Developed sampling methods
to predict human behavior*

George Gallup, the original sampler. Photo courtesy of George Gallup, Jr.

S*ir, do you mind if I ask a few questions?"*
Startled Iowa Citians in the 1920s weren't used to intense
people coming up to them and asking questions. Being
this bold invaded another person's space and in a Victorian-based society that just wasn't done. It wasn't done until a
young Iowan dreamed up the idea and carved a niche for himself
in the process.

George "Ted" Gallup believed that survey research brought
out the truth and truth was vital for needed reform in society. He
used that conviction as foundation not only for his personal career and business but to inaugurate a new sociological dimension
to human life. The industry he founded came to be known as public opinion research, an effort that brought opinion polls into being.

Born on an Iowa farm near Jefferson, Ted attended the University of Iowa. During his sophomore year, his family suffered
severe financial reverses and so for the remainder of his college
days he supported himself by means of scholarships and by operating the towel concession in the UI swimming pool. Ted also
found time to act as editor of the *Daily Iowan,* which he extended
from a campus newspaper into a newspaper that served the entire
Iowa City community.

49

Iowa Pride

Following graduation, he became a UI instructor in journalism, while pursuing an M.S. in psychology and a Ph.D. in journalism. His doctoral thesis, "A New Technique for Objective Methods for Measuring Reader Interest in Newspapers," contained the germ of the idea that he later developed into the Gallup Polls.

After receiving his doctorate, Ted became professor of journalism at Drake University in Des Moines. After two years, he accepted positions of professor of journalism and advertising at Northwestern University and as visiting professor in the Pulitzer School of Journalism at Columbia University.

Meanwhile, the theories he advanced were being tested in newspapers beginning with *The Des Moines Register.* Two of his important findings in his research led to the use of comics in advertising and the publication of *LOOK* magazine by the Des Moines Register and Tribune Company.

In 1932, Ted accepted a position as director of research for Young & Rubicam, a major New York City advertising agency. While there, he worked out methods for measuring reaction to advertised products, using the same techniques he had devised to measure response to radio programming.

In 1935, founding the American Institute of Public Opinion, he established the Gallup Polls. The avowed purpose of his organization was "to impartially measure and report public opinion on political and social issues of the day without regard to the rightness or wisdom of the views expressed."

Today, an affiliated Publisher's Syndicate distributes the results of Gallup Polls to hundreds of newspapers. An associated Audience Research Institute, Inc., evaluates movie titles, casts and stories.

Iowan Dr. George Gallup redefined the way people understand each other. In doing so, he shouldered a large share of the responsibility, and shares much of the credit, for acting as the impetus of social reform in the world.

All his life George "Ted" Gallup proclaimed his pride in his Iowa origins and his love of farming. He once said, "I'm from Jefferson, Iowa, and I'll always be from Jefferson, Iowa."

DEVELOPED the first scientific method of measuring reader interest in the content of a newspaper and developed the coincidental method for measuring radio audiences. Established the first continuing nationwide method of measuring radio audiences via the coincidental method. Developed the first full-fledged copy research department. First systematic use of "group sessions" to determine the entertainment value of radio programs and their component parts. Developed the impact method of measuring advertising effectiveness based upon recall principles. Formed a firm, Gallup and Robinson, to measure advertising effectiveness. Introduced the Activation system for measuring advertising effectiveness. Gallup's studies led to the formation of: *LOOK* magazine, Hooper's radio rating service and Starch commercial service. Founded Quill and Scroll, an international honorary society for high school journalists.

Born: November 18, 1901, Jefferson, Iowa. *Educated:* B.A., M.S., Ph.D., UI. *Family:* Ophelia, wife; Alec and George Jr., sons; Julia, daughter. *Iowa Connection:* born, raised, educated, developed his research thesis and performed his first studies in Iowa.

Honors: 1934, President, Market Research Council. 1935, Annual Advertising Award, "in recognition for a distinguished contribution to advertising research." 1964, Advertising Gold Medal Award. 1965, The Parlin Award, American Marketing Association. 1975, Distinguished Achievement Award, first recipient, New Jersey chapter of the American Marketing Association. 1977, elected to Advertising Hall of Fame. 1983, elected to the New Jersey Advertising Hall of Fame. Honorary Doctor of Laws degrees from Northwestern University, Drake University and Boston University, and honorary doctorates from Tufts College and Colgate University. The Missouri Honor Award, University of Missouri.

Burt

GRAY (1871–1962)
Invented (?) the hamburger

Burt Gray. Hold the pickle! Photo courtesy of Gloria Lake.

Have you noticed how some-body always wants to sandwich in on another person's fame? Especially if you invented the world's most popular anything.

Iowan Burt Gray claimed he invented the hamburger. He just might have, at that. The facts seem fairly clear, if not the date of first invention. Here is the story as later reported in newspaper accounts.

Burt was an experienced restaurateur in Clarinda. One day he walked next door to his restaurant to visit his friend Al Wall (the name could have been Wahl), who ran a butcher shop. Al was stuffing wieners with ground pork. As they chatted, Al suggested that a sandwich might be made out of ground beef. Burt agreed to give it a try.

The big question was how to make ground beef hold to-gether during cooking. Ground pork was held together with sausage skin, but there was no beef skin to hold ground beef the same way.

Burt took some ground beef back to his restaurant. Reasoning that he needed a matrix, or glue, to hold the beef together during cooking, he mixed egg batter in with it. Not only did that prove to be messy, but the taste was less than wonderful.

Burt then decided to form the beef into a patty shape, after mixing it with flour. He dropped the patty into hot fat and fried it well, then placed the cooked patty between two slices of bread. He and Al ate and nodded approval. Hmmm. Not bad. Maybe a pickle and some catsup and onion would make it even better.

They knew that Burt had invented something pretty special, but it was a sandwich that needed a name. They talked about that for a while, until Al suggested "Hamburger." Burt objected that the sandwich had no ham in it, but, unable to come up with a better name, he let that one ride.

Some people later said that Al named the sandwich as a tribute to his mother, who still lived in Hamburg, Germany. That seems unlikely, even though Hamburg was Al's birthplace, too.

It is possible that Al thought of this new sandwich as the leading sandwich of all time. A leader (or mayor) of a German town is called a burgher. Putting together a clever contraction of two German words—the city, Hamburg, and the leader, burgher—produces "hamburger."

Recall that the immigrant Al Wall still thought in German. However, any guesses about the origin of the name are just that, guesses.

Once word got out about Burt's great new hamburger sandwich, Clarindans rushed to Burt's cigarette and sandwich shop on the north side of the city square. Business boomed. People loved Burt's 'burgers.

Later, when he introduced the hamburger into his restaurant in Rockwell City, the townspeople at first refused to buy it. They said they didn't like cheese! The cheeseburger hadn't been invented, so that response seems strange, until we recall that the townspeople knew about limburger cheese, with its world-class stench.

Burt's first hamburgers contained a half-pound of hamburger, an onion slice, pickles and catsup. They sold for a nickel. Times and prices have changed, but Burt Gray and Al Wall's hamburger lives on, by the billions.

And pretenders to the throne of hamburger kingdom continue to arise. Go figure.

RESTAURATEUR, introduced the hamburger.

Born: December 21, 1871, Clarinda, Iowa. *Family:* Sadie, wife; Vern, Max, Gilbert, sons; Ruth, Lucille, Doris, daughters. *Iowa Connection:* born, raised, lived, worked and invented in Iowa.

Beulah
GUNDLING (1916–)
Invented aquatic art

Beulah Gundling, good strokes.
Photo by John W. Barry; courtesy
of Mrs. Henry Gundling.

First she almost drowned, second she learned to swim from a book, and then she went on to make swimming history.

Fourteen-year-old Beulah Gundling slunk home from the Cedar Rapids pool red-faced with shame after nearly drowning during a swim lesson. She vowed to do better and got a book on swimming written by Olympic champion and movie Tarzan Johnny Weissmuller.

When she was 24, Beulah won a half-mile river race, eventually winning an Iowa AAU gold medal in the backstroke. Tiring of racing, she took up ballet, until one day, on reading a book about rhythmic swimming, she conceived a routine of swim strokes set to music. Her swimming and ballet skills merged to create her act.

During this time she met her husband Henry who urged her to enter a race held at the Aquatennial Water Show in Minneapolis. Her surprising high placement prompted her to study the sport until she heard of a national synchro swim meet in Des Moines. Henry again egged her into competing in the duals and, together with a friend, she placed 10th out of 14 places. Not a bad start for someone who had never seen a synchronized swim meet.

When Beulah learned of the Canadian Dominion Synchro Championships, she entered as a soloist and stunned the synchro swimming world by winning first place with a routine she called "The Swan," inspired by Pavlova's "Dying Swan" ballet solo. She also discovered she had become the first Solo Synchronized Swimming champion in the world.

Beulah's success in solo synchro swimming prompted U.S. swim officials to include the event in future AAU national competitions. After her Canadian triumph, Beulah conquered the synchro swimming world, reigning supreme for seven years.

Between competitions, Beulah and Henry toured the world demonstrating the synchro sport and acquiring adherents for it on four continents. It was a heady time of achievement and accomplishment, travel and triumph, holding international championships for seven years and winning the first Gold Medal for synchro at the Pan-American games.

Tired of what had become cutthroat competition, Beulah and Henry decided that synchro should be an art form rather than an athletic competition. With others interested in the art aspects of swimming, they founded the International Academy of Aquatic Art (IAAA), encompassing water ballet, water pageantry, and synchronized swimming.

Its purpose was to develop swimming as a performing art. Henry was chosen as its first president and served for 25 years in this capacity.

The following years saw Beulah and Henry busy building the art form that they had created. They again toured the world, putting on demonstrations, enlisting adherents and receiving the acclaim that was their due.

In 1965, 35 years after reading Johnny Weissmuller's book on how to swim, Beulah Gundling became one of the first 20 Honorees to be inducted into the International Swimming Hall of Fame.

Another of the first 20 Honorees was ... Johnny Weissmuller. Beulah and her swimming teacher finally met.

AUTHORED AND COAUTHORED numerous texts on aquatic art. Advanced synchronized swimming through additions to its vocabulary and figures. Helped establish synchronized swimming as an event in the United States and abroad.

Born: Beulah Detwiler, February 13, 1916, Cedar Rapids, Iowa. *Education:* B.A. magna cum laude, majoring in physical education and zoology, Coe College, Cedar Rapids, 1938; Cedar Rapids Business College, 1942. *Iowa Connection:* born, educated, lived in and swam out of Iowa.

Honors: After winning numerous prizes and awards through her primary and secondary education years, she became the first Solo Synchronized Swimming world champion (Canada, 1951), then during the next few years won virtually all synchronized swimming awards available. She was the first to exhibit synchronized swimming at the Olympic Games (Helsinki, Finland, 1952) and won Gold Medals and various firsts in numerous competitions, including the Pan-American Games in Mexico City, 1955. Following this aspect of her career, she won 35 top ratings in Aquatic Art Festivals. In 1965, she was elected to the International Swimming Hall of Fame and, in 1974, to the Aquatic Art Hall of Honor. The citation on one of her many gold medal awards reads, "To Beulah Gundling, who, more than any other performer, made water ballet into an aquatic art." In 1980, she was the first woman athlete to be inducted into the Coe College Athletic Hall of Fame.

Jesse
HIATT (1826–1898)
Discovered the Delicious apple

Jesse Hiatt, discovered something delicious on the most famous fruit tree since the Garden of Eden. Photo courtesy of the Madison County Historical Society and Stark Brothers Nurseries and Orchards.

J esse Hiatt knew and loved apples, but he surely had never seen anything like this one. But that's putting the apple before the tree.

Responsibility often came early in pioneer days. When Jesse Hiatt was 17, he took over the family farm in Pennsylvania to support his parents. When they died he moved to Madison County in Iowa and bought a section of land near his brother's place.

Soon Jesse planted an orchard to replace the one he left behind and began to grow beautiful fruit for his family and neighbors. To be certain his orchard started with good stock, Jesse and his brother hauled a wagonload of trees from Oskaloosa, 77 miles away.

One day Jesse noticed that an aggressive little shoot had sprung out of the root of a Bellflower apple seedling that had died. Since he couldn't make the trip to buy another seedling just then, he decided to let it grow. The shoot blossomed and grew into a handsome apple tree. But Jesse had never seen fruit like this.

The apple was elongated, streaked with red and yellow, firm and lovely and with a quintet of well-defined, rounded knobs on the flower end. Its wonderful aroma was matched only by an incredibly good taste. Jesse named it the "Hawkeye" in honor of his adopted state of Iowa.

Over the next 11 years Jesse traveled far and wide, extolling the virtues of the decidedly superior Hawkeye apple. But there was little interest and few farmers wanted to grow them for themselves.

At this same time, an enterprising nurseryman, Clarence Stark of Louisiana, Missouri, was seeking the best apple he could find. The currently popular apple was the Ben Davis, a hardy grower but not a good-tasting apple. Stark conceived the idea of an Apple Show and Contest, to find the best apple in the world. Letters were sent to growers around the nation and soon apples arrived to be judged by Professor H.D. Van Deman, the United States Pomologist from Washington, D.C.

Jesse entered his apples and immediately they captured the fancy of Stark and of the judge, who called them the best apples he had ever seen or tasted. There was only one small problem. The entry card was missing and a frantic search failed to find it.

Stark could only send out letters again, offering another contest the following year. Patient and persistent Quaker that he was, Jesse dutifully entered once more, not realizing he had already won the prize. When Jesse's new apples arrived at the contest the following year, Clarence Stark, owner of Stark Brothers Nursery, immediately traveled to Peru, Iowa, and bought the sole right to propagate and disseminate the Hawkeye apple from Jesse.

Stark thought the aberrant tree might have occurred from an accidental cross between two old-timer apple trees, the Bellflower and the Winesap. Stark loved the apples, but thought the name wouldn't sell. So he decided this was the perfect fruit that awaited the perfect name, which was "Delicious."

To promote the apple, Stark placed a bundle of 10 trees marked "Key Z26 for experimental test only" into every order for apple trees. In three years, when those experimental trees bore fruit, apple growers from around the nation clamored for more.

Orchardists learned that the Delicious apple tree required very little pruning and shaping, always growing with a perfect head of strong hardy branches, capable of bearing enormous loads of fruit. The branches bent with the weight of the fruit, but didn't break.

Iowa Pride _____

The Delicious apple tree came into bearing young, flowered later in the spring, avoiding many killing frosts, and predictably grew and yielded good crops in diverse climates and soils.

One hundred years later, from the root of Hiatt's original Delicious apple tree, another apple tree has sprouted which amazingly still produces fine fruit.

From this single tree, over fifteen million apple trees have been produced. In only a few years, the Delicious apple produced more income than any other apple, with modern annual production exceeding $100 million in value. This, from one ageless Iowa tree.

Over 60 percent of all apple trees in the world today have come from this single Iowa apple tree, known appropriately as the "Mother of Millions." Red Delicious and Golden Delicious apples—offshoots of the original Delicious apple—are Nos. 1 and 2–producing apple trees in the world.

Iowan Jesse Hiatt discovered the most important fruit tree since the Garden of Eden.

_____

GREW the Delicious apple.

Born: February 16, 1826, Randolph County, Pennsylvania. *Educated:* elementary schools; father taught him how to plant, prune, graft and grow fruit. *Family:* Rebecca Jane, wife; 10 children. *Iowa Connection:* lived and worked in Iowa from age 29 on.

Honors: The Best New Apple prize, 1893. A posthumous monument in Winterset Park, Winterset, Iowa, 50 years following his apple discovery. Recognized in such magazines as *The American Fruit Grower* and by world-renowned pomologists as the discoverer of the world's finest apple.

Cora Bussey

HILLIS (1858–1924)

Child welfare advocate, founded the first Child Welfare Research Station

Children should have a safe place to swim in the river, Cora Bussey Hillis decided, and so in 1894 she helped organize the first public bathing house on the banks of the Des Moines River. The idea of public swimming pools, at the time, had barely begun and certainly not crossed the Mississippi River from the east.

Helping children was to be the pattern of Cora's life, perhaps inspired by the five children of her own whom she raised with her husband Isaac Hillis.

Born in Bloomfield in 1858, she attended a private school in New Orleans before marrying and moving to Des Moines. While attending the National Mothers Congress in Washington, D.C., in 1899, she extended an invitation for the group to convene in Iowa the following year.

The officers accepted and for a year Hillis went about the state speaking at organizational meetings of Mothers Clubs. By the time the opening gavel sounded, on May first of 1890, representatives of 644 Iowa Mothers Clubs packed the 4,500-seat Des Moines auditorium to overflowing. When the closing gavel came down, Hillis was elected president of the Iowa Congress of Mothers.

The following year, Hillis worked to establish a free chil-

Iowa Pride ————————————————

dren's ward at Iowa Methodist Hospital in Des Moines. The next year she lobbied for passage of a bill which founded the Iowa juvenile court system, a bill she helped write.

President Theodore Roosevelt appointed her to serve on the Country Life Commission, the first of several national commissions and boards for Hillis. She also helped found the Iowa Child Welfare Association as a branch of the Department of Public Safety. The Association sponsored benefits to help children, such as the Baby Saving Campaign to counteract high infant mortality rates. Other Association activities included free ice, pure milk distribution, visiting nurses, and a fresh air camp for mothers and sick babies.

For years Hillis, who was tireless in speaking out for child welfare, worked for the establishment of the Child Welfare Research Station at the University of Iowa. In 1917, it became the first of its kind in the nation.

CHILD WELFARE ADVOCATE.

Born: August 8, 1858, Bloomfield, Iowa. *Education:* in a private girls' school in New Orleans, Louisana; the Sylvester Larned Institute. *Family:* Isaac Hills, husband; Ellen, Doris, daughters; Cyrus, Philip, Isaac Jr., sons. *Iowa Connection:* born, organized groups in Iowa.

Honors: Helped incorporate the Des Moines Club in 1887. In 1900, was unanimously elected president of the newly formed Iowa Congress of Mothers. In 1901 worked to establish a free children's ward at Iowa Methodist Hospital in Des Moines. Served on President Theodore Roosevelt's Country Life Commission; founded the Iowa Child Welfare Association as a branch of the Department of Public Safety. Hillis Elementary School in Des Moines, Iowa, was named in her honor. Inducted into the Iowa Women's Hall of Fame in 1976.

Arthur L. ─────────
HUBBARD (1921–)

*Refined the mechanical
cotton picker*

*Arthur Hubbard, revolutionized
cotton pickin' cotton picking.
Photo courtesy of Arthur L.
Hubbard.*

Iowan "Blackie" Hubbard freed the
slaves. No known report puts it just that way, but
read his story and you decide.

As a 16-year-old, Blackie Hubbard from
Almartha, Missouri, went to work as a mechanic in the Illinois
John Deere factory. It was the time of the Great Depression, but,
because his father had trained him in the family blacksmith
shop—where Blackie picked up his nickname—he had marketable skills.

During his first months on the job, he saw workmen scrap-
ing paint from a metal part. On the spot he invented a scraper that
shrank an hour's job to seconds. When management heard of this,
Blackie was assigned to a creative group tasked to dream up new
products for the company. A working cotton picker was their No.

Iowa Pride

1 priority. In 1950, Blackie moved to Des Moines to continue his work for John Deere.

Cotton pickers of the day picked up trash along with the snow-white bolls of cotton. Trash in cotton equals less money from cotton buyers. Growers were desperate for a way to pick clean cotton mechanically.

In the meantime, tens of thousands of Southern blacks toiled in the cotton fields from dawn to dusk. The pay was pitifully low, hours were so long that there was almost no family life, the children often had to work instead of attending school. Cotton pickers lived lives of harsh servitude.

To learn about cotton, Blackie went into John Deere's experimental cotton fields in Texas and Arkansas where he worked seven-day weeks. As the months rolled past, Blackie applied for patent after patent on concepts to solve the problems. Eventually, he created the revolutionary John Deere 9900 Cotton Picker, AirTrol System.

The 9900 worked. Suddenly, tens of thousands who had lived lives subservient to the cotton crop, found a new freedom that even Abraham Lincoln had never given them. They could seek better-paying jobs in factories or driving the cotton pickers. Their children could attend school. They could eat more healthful diets. And families suddenly had family life.

When Blackie Hubbard, the eighth-grade dropout, was called by the American Society of Mechanical Engineers to receive their highest award, the Leonardo da Vinci prize, Blackie said, "I think you've probably made a mistake. I not only don't belong to your society, I'm not even an engineer."

The society of engineers had made no mistake. Blackie Hubbard, who had patented more ideas than all of John Deere's cadre of college-trained engineers had ever patented, received an honor duly earned.

REGISTERED over 70 patents, mostly for cotton harvesting.

Born: Almartha, Missouri, February 9, 1921. *Educated:* to the eighth grade in Sherrard, Illinois. *Family:* Alice, wife; Gary, Bruce, Brian, sons. *Iowa Connection:* worked, lived, invented in Iowa.

Honors: 1979, Leonardo da Vinci Award, American Society of Mechanical Engineers. 1979, Iowa Inventors Hall of Fame. Professionally recognized by the National Cotton Council, Cotton, Inc., and many research and experimental station personnel of the United States Department of Agriculture as the world's leading authority on cotton harvesting.

W.A.
JENNINGS (1898–1980)
Invented a portable concrete form

W. A. Jennings tried to give away a multimillion-dollar idea, but his boss would have none of it.

In the 1930s, W.A. took four tries before he could find a job that made sense and earned a few bucks. In those Great Depression times, green civil engineer grads from ISU weren't worth much in the marketplace. Nor was anyone else.

His first job was with a Des Moines steel company, but no one was building and that meant steel wasn't selling. He took his talents to an Oklahoma steel company with the same depressing results. Then he headed to Milwaukee to work for a company that sold metal forms to contractors for use in erecting concrete structures.

But the form he sold was too bulky and heavy for workmen to comfortably use. Even with the cheap labor of Depression times, the cost of using the form exceeded the cost of buying the form. Problems beg solutions, and innovative W.A. didn't have to be begged twice.

He quickly invented a small 30" × 30" form that one man could easily carry and interlock with other forms, to create the master mold for concrete to be poured into. As a good employee, he offered his idea to his Milwaukee boss. The boss wasn't buying, so W.A. returned to Des Moines and opened a factory, first in his basement, then expanded to his garage.

Not only was his idea of a portable form revolutionary, his business sense told him he needed a sweetener, a business edge, to get his form used over others. As an added incentive, he offered to lease the form to cash-strapped builders.

As W.A. started his business, the government entered the building business, through the Works Projects Administration (WPA). The WPA was designed to create jobs by employing men to work on the infrastructures of public buildings and other building projects such as highways. Leased forms not only meant easier work and faster finished buildings, but were an incentive to contractors squeezed for cash.

It was a win-win situation that W.A. shrewdly capitalized on, expanding his business year after year until EFCO, Economy Forms Company, penetrated world markets, even building plant facilities in foreign countries.

The original form was supplanted by another, larger form. This 24" × 48" form could be either purchased by the contractor or rented. This move brought even more growth to the company.

Since W.A.'s death, the company has expanded its product line to ease project problems in various building areas, making construction still more profitable for contractors and providing additional business.

Today, when you see a large building project almost anywhere in the world, chances are its construction was made possible by an Iowan who didn't know it couldn't be done. That bit of construction might be a gigantic church, office building, concrete barge, tunnel, dam, factory, warehouse, waterway or sewage treatment plant.

It might even be the Houston Astrodome or Texas Stadium, home of the Dallas Cowboys. Inventive Iowan W.A.'s forms built them both.

BUILT the world's largest concrete forms business. Holder of 25 patents related to concrete forms.

Born: 1898, Des Moines, Iowa. *Educated:* ISU, civil engineering. *Family:* Lillian, wife; Al, Ralph, Don, sons. *Iowa Connection:* born, educated, worked and invented in Iowa.

Honor: 1985, Iowa Inventors Hall of Fame.

MacKinlay

KANTOR (1904–1977)
Novelist specializing in the Civil War

My stories have appeared in an appalling number of magazines, sublime, ridiculous and penny-dreadful.

I used to write a great deal of stuff for the pulp detective and crime story magazines, in the years when I made my living that way, and I don't think my rather complicated talents were harmed in the least.

—MACKINLAY KANTOR

Mack Kantor confessed that he wrote an awful lot of junk. He wrote some of it "learning to push thousands of words around" in Webster City, where his mother edited the local newspaper. His job as the paper's ace reporter became his college career.

When the Webster City paper folded, Mack took a job on the *Republican* newspaper in Cedar Rapids, and when it was sold he first drifted to Des Moines to work on the *Tribune,* and then to Chicago where he hacked words by the pageful.

To learn of life, Kantor took hobo trips through the Midwest. Many of his 40 novels reflect his observations on these travels. The acclaimed novel *Signal Thirty-Two* was born of two years' duty as a uniformed policeman in New York City.

To learn about the World War II bursting around him, he became an accredited war correspondent. After some months of traveling with the Royal Air Force from England, then the U.S. Air Force, MacKinlay's writings and insights were so highly thought of that General H.H. "Hap" Arnold commissioned him to perform studies of high-altitude aerial bombardment. Incredibly, Hap appointed Mac, a man who never attended college, to make this important study. After the war, General Curtis LeMay chose MacKinlay to co-author his autobiography.

When the Korean war broke out, some years later, MacKinlay returned to the military, this time with a rank of Lieutenant General. He flew with the 92nd Bombardment Wing in the Far East, probably being the last of the genre of generals who had no college degree.

Between those war episodes, Kantor went to Hollywood as a scenario writer for Paramount Pictures. Here he scripted his book *Glory For Me* into the motion picture that makes everyone's list of all-time classic motion pictures. Its new title was *The Best Years of Our Lives*.

MacKinlay Kantor's life should inspire us when we feel life hasn't dealt enough favors our way. For this hardy Iowan, MacKinlay Kantor, just up and made it on his own.

Best-Known Books: The Voice of Bugle Ann, Books, Inc., 1935; *Glory for Me,* Coward-McCann, 1945; *But Look, the Morn,* Coward-McCann, Inc., 1947; *Lee and Grant at Appomattox,* Random House, 1950; *Signal Thirty-Two,* Random House, 1950; *God and My Country,* The World Publishing Co., 1954, retitled for the cinema *Follow Me, Boys!; Andersonville,* The World Publishing Co., 1954; *Lobo,* The World Publishing Co., 1957; *If the South Had Won the Civil War,* Bantam Books, 1961; *Spirit Lake,* The World Publishing Co., 1961; *Valley Forge,* M. Evans and Company, Inc., 1975.

Born: February 4, 1904, Webster City, Iowa. *Educated:* Webster City High School. *Family:* Florence Irene, wife; Layne Kantor, daughter; Thomas MacKinlay, son. *Iowa Connection:* born, educated, and worked in Iowa.

Honors: O. Henry Award, 1935, for "Silent Grow the Guns." Pulitzer Prize, 1956, *Andersonville.* Medal of Freedom, Freedom Foundation, 1956. Honorary D. Litt. Grinnell College, 1957. Honorary D. Litt. Drake University, 1958. Honorary D. Litt. Lincoln College, 1959. Honorary D. Litt. Ripon College, 1961. Honorary D. Litt. Iowa Wesleyan College, 1961.

Karl L.
KING (1891–1971)
World-renowned band music composer

Karl L. King, America's march king. Photo courtesy of Fort Museum and Frontier Village, Fort Dodge.

Bandleaders say that somewhere on this planet, at any given time, some band is striking up one of Karl King's tunes.

Karl King wasn't a child prodigy in music. In fact, Karl was 14 years old before he had saved enough money to buy a trumpet. But once he had a horn, the music never quit. In a few months he had composed his first march. But when he discovered he didn't have what musicians call a trumpet lip, he bought a baritone horn and continued writing band music.

By the time Karl was 17, a publisher accepted one of the stream of band marches that flowed from his prolific pen. Over the next-half century, Karl King wrote between 300–400 band marches, waltzes, overtures, intermezzos, serenades, dirges, rags and galops. But his greatest specialty was the band march, especially the march that fueled the circus.

At 19 Karl left Ohio to join the circus band of Robinson's

Famous Circus. In two years he moved on to the Sells-Floto Circus, and the following year he played baritone horn with Barnum & Bailey's Circus. Two years later Karl became bandmaster for the Sells-Floto and Buffalo Bill Combined Show; a year after that, he rejoined the Barnum & Bailey Circus as bandmaster. His classic "Barnum & Bailey's Favorite," was written during this time.

In 1920 newly married Karl King went shopping for a band position where he could settle down, compose, maybe sell some music and raise a family. An ad placed in *Musician's Journal* was spotted by an alert Fort Dodger who invited King to guest-conduct the Fort Dodge Municipal Band.

Both King and the city liked each other, and he settled in for a half-century stint to write the music that has been said to "express the spirit of America." On the surface it appears that Karl King joined the circus, but what really happened was the circus joined Karl King.

FOUNDING MEMBER of the American Bandmasters Association and the Iowa Bandmasters Association. Played an important role in regard to the Iowa Band Law. Director of the Iowa State Fair Band for over 50 years.

Born: February 21, 1891, Painterville, Ohio. *Educated:* high school in Ohio; mostly self-taught musically. *Family:* Ruth, wife; Karl, Jr., son. *Iowa Connection:* lived and composed in Fort Dodge for over half a century.

Honors: 1971 Edwin Franco Goldman Award from the American School Bandmasters Association (despite having never taught in schools). 1967 Distinguished Service Award, Kappa Kappa Psi, National Honorary Band Fraternity. 1966 Elected to the Society of European Stage Actors and Composers. 1962 Elected to the Academy of Wind and Percussion Arts, the highest honor that can come to a band director. 1962 Karl L. King Viaduct, spanning the Des Moines River in Fort Dodge, named for him. 1953 Honorary Doctor of Music, Phillips University, Enid, Oklahoma.

Nile

KINNICK (1918–1943)

Heisman trophy winner

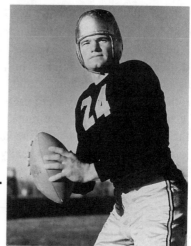

*Nile Kinnick, the cornbelt comet.
Photo courtesy of University of
Iowa Photo Service.*

The smallest guy on the football squad won a Heisman Trophy in exactly 480 minutes.

Nile Kinnick was the smallest guy in about any room. He weighed only 170 pounds, stood 5'7" tall, was the slowest running back on the Iowa football squad and played almost every minute of eight football games. When the final gun sounded, he had earned a clean sweep of every major football award in America.

Nile Kinnick was the date for the girl next door, for he was the boy next door—handsome, bright, shy, unassuming, clean-cut—the kind of young man every father wishes his daughter would find. Nile's career in high school was filled with winning, both on the football field and in the classroom.

After high school graduation, Kinnick was undecided where to pursue college. He finally narrowed his choices to the Universities of Minnesota and Iowa. Iowa won the toss, not because it had a great football team, but because its football program was as depressed as the economy of the Great Depression gripping the nation.

Minnesota's program, on the other hand, was flush with success. Shrewdly, Kinnick reasoned that there was more to gain in turning a losing program around than in riding the coattails of a winning program.

His freshman year was promising, but hidden from the public behind a ban on first-year players competing at the varsity level. His sophomore year was a triumph, ending with being named to the United Press All Big Ten Team. Kinnick's junior year was a failure, for he injured an ankle in the opening game, and the year's record of 1–7 recovered no better than he did.

Many teammates thought Kinnick's sprained ankle was broken, but no one knew because he was a Christian Scientist and refused to allow his ankle to be examined, X-rayed or treated. Despite that hindrance he punted 41 times during the year, averaging 41.1 yards per punt, good enough for fourth best in the nation.

The winds of change were upon Iowa football, and in November of 1938 Iowa fans cheered the news that Dr. Eddie Anderson had accepted the Iowa coaching challenge. Anderson had been born and raised in Iowa, educated at Notre Dame, and had led Holy Cross to national recognition. He brought with him not only impeccable credentials but a new spirit of winning.

The Anderson formula worked. During the first two games of the 1939 season, Iowa scored more points than it had in the entire previous year. Then came the single loss, in the third game, which was a respectable loss to a Michigan team headed by Tom Harmon, the Heisman trophy winner in 1940. Then came four wins in a row, with especially sweet victories over nationally acclaimed Notre Dame and the vaunted Minnesota team.

During most of the games, many of the players went the full 60 minutes, earning the team title of the "Iron Men." But Nile Kinnick became the center of attention not only for the eyes of Iowans but for those of the nation. Sportswriters knowing good copy when they heard it printed reams of stories about this phenomenal player who did it all—punt, pass, kick, tackle, intercept, run and play—as though he were the biggest man on the field instead of the smallest.

The '39 football season was the stuff of legends, and the Kinnick square-jawed grin reflected a persona the public loved. He was a genuine hero, and every accolade that could be heaped, every prize that could be given, every award that could be granted cascaded onto his small but solid shoulders.

After a hectic year of awards ceremonies, Nile entered Iowa Law School, just as World War II entered the world's consciousness. In September 1942, after two years of law school, Nile Kinnick entered the Naval Air Corps to become a fighter pilot.

At 10 o'clock on Monday morning, June 2, 1943, off the Gulf of Paria between Venezuela and Trinidad, after experiencing an oil leak, Ensign Nile Kinnick made a routine wheels-up landing on a calm sea, within four miles of his carrier, the *Lexington,* and in full view of other pilots. A fellow pilot saw him emerge from the cockpit, and radioed that all seemed well.

Within a minute the plane sank, leaving only a few paint chips and an oil slick for the rescue party which arrived in minutes. America had lost one of its greatest All-Americans.

In 1972, the University of Iowa accorded Kinnick its highest honor. University officials renamed the UI football stadium *Kinnick Stadium,* a fitting tribute to one of the greatest players ever to play on its turf.

_____

FOOTBALL LEGEND.

Born: July 9, 1918, Adel, Iowa. *Educated:* B.A. in economics, UI, 1939. *Iowa Connection:* born, raised, educated, and earned all his awards in Iowa.

Honors: Phi Beta Kappa. Captain of the All-Americans, football, 1939. Maxwell Award, 1939. Walter Camp Trophy, 1939. AP Athlete of the Year award, 1939 (finishing ahead of baseball player Joe DiMaggio and heavyweight boxer Joe Louis). Chicago Tribune Silver Football Award, 1939. College All-Star game (top vote-getter), 1939. Order of Artus, school of commerce honor society, 1939. Senior Class President, College of Liberal Arts, UI, 1939. Iowa Athletic Board Cup, for excellence in scholarship and athletics, 1939. President of all the 10 colleges at UI, 1939. Athlete of the Year, UI, 1939. Most Valuable Player, voted by teammates, 1939. John P. Laffey law scholarship, UI, 1939.

Mauricio

L ASANSKY (1914–)

World-renowned printmaker

If Mauricio Lasansky hadn't gone deaf you might be listening to his musical genius today, rather than viewing his printmaking.

Engraving bank notes kept bread on the Lasansky table and provided table talk, as well. But young Mauricio failed to allow talk of the artistry of engraving to sway him from his wish to follow the musical arts. Then tragedy struck—Mauricio developed a hearing problem so severe his musical career faded into quiet.

Mauricio turned to sculpting and, upon graduation from art school in Argentina, studied printmaking. By the time he was 22 he had moved to Cordoba, Argentina, to direct the Free School of Fine Arts and attain national prominence. Fortunately, he exhibited often, and during one exhibit, the director of the Metropolitan Museum of Art in New York City recommended him for a Guggenheim fellowship.

Mauricio seized the opportunity for study in New York, and on arrival, began combing through the entire print collection of the Guggenheim museum, something no one had done before. After a year, Mauricio petitioned for a second year's Guggenheim, an unusual request that was granted at once. He sent for his wife and children and began a second year of mastering his metier.

In the early 1940s there were few printmaking opportunities for talented printmakers. But Virgil Hancher, head of the University of Iowa, had already decided that the arts were worthy of graduate pursuit and had commissioned a search to replace the head of the UI printmaking department, Emil Ganso, who had died suddenly.

Fortunately Mauricio wanted time and quiet to develop his talent, and despite offers from Albuquerque and Chicago, chose Iowa, saying, "Now that's America!" Mauricio accepted a two-year appointment.

In his first years at Iowa Lasansky developed his talent in two directions. One dealt with portraits depicting the different aspects of human dignity, a whimsical, warm, playful series of prints that evoke smiles and good feelings. The other was an approach to deeper emotions, with prints that touched on brooding themes or social commentary.

In his teaching he revamped the department, equipped it with new presses and studios, worked with students to help them find their own method of making a statement through mastery of the craft, and taught his students the appropriate habits and attitudes to succeed as a printmaker.

In the 1960s Lasansky felt a need to express a statement that had been boiling within him. He had shared the world's outrage at the Nazi Holocaust of World War II, and ideas that had been working in his mind began to take shape in his drawings.

As a result a series of 30 drawings was assembled which read, much as a cartoon serial, from first to last. An additional three-panel triptych concludes Lasansky's powerful statement. This series has been exhibited throughout the world as the *Nazi Drawings*. Probably no other series of drawings ever evoked the emotional flow that these powerful works command.

There can be no doubt, weighing the creative genius of this man, that had events turned out differently, we would be currently listening to his compositions in music as avidly as we view his compositions on paper. True genius is never stifled and Iowan Mauricio Lasansky is pure genius.

> Dignity is not a symbol bestowed on man, nor does the word itself possess force. Man's dignity is a force and the only *modus vivendi* by which man and his history survive. When mid-twentieth century Germany did not let man live and die with this right, man became an animal. No matter

how technologically advanced or sophisticated, when a man negates this divine right he not only becomes self-destructive, but castrates his history and poisons our future. That is what the *Nazi Drawings* are about.

—MAURICIO LASANSKY

PRINTMAKER OF RENOWN.

Born: October 12, 1914, Buenos Aires, Argentina. *Educated:* sculpturing studies to age 19 in Buenos Aires; graduate work in printmaking at the Superior School of Fine Arts; studied the entire print collection of the Metropolitan Museum of Art, New York City. *Family:* Emilia, wife; William, Leonardo, Phillip and Tomas, sons; Rocio, Jimena, daughters. *Iowa Connection:* lived, taught, drew and printed for a half-century in Iowa.

Honors: His work is displayed in hundreds of public and private collections around the world and he has exhibited in scores of museums worldwide. The many prizes and honors he has won include five Guggenheim Fellowships (1943, 1944, 1945, 1953 and 1963) more than any other recipient, dozens of Purchase Prizes, and Citations from art groups around the world. He has received Honorary degrees from Iowa Wesleyan College, Pacific Lutheran University, Carleton College, Coe College and the Associated Colleges of the Twin Cities. The Lasansky Wing at the Cedar Rapids Art Museum and the UI Lasansky Room house permanent collections of his works. He was installed as an Academician of the National Academy of Arts and Design, New York City, 1990. He has been cited numerous times by the Governor of Iowa and in 1991 was awarded the Certificate of Recognition for Distinguished Service to the State of Iowa. He has been named the UI Virgil M. Hancher Distinguished Professor of Art and Professor Emeritus.

Dave
LENNOX (1856–1947)
Invented the sheet metal furnace

Dave Lennox, a fire in his furnace.

Dave Lennox loved simple solutions and hated boring repetitions.

That's why he invented ingenious things and let others set up production lines. Dave never wanted his days bogged down by doing something he thought was dumb, like making the same product over and over just because a person could get rich doing it.

Dave was an idea man, a right-side brain guy who could create ideas and translate them into products. Left-side brain people could take over the factories, and deal with production schedules and sales strategies, as far as Dave was concerned.

When most children were in the fourth grade, studying spelling and arithmetic, Dave was a rivet beater in a railroad boiler shop in Aurora, Illinois. Dave's father had died in action during the Civil War.

When the family moved to Chicago, where his mother ran a grocery, young Dave repaired sewing machines in a shop behind his mother's store. That job kept him busy until two of his mother's customers appealed to the restless nature of a 24-year-old man and induced Dave to move to Marshalltown, Iowa.

Dave set up a repair shop and hunted business to help him meet the $7 a month rent. His first job was right around the corner. A Marshalltown businessman ran a barbed wire plant and was looking for someone to swiftly cut staples, which are the spurs on a barbed wire fence.

Dave took on the challenge by perfecting a machine to build the staples. He then took the barbed wire production plant apart and put it together in a way that made it work better than ever. Word spread quickly that Dave Lennox could fix about anything.

A stonemason placed an order for a trowel for Dave to make. The trowel was made so well that masons from far and wide began ordering Dave's incredibly good trowels. But, having created the technique, Dave tired of the production end of the business. He turned it over to two employees and went on to grander goals.

Other business came his way. Alternately, Dave's creative genius focused on steam boilers, the gasoline engine, and various manufacturing opportunities that people brought to Dave. By now he had brought his mother and his brother to Marshalltown to enjoy his success.

In 1895, two men from Oskaloosa established a heating company in Marshalltown with the intent of making central heating furnaces for homes. This was a novel concept in those days, held back largely due to the inefficient cast iron furnaces in use. A cast iron furnace warped under constant heating and cooling, cracking open joints and allowing fumes and soot to enter the system and spread through the house.

The two men had an idea for a sheet metal furnace that couldn't leak. They came to Dave for help and Dave obliged. Soon the two would-be entrepreneurs found themselves underfinanced and had to give up their business to Dave in payment for his work. Dave promptly redesigned the furnace so that it worked as intended and could be produced profitably.

Once more, Dave took no interest in selling the same item again and again, so he sold one item, one time: the furnace company that bore his name. In 1904, Dave sold the Lennox Furnace Company for $40,000, a fortune by any standard of the day.

The rest of his life, Dave continued to work in a small shop behind his home. He died, in Marshalltown, in 1947 at the age of 90. Dave Lennox was personally responsible for most of the manufacturing community that grew up in Marshalltown. The two men who sold him on coming to Marshalltown did Iowa, and Dave Lennox, one enormous favor.

INVENTED a machine to make barbed wires. Founded the Marshalltown Trowel Company. Pioneered work on building steam boilers. Invented the first gyratory rock crusher. Invented numerous machines. Designed a revolutionary sheet metal furnace.

Born: April 15, 1856, Detroit, Michigan. *Educated:* only a few years of grade school. *Family:* a wife, 2 sons and 2 daughters. *Iowa Connection:* lived, worked and invented in Marshalltown.

Monsignor Luigi

L IGUTTI (1895–1983)

Founded the National Catholic Rural Life Conference

It was 1912, and the monsignor got off the train in Des Moines.

Actually, he wasn't yet a monsignor. He was a scared 17-year-old Italian lad eager to become a Catholic priest, frightened to be so far from home. Within five years he had accomplished his immediate goals, being ordained at the incredibly early age of 22 years.

Father Luigi was assigned to Des Moines Catholic High School, which later became known as Dowling High School. After several years of teaching, he accepted a three-point charge, serving Magnolia, Woodbine and Logan parishes in Harrison County.

It was a fortunate placement, for Luigi learned the problems of rural Iowans during the years after World War I. He was then sent to Granger, Iowa, a parish that served not only rural and small-town Iowans but people from the county coal camps. Here Luigi saw squalid living conditions forced upon mining families, where opportunity for the young was unheard of.

He saw people existing on unwanted but urgent welfare relief. He saw these pockets of poverty become seedbeds breeding crime. He saw failed opportunities for young people to climb out of their squalor. And he was struck by the incredible juxtaposition of the rich Iowa soil and the bleak lives growing on it.

In 1932 Luigi addressed a conference of Catholic Church officials in Omaha in which he described "the horrible situation in the Iowa mining camps." He suggested the government should

81

Iowa Pride

enable these people to live on a plot of ground where they could grow vegetables and healthier families. He called for the government to make suitable homes available on that plot, where miners could give their families decent opportunities for their lives.

Word of the idea reached Eleanor Roosevelt, who immediately urged the President to approve the novel proposal. The Granger Homestead project was the result, and, within a year, 51 families were relocated, each on about five acres of ground surrounding a sturdy house, which they lease-purchased from the government. The repayment rate on these federal loans was almost 100 percent, an astounding record.

Word of this project spread across the land and Monsignor Ligutti became the most famous priest of his day. During this time, he helped found, and for 18 years headed, the National Catholic Rural Life Conference, headquartered in Des Moines. From this platform he advocated the small family farm, soil conservation, fair prices for farmers and efforts to feed the world's hungry from the bounty of Iowa crops.

Monsignor Ligutti went on to become an advisor to three Popes, who called him their "County Agent" after they heard the role Iowa County Agents play in serving people in rural areas. In his papal advisory role, Monsignor Ligutti became the Vatican's permanent observer to the United Nations Food and Agricultural Organization.

Over the door of his home in Rome, Monsignor Ligutti displayed a bumper sticker that proclaimed one of his profoundest beliefs. It said, "I'm Proud to be a Farmer!"

Monsignor Luigi Ligutti grew more than crops in the Iowa soil he tilled.

FOUNDED THE Granger Homestead Project.

Born: March 21, 1895, Province of Udine, Italy. *Educated:* St. Ambrose College, 1912. Ordained a Roman Catholic Priest, St. Mary's Seminary, Baltimore, Maryland. *Iowa Connection:* educated, worked, lived and served the poor in Iowa.

Honor: 1980, The Iowa Award.

E.F. LINDQUIST (1901–1978)

Created the Iowa Tests of Basic Skills

All the kids in Iowa take the Iowa Tests of Basic Skills. The kids in other states take the same test and call it the same thing.

The Brain Derby began and died in Iowa, but it left a legacy that has never stopped growing. The Derby began as a contest between schools, pitting students' minds against one another, to win glory for the students, their teachers and their schools.

The time: the early 1930s. The place: UI. The participants: 1,000 students annually. The cofounder, author of the original tests and program director: Dr. E.F. Lindquist.

Like many terrific ideas, this one became mired in its own success. Winning the championship became such a coveted prize that soon teachers were teaching for rote memory and accumulation of facts, instead of teaching students how to think.

Despite the program's success at stimulating learning in A and B students, E.F. was startled to learn that some C, D and F students astounded their teachers by scoring at the top in the objective tests of these competitions. This showed that objective testing could earlier identify students who were capable of greater academic promise.

Basing his work on this finding, E.F. used the tests as a proving ground to improve techniques of objective testing. The Iowa Every-Pupil Test grew out of these findings and soon began to attract interest from around the nation. The new tests emphasized understanding concepts and downplayed testing for detailed data.

In the fall of 1935, the Iowa Tests of Basic Skills (ITBS) were introduced across Iowa, at the junior high level. For the first time, norms were developed and the pupil's progress could be plotted against those statistical values. The program was an immediate success. In 1940, the tests were extended to grades three through five, and by now were being published nationwide.

The next test to develop was the Iowa Tests of Educational Development (ITED) which gave unique teaching advantages along with the opportunity to estimate the growth in a student's development from year to year.

With all that testing, tests by the carload poured in, prompting E.F. to conceive of a grading machine. Within several years, a prototype machine graded 4,000 tests an hour. Later improvements pushed that number up to 100,000 sheets of tests graded in a single hour, even when the tests were in 40-page booklets.

Early in World War II, the military wanted a general test for service personnel who had not finished high school, but had an equivalent education. The General Educational Development (GED) test was born under Dr. Lindquist's guidance.

In 1957, the National Merit Scholarship Corporation used Lindquist's testing techniques to award scholarships to college-bound students. As a spinoff of the Iowa Testing Program, the American College Testing (ACT) program was founded under Dr. Lindquist's leadership. He had already served on the Board of Directors of the College Board for the Scholastic Aptitude Test (SAT).

Many educators give Dr. Lindquist credit for bringing Iowa to these academic heights among the 50 states:

• Since 1910, Iowa has the nation's highest literacy rate.
• Iowans read more books per capita.
• Iowa students score in the top 2 percent in SAT tests.
• Iowa students top the nation in math skills scores.
• 88 percent of Iowa high school students graduate.
• 68 percent of Iowa high school grads go on to college.
• A higher percentage of Iowa high school graduates attend college than in any other state.

DIRECTED the Iowa Testing Program. Invented a high-speed test scoring machine. Directed development of the General Education Development tests (GED) for the United States Armed Forces Institute. Editor of the National Merit Scholarship Qualifying Test. Founded The American College Testing (ACT) program. Director of the College Entrance Examination Board (CEEB), the ruling body for the Scholastic Aptitude Test (SAT). Author of a half-dozen texts on testing procedures. Organized the Measurement Research Center (MRC), the world's largest processor of educational tests. Inaugurated the Iowa Educational Information Center (IEIC). Established the Iowa Measurement and Research Foundation (IMRF).

Born: June 4, 1901, Gowrie, Iowa. *Educated:* A.B., Augustana College, 1922; Ph.D., UI, 1927. *Family:* Mary Liebig, wife. *Iowa Connection:* born, raised, educated, taught, and created in Iowa.

Honors: 1970, The E.F. Lindquist Wing, in the American College Testing building. 1970, The E.F. Lindquist Chair in Educational Measurement, UI. 1967, Educational Leadership Award, jointly presented by the American Education Research Association and Phi Delta Kappa. 1964, Honorary Doctor of Letters, Augustana College. 1960, Outstanding Achievement Award, Augustana College. 1956, Phi Delta Kappa, honorary professional fraternity, named him one of 31 outstanding educational leaders from 1900–1956.

Lester
MARTIN (1895–1963)
Invented direct mail advertising

In 1919, Lester Martin had an itch for success but he really didn't know how to scratch it.

Lester viewed his job as a clerk in the Story County treasurer's office as a dead end. Until one day a Detroit auto maker asked for a list of car owners who had applied for licenses in Story County. The county treasurer didn't want to be bothered by the request and turned it over to Lester.

As Lester typed up the requested data, his big idea struck. If a car manufacturer was interested in car owners' names in Story County, why wouldn't he be interested in names from other counties? And wouldn't other merchants like those same lists?

Lester confided his great idea to A.M. Anderson, a friend who was home from college. Anderson brought avid enthusiasm to the venture. After a few months, Donald Fowler joined the two, and soon they were compiling lists from adjoining counties, gradually spreading their operations across the state, then across the Midwest, doing business as the M & F Mailing System.

Within two years salesmen were hired to compile and sell lists all around the country, and the direct mail concept of advertising was born.

The cash-flow problems that plague fast-growing businesses also hit Lester, who had taken over sole ownership of the company. To solve this problem he sold a half-interest in the business to his brother-in-law, D.L. Harrington. Within months the company employed hundreds of people to hand-address mailing pieces. In 1921, the company posted 30,000,000 pieces of mail.

In February of 1922 the Reuben H. Donnelley Corporation of Chicago spotted the growing company and negotiated a purchase. With the advent of the direct mail advertising business, the United States Post Office was forced to expand and adopt new techniques of mail handling, all because an Iowa entrepreneur put his own stamp on a new industry.

USED LISTS of car owners to launch direct mail advertising.

Born: August 24, 1895, Nevada, Iowa. *Educated:* Nevada public schools. *Family:* Florence, wife; Jean, daughter. *Iowa Connection:* born, raised, educated, worked and invented in Iowa.

Fred L. MAYTAG (1857–1937)

Developed the agitator washing machine

Fred L. Maytag, brightened the Monday blues. Photo courtesy of the Maytag Archives.

Because it hasn't been done is no reason to believe it can't.
—F.L. MAYTAG

Fred Maytag always believed he could do anything he set his mind to. In the 1880s Fred got a job in a farm implement store, and before the year was out he bought part ownership. After several years spent selling farm implements Fred bought a lumberyard.

One day his friend G.W. Parsons came to buy lumber for a new invention he was working on, an invention that would save farmers' hands from harm during reaping. Fred and G.W. put together a sample. When it worked, together with A.H. and W.C. Bergman, F.L.'s brothers-in-law, they formed a company to market the invention.

The financial panic of 1894 and 1895 gripped the nation so hard that The Parsons Band Cutter and Self Feeder Company barely survived. But by 1901, the company had ridden out the depression and had become the world's largest manufacturer of threshing machine feeders. Other farm implements were added to the product line and in a few years the company had a work force of almost 100 people and was the largest employer in Newton.

In Minnesota Howard Snyder was such a fine salesman and mechanic for Fred that he was hired to develop new products for the Maytag Company, as Fred called his new wholly owned entity. While business was great, winter downtime hurt his workers, so Fred and Howard scoured for year-round products.

Since his whole focus had been toward the farmer, Fred looked at various farm jobs, trying to find a need to fulfill. It was not long until he and Snyder found opportunity. They built a washing machine to take the backbreaking Monday blues of scrubbing boards and lye soap–soaked hands away from farmers' wives.

The Pastime washing machine debuted in 1907. It featured a tub of cypress wood. On top of the washer was a lid with a crank on the outside and four wooden pegs beneath. When the lid was closed, the turning crank dragged the clothes through soapy water, against the corrugated sides of the tub.

In 1909 the Hired Girl replaced the Pastime. It included a wringer on top, and a belt and pulley arrangement allowed this washer to be operated by a belt from an engine. In 1911, Fred and Howard brought out the Maytag Power Washer which boasted another company first, a wringer that could be swung over rinse tubs.

Finally, in 1911, Maytag introduced its first electric washer. Four years later, the gasoline-powered machine was added to the product line. By then, Snyder and Maytag had focused their attentions on how to build a better washing machine, their goal being a 30-inch, 40-pound tub that the industry said could not be cast. "Saying that it can't be done is only an acknowledgement that there is still left an obstacle for someone else's ingenuity," Fred noted.

At the end of the decade the "washer that couldn't be built" rolled off Fred's assembly lines and the Maytag Company vaulted to world dominance. In 1917, Fred and Snyder stunned the industry, and reversed all washing principles, by inventing a bottom agitator which dragged the water through the clothes, not the clothes through the water. Production began in 1922 and sales soared.

Within 600 days the Maytag Corporation grew from one of the leading American washing machine manufacturers to first place in the world. Sales established new records almost daily. By 1924 the Maytag Corporation was twice the size of its nearest competitor.

On October 12, 1926, five solid trainloads of Maytag washers were shipped from Newton to Philadelphia in the world's largest single shipment of merchandise. In May of 1927, that record was eclipsed by an eight-trainload shipment to the same destination.

The Maytag Corporation endured on the principles Fred Maytag established in the beginning. Find a need. Solve the problem. Put the highest quality goods in the users' hands. And have one of the highest-recognition advertising programs ever created in Ol' Lonely, the Maytag repairman who hasn't much to do because Maytags just don't break down.

> Nothing is sold until it is in the hands of a satisfied user.
> —F.L.M.

BROUGHT TOGETHER the team to change America's home-laundering habits. Coinvented many farm implements.

Born: July 14, 1857, Independence, Iowa. *Educated:* 1869–1874 attended school for 20 months. Found school difficult. Possibly attended Northwestern College in Naperville, Illinois, for one term. *Family:* Dena Bergman, wife; Elmer and Lewis, sons; Freda and Louise, daughters. *Iowa Connection:* born, raised, educated, worked and created in Iowa.

Honors: 1926, Doctor of Laws, Parsons College, Fairfield. 1926, Gold Medallion, Home Appliance Dealers of America, for "his outstanding services in originating and manufacturing home appliances."

James Alan

McPHERSON (1943–)

Pulitzer Prize-winning author,
Guggenheim Fellow and
MacArthur Fellow

It was heavy-duty preparation for writing grim stories of desperate characters, people who deal with their situations by raging impotently against factors out of their control. All it took McPherson to reach that writing level was a Bachelor of Arts degree from Morris Brown University, an LL.B. from Harvard University Law School, and a UI Master of Fine Arts degree.

Actually, his writing talent surfaced during law school, when McPherson carried off the first prize in a contest sponsored by the *Atlantic Monthly* and garnered national publication status. He later became a contributing editor of the *Atlantic Monthly,* and the magazine, in conjunction with Little, Brown, also published two of his early books.

His first collection of short stories, *Hue and Cry,* was thought by the *Times Literary Supplement* critic to unveil "mostly desperate ... mostly lost figures in the urban nightmare of violence, rage, and bewilderment that is currently America."

Irving Howe, wrote in *Harper's* that McPherson "maintains a healthy distance between himself and his characters, a feat not noted in many story-tellers." Granville Hicks, in *Saturday Review,* agreed, but saw that McPherson sympathizes deeply with the victims.

Iowa Pride ─────────────────

James Alan McPherson is a rare person, an Iowan who is one of the nation's foremost African-American authors.

──────────────────────────────

PULITZER PRIZE-winning author.

Born: September 16, 1943, Savannah, Georgia. *Education:* Morgan State University, 1963-64; Morris Brown College, B.A., 1965; Harvard University, LL.B., 1968; University of Iowa, M.F.A., 1969; Yale Law School, visiting scholar, 1978. *Iowa Connection:* Educated and taught in Iowa.

Honors: First prize, *Atlantic* short story contest, 1965, for "Gold Coast"; grant from Atlantic Monthly Press and Little, Brown, 1969; National Institute of Arts and Letters award in literature, 1970; Guggenheim Fellow, 1972-73; Pulitzer Prize, 1978, for *Elbow Room: Stories;* MacArthur Fellowship, 1981. *Writings: Huse and Cry: Short Stories,* (editor with Miller Williams) *Railroad: Trains and Train People in American Culture, Elbow Room: Stories, The Stories of Breece D'J Pancake.* "We Will Go Down the Line Together", essay in *Yale Review,* "Saturday Night, and Sunday Morning", essay in *Witness Magazine,* "Listening to the Lower Frequencies", essay in *World Literature Today,* "Ivy Day in the Empty Room", essay in *The Best American Essays,* "Crabcakes" in *Double-Take.* Essays, stories and reviews in *Atlantic, The Harvard Advocate, Ploughshares, Nimrod, University of Toledo Law Review, New York Times (Magazine and Op-ed page), The Nation, Playboy, Harvard Magazine, Esquire, Reader's Digest, Newsday, Tikkun, The Atlanta Constitution, The Washington Post, Atlanta Magazine, World Literature Today, Subaru (Japan), Double-Take.* Other essays and stories appear in anthologies such as *The Best American Short Stories, O'Henry Prize Stories, The Best American Essays, The Prevailing South, Southern Magazine, A World Unsuspected, Lure and Loathing.* Contributor to *Cutting Edges, Black Insights: Significant Literature by Afro-Americans, Book for Boston, Speaking for You, A World Unsuspected.* Also contributor to *New Black Voices, Atlantic, Esquire, New York Times Magazine, Playboy, Reader's Digest, Callaloo.* Editor of special edition of *Iowa Review,* Winter, 1984.

E.T.

MEREDITH (1876–1928)

Created national magazines

E.T. Meredith, publishing pioneer and magazine mogul.

Whose they got married, they received a magazine as a wedding gift, with the intriguing and cryptic notation: "Sink or swim."

The gift wasn't a single issue of the magazine, it was the entire *Farmer's Tribune,* a small Populist publication that E.T. Meredith had worked on while attending school. The paper had enjoyed lackluster success, and E.T.'s uncle knew that the *Tribune* could as easily fail as survive. The challenge was a sporting dare to E.T. and his bride.

E.T. promptly dropped the *Tribune's* Populist views, redesigned the layout and format, and blanketed the state with free copies as a promotional device. Circulation responded and, while the magazine didn't enjoy huge success, the paper at least kept its head above water. But E.T. had his editorial visor set on higher sights—a publication of more significance. The *Tribune* was sold and the first issue of *Successful Farming* was published in October 1902.

E.T.'s wife Edna shouldered her share of the struggle to turn *Successful Farming* into successful publishing. As the months rolled by, the pair began growth that finally reached a point where a new building was needed, one dedicated to publishing the young couple's dream.

Going into heavy debt, E.T. and Edna built their core building and now *Successful Farming* began to live up to its name. Once he brought two successive trainloads of Eastern advertising people to see at close range the great advertising opportunities his magazine, now with a million subscribers, presented to their businesses.

As *Successful Farming* grew, E.T. questioned why he and Edna were missing the urban families. While *Successful Farming* gave service information to farm families, why not have a companion publication offer the same information to people in the cities?

Why not indeed? In September 1922, the first edition of *Fruit, Garden and Home* was born in their new building, with 150,000 copies of 52 pages each flowing off the presses. By August, 1924, the magazine was renamed and *Better Homes and Gardens* made its first appearance. By the 1990s 7,600,000 copies monthly, of 200 pages each, were reaching the homes of America.

At age 44, E.T. Meredith had founded one of the largest publishing houses west of the Mississippi. He had served as president of the Associated Advertising Clubs of the World. He had served a term as Secretary of Agriculture under President Woodrow Wilson.

He had lent his prestige, power and resources to the 4-H movement, founded by fellow Iowan Jessie Field Shambaugh. To spur 4-H growth, E.T. loaned thousands of dollars to deserving youngsters—taking as collateral their signatures alone—for them to buy livestock and gain firsthand farm experience.

At the time of his death, at age 51, E.T. Meredith was being considered as the Democratic presidential candidate.

One feature of the advertising policy that E.T. laid down, early in the growth of his two flagship magazines, set his publishing empire apart from others. In the very first issue of *Successful Farming,* E.T. wrote: "We believe ... every advertisement (in this magazine) ... is backed by a responsible person. But to make doubly sure, we will make good any loss."

For the first time in history, a magazine publisher accepted direct responsibility for his advertisers. Meredith's unique guarantee has remained unchanged through the years and has fostered the credibility of America's favorite home magazine.

Iowan Edwin Thomas Meredith knew what makes an American magazine tick.

SERVED AS Secretary of Agriculture under President Woodrow Wilson. President, Associated Advertising Clubs of the World. Helped establish the 4-H movement (see Jessie Field Shambaugh).

Born: December 23, 1876, Avoca, Iowa. *Educated:* Marne, Iowa, High School, attended Highland Park College in Des Moines. *Family:* Edna, wife. *Iowa Connection:* born, raised, educated, worked and lived in Iowa.

Honor: Advertising Hall of Fame: one of the first 10 men so named.

Viola Babcock

MILLER (1871–1937)

Founded the
Iowa Highway Patrol

W hen "Ola" Miller's husband Alex died, she took up the reins he had held in the Iowa Democratic Party. She thought she was being a "martyr for a cause." Her husband had been an unsuccessful candidate for governor. But in 1926 the Democratic landslide swept her into office as Iowa's Secretary of State, and she became the first woman to sit on the Iowa executive council.

Ola was born on a farm in Washington County in 1871. After she graduated from Iowa Wesleyan College in Mt. Pleasant, she married Alex Miller, editor of the *Washington Democrat*. An ardent leader in the suffrage movement, she became prominent in local affairs, including the PEO sisterhood, which she served as both state and national president.

As Secretary of State, Ola developed a deep concern for highway safety, spearheading efforts to establish driver's license exams and automobile safety programs. In 1934 she expanded the duties of the 15 motor vehicle inspectors to include enforcement of safety regulations.

The following year, the state legislature created the Iowa Highway Patrol, with 50 men patrolling the state in 30 autos and 12 motorcycles. Her third term was cut short in 1937 when she died of pneumonia. The entire Iowa Highway Patrol honored her memory by attending her funeral as a group.

Iowa's Secretary of State and founder of the Iowa Highway Patrol.

Born: March 1, 1871, Washington, Iowa. *Education:* Iowa Wesleyan College, Mt. Pleasant, Iowa. *Family:* Alex Miller, husband; Barbara, Ophelia, daughters. *Iowa Connection:* born, raised, educated in Iowa.

Honors: First woman ever elected to office of Secretary of State of Iowa, 1932. Established the first Iowa Highway Safety Patrol. National president of the P.E.O. Sisterhood. Was inducted into the Iowa Women's Hall of Fame in 1975.

Clark R.

MOLLENHOFF (1921–1991)

Nationally known
investigative reporter

He was a big booming man, the kind of person people call a "take charge" kind of guy.

That may have been why his teammates chose him to captain the Drake football team. By contrast, he wrote poetry good enough that President Ronald Reagan quoted him, twice! Clark Mollenhoff, all 6'4" and 250 pounds of him, was a giant among Iowans in many ways.

As a youngster Clark read an investigative book, *Shame of the Cities,* and at once planned the direction of his life. He never wavered from that course.

To learn his reportorial skills while attending Drake law school, he worked for *The Des Moines Register.* After naval service in World War II, he spearheaded investigations of mismanagement and corruption in Polk County. From there Mollenhoff went on to study American government and history as a Nieman Fellow at Harvard University.

These credentials propelled him into Washington, D.C., where his investigations included in-depth studies of virtually every government department, as well as six regulatory agencies. His dogged obstinance, and brilliant insight, resulted in the ultimate prize for journalism, a Pulitzer Prize.

In 1969 Mollenhoff surprised his colleagues by taking a leave of absence to become a Presidential Ombudsman for President Richard Nixon. He reportedly left that job because he did not believe his ideas were being received with the same conviction that he felt for them.

For six years Mollenhoff was then chief of the Washington Bureau for *The Des Moines Register,* finally leaving for a position as Professor of Journalism at Washington and Lee University. In his professorship, he wrote a syndicated column and collaborated with columnist Jack Anderson on investigative writings.

For the remainder of his career, Mollenhoff wrote expose books about government, focusing upon presidents Nixon, Ford, Carter and Kennedy. His next-to-final book, which many considered to be his finest, revealed the little-known fact that Dr. John Atanasoff, of ISU, contrary to others' claims, was the father of the digital computer (see the chapter on John Vincent Atanasoff). His last book, interestingly, was a volume of poems.

Clark Mollenhoff was a literary giant among investigative reporters.

AUTHORED 11 political investigative books. Syndicated columnist, political lecturer, Washington correspondent.

Born: April 16, 1921, Burnside, Iowa. *Educated:* Webster City High School; Drake University, 1944, LL.B.; 1968, J.D. *Family:* Georgia, wife; Gjore Jean and Jacquelin, daughters; Clark, son; Jane, wife. *Iowa Connection:* born, raised, educated, and worked in Iowa.

Honors: National Collegiate Who's Who, Drake University, 1944. Nieman Fellow, Harvard University, 1949–50. Sigma Delta Chi Award for Washington Correspondence, 1952, 1954. Raymond Clapper Memorial Award for Washington Correspondence, 1955. Heywood Broun Memorial Award, 1955. Drake University Distinguished Alumni Award, 1956. Sylvania Television Award for commentary on the Senate Committee investigation of labor and management practices, 1957. Pulitzer Prize for national reporting, 1958. Sigma Delta Chi Award for Public Service in newspaper journalism, 1958. Colby College, Lovejoy Fellowship and Honorary LL.D., 1959. National Headliner Award for magazine writing (*Atlantic*), 1960. Cornell College, honorary L.H.D., 1960. Eisenhower Exchange Fellow, 1960–61. Drake University, honorary Litt. D., 1961. University of Arizona, John Peter Zenger Award, 1962. Freedom Foundation, George Washington Medallion, Public Address, 1963. William Allen White Award, University of Kansas, 1964. National American Legion, Fourth Estate Award, 1965. Buena Vista College, Honor Iowans Award, 1966. Iowa Wesleyan

College, honorary Litt. D., 1966. New York University, Kappa Tau Alpha Award, 1967. Drake University "Double D Award" for outstanding former athlete, 1968. Ohio University Honor Award, 1969. National Collegiate Athletic Award for professional achievement as a journalist, 1972. Drew Pearson Foundation Award—special award for sustained and significant contribution to investigative reporting, 1973. Freedom Foundation, George Washington Medallion, Published Article, 1974. Simpson College, Honorary Litt. D., 1974. *Washingtonian* magazine list of 10 best investigative reporters in Washington, 1975. Buena Vista College, Honorary Doctor of Journalism, 1976. Washington Correspondents "Hall of Fame" of Washington Chapter, Society of Professional Journalists—Sigma Delta Chi, 1979. Elected Fellow of the National Society of Professional Journalists—Sigma Delta Chi, 1980. Walter Wood Hiteman Lecturer, Louisiana State University, 1984. Drake University Law School, Alumnus of the Year Award, 1986. George Mason, Virginia Journalist Award, Richmond SPJ-SDX, 1987.

Thomas D. —————

M URPHY (1866–1928)
Founded the art calendar industry

How do you suppose it happened that so-called hayseed Iowans, who live in the boonies, improved the cultural level of America?

Red Oak is about as close as one could find to a town barely big enough for its own water tower. T.D. Murphy hadn't planned to live in Red Oak. But his college chum Edmund B. Osborne's father-in-law had owned a newspaper in Red Oak, and one day the editor was found dead in his office chair. Edmund went to help dispose of the newspaper but soon found himself running it instead.

Edmund then bombarded Tom with letters asking him to come dip into the untold riches that awaited their joint management of their newspaper, the *Independent*. This little paper was one of several Red Oak newspapers which were in rough competition with one another. Since T.D. didn't want to farm, his father staked him to a small loan which T.D. used to buy into the decrepit newspaper.

Times were tough for the two, despite their exuberance. They struggled along until in 1889 a new county courthouse was erected. They wanted to publish a picture of it in their newspaper, but the cost of the only available process—a woodcut—would have cut into an entire week of profits. Osborne had an idea: make a woodcut, surround it with advertising and sell spaces to local businesses.

The idea worked and they immediately took it to nearby towns and doubled their profits. They decided to branch into

101

other cities as fast as they could. It was a grand idea, except it didn't work out that way.

The new Gage County courthouse in Beatrice, Nebraska, was the first target of their scheme. But three days of solid sales effort produced only one advertiser, and gloom settled over the two entrepreneurs. The next venture in Denver produced little more to cheer their sagging finances and spirits.

But a germ of an idea sprang from the Denver loss: A company in Boston sent the men an art calendar which gave them the idea to convert their Denver Capitol building woodcut into an art calendar, which they then sold to an insurance company. They lost money, but not a particle of enthusiasm, for they now believed they were on the right track.

Borrowing money to the limit, and stretching their credit past the absolute limits, Edmund and T.D. equipped their shop with state-of-the-art presses. With Osborne selling and Murphy at home running the business, the company began to show steady growth.

A difference of opinion about how fast to grow—Osborne wanted a no-holds-barred expansion, while Murphy was ultra-conservative—finally resulted in Murphy selling the business to E.B. and agreeing to stay out of the calendar business for five years.

After several years, Edmund became restless and moved his operation to the East Coast where he continued modest success. Murphy immediately opened the Thos. D. Murphy Co. and within half a decade, in a remarkable series of business successes, created the world's largest and most innovative art calendar company.

Murphy established the art calendar industry's first national and international sales force. He introduced equipment and techniques that produced products of such high quality that their duplication today, even with the advent of high technology, is difficult.

T.D. Murphy sought and bought fine works of art from renowned artists, such as Frederick Remington, Thomas Moran and Charles M. Russell. These he knew would find welcome homes, gracing the walls for people who had little chance for exposure to fine art.

The art calendar industry phenomenon, spawned by T.D. Murphy, counted cultural fulfillment as its real mission. Fittingly, a major force in the cultural enrichment of small-town America came from small-town Red Oak, Iowa.

CREATED the Thos. D. Murphy Co. Wrote and published an extensive series of travel books.

Born: July 10, 1866, Monroe, Iowa. *Educated:* Simpson College. *Family:* Ina, wife; Thomas Culbertson, son. *Iowa Connection:* born, raised, educated, invented, and worked in Iowa.

John L.
NAUGHTON (1915–)
Invented sit-down dentistry

John L. Naughton, wouldn't stand for bad dentistry. Photo courtesy of Mrs J. Naughton.

The next time you see your dentist sitting by your side, thank Iowan John Naughton. Your dentist does. Here's why.

Few professional revolutions have been spurred by a single person, especially by an outsider to the profession. Fortunately, John Naughton didn't know that.

John was raised on a farm near Williamsburg and always had a knack for people relationships. After high school, John found a variety of selling jobs, finally landing in Des Moines as the state distributor for the Niagra Massage company. John then combined the Niagra Massage unit into a chair he called a Comfa-Lounge®, which he sold to stressed professional people as the ideal way to relax after a hard day at the office.

John displayed his chairs at professional conventions, including the Iowa State Dental Convention where he offered a moment's respite to weary conventioneers. Two of his dentist customers, Dr. Bernard "Barney" Morgan of Britt, Iowa, and Dr. Meigs Jones of Kansas City, cornered John and asked him to build a chair as comfortable for patients as the one for the visitors to the convention. John thought that sounded rather interesting.

He constructed a crude prototype of what he thought a dental chair should be. The chairs of the day were monstrous metal frames, upon which a pair of rock-hard seat and back cushions were fixed. Dentists stood by these thick chairs and leaned awkwardly against them in working positions. John built his chair and took it to Barney Morgan's dental office to watch it in use.

John sat in the hallway all morning, watching the tall Dr. Morgan work with even greater discomfort than with his old upright chair. But Dr. Morgan knew his patients loved the new chair and he asked how soon he could get another. John parried that question and went back to his shop to make a chair that comforted both the patient and the dentist.

John next plowed through a blizzard to Kansas City to show the concept to the nationally known Dr. Jones. This second chair had an upper iron infrastructure that allowed the patient to be lowered into a reclined position. Dr. Jones loved the chair and the next day the *Kansas City Star* carried a feature on the novelty of dental patients lying down in a dental office.

John went home and formed the Den-Tal-Ez® dental chair manufacturing company, and began a scramble for dentist recognition. At first, dental supply houses refused to show and sell this strange chair.

But an even greater problem was the resistance John encountered with dentists entrenched in the stand-up concept of dentistry.

Backed by John, teams of salespeople fanned out across the nation teaching dentists the new technique of "four-handed dentistry," which counted the two hands of the doctor and the two hands of his ever-present assistant.

When dentists objected to patients lying flat while they worked, saying that materials would drop down the patients' throats, John—who had no medical training—pointed out that the throat closes when a person is supine. The doctors were amazed to learn that truth from John.

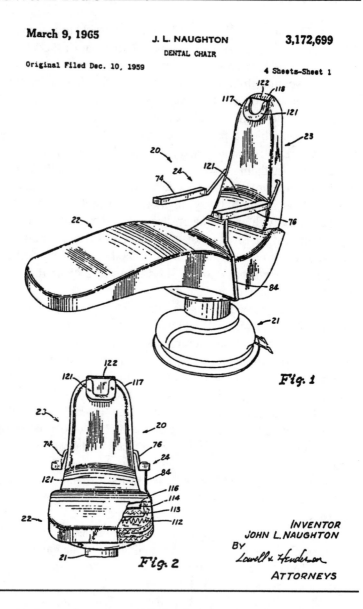

March 9, 1965

J. L. NAUGHTON
DENTAL CHAIR

3,172,699

Original Filed Dec. 10, 1959

4 Sheets-Sheet 1

Fig. 1

Fig. 2

INVENTOR
JOHN L. NAUGHTON
BY
Lowell & Henderson
ATTORNEYS

In just a few years, John's chair became the most popular chair in dental history. And the sit-down dental concept John invented became entrenched as the standard of care in the profession.

Studies have shown that dentists who work sitting down live 17 percent longer than dentists who worked standing up. That just gives those dentists a few more years to extend profound thanks to the outsider who changed dentistry, four-handedly.

INVENTED the lie-down dental chair. Introduced one of the most revolutionary concepts in dentistry in all history. Responsible for the introduction of instruments and systems supportive of sit-down dentistry. Formed and managed the largest dental chair manufacturing company in the world.

Born: October 27, 1915, Williamsburg, Iowa. *Educated:* Parnell, Iowa, High School. *Family:* Mary Dolores, wife; Mary, Jeanne, daughters; Thomas, Michael, sons. *Iowa Connection:* born, raised, schooled, worked, invented, and lived in Iowa.

Honors: 1970, Certificate of Recognition, Minnesota State Dental Association. E Award from the President of the United States for excellence in manufacturing and export. 1982 Honoree of the Iowa Regional National Conference of Christians and Jews for distinguished human relations and community service. 1982, Original and 100,000th Den-Tal-Ez® chairs placed in the Smithsonian Institution in Washington, D.C. 1989, inducted into the Iowa Inventors Hall of Fame.

Christian K. _____
NELSON (1893–1992)
Invented the Eskimo Pie®

Christian K. Nelson, changed the way America screamed for ice cream. Photo courtesy of Loess Hills Historical Society of Monona County, Onawa, Iowa.

I Scream, You Scream, We All Scream for Ice Cream.
—POPULAR SONG OF THE 1920s

The two men grunted under the weight of the huge tub of ice cream that they hoisted aboard the train.

Young Christian Nelson, riding the same train home from college to Onawa, watched the scene with interest. He decided to ask his dad to go into the ice cream business. The next year, the Nelson Creamery sold 10,000 gallons of ice cream.

When Chris graduated from college, he returned to Onawa to teach and to open his own ice cream store. One day, a lad entered Chris's store and asked for a candy bar. Chris was out of the brand he asked for, so the boy ordered an ice cream sandwich. As the ice cream was layered onto the wafer, the lad said he had changed his mind and now wanted a candy bar instead.

When Chris put down the ice cream and went to the candy counter, he asked the lad if he really knew what he wanted. The boy said, "Yes, I want 'em both, but I only got a nickel."

The more Chris thought about the boy's dilemma the more

he believed that if he could wed chocolate candy to ice cream he could create the perfect confection. The problem was, how to get something hot to stick to something frozen.

Chris began to experiment, but failure after failure convinced him that this was no easy problem. A chance remark by a chocolate salesman triggered the winning try. The salesman mentioned that chocolate used in candy held more cocoa butter than cocoa. So Chris increased the cocoa butter proportion and late one night the frozen bar and hot chocolate wedded instantly.

Chris named his new ice cream confection the I-Scream bar, secured patent rights to it, then tried to figure how to sell it. Needing capital and know-how, he visited an ice cream manufacturer in Omaha, who made one of history's worst business decisions. He turned it down.

Chris took his bar to another manufacturer who was out of town. The manufacturer's foreman, Russell Stover, took one look at the ice cream bar, quit his job and negotiated a deal with Chris. Chris and his new partner began their search for a new name for the confection. When they happened onto the name Eskimo, Chris suddenly blurted out "Eskimo Pie," and the name stuck like chocolate on ... well, on an Eskimo Pie®.

For a test market, the two men made up thousands of pies wrapped in aluminum foil, took them to Des Moines and became the instant talk of the town. Long lines queued up to taste this wonderful treat. In days, nearly every ice cream manufacturer in Iowa had signed up to manufacture and distribute Eskimo Pies®.

Flushed with this success, Nelson and Stover went to Chicago and within four months sold 2,700 franchises. By the following spring sales averaged one million Eskimo Pies® daily. Within 19 months one billion pies had been sold.

Then the imitators moved in and the war to protect the patent began, costing thousands of dollars monthly. Stover soon caved and offered to either buy out Chris or sell out to him. Chris bought but soon needed cash to keep his company running and approached R.S. Reynolds, Sr., who had sold him 500 million wrappers for his bars in the first six months alone.

Nelson and Reynolds struck a deal by which Reynolds would own and manage the company and Nelson (and two new

Iowa Pride _____

partners he had taken in to help with financing) would receive royalties. Nelson also would be technical advisor for the Eskimo Pie division of the United States Foil company.

After a time, R.S. Reynolds, Sr., decided he would take the patent to court and bring suit against one of Eskimo's imitators. The lawyer for the defendant was able to cast doubt on Nelson's originality and the court threw out the patent.

Nelson immediately retired at age 35. He had twice shaken the foundations of the ice cream industry, first with Eskimo Pie® which made the industry a year-round business, and then with his dry ice revolution in distributing and marketing techniques.

Not only did Chris Nelson change the eating habits of the nation, but countries like Ecuador—a nation whose economy was based upon the cocoa bean—sent special thanks to Christian Nelson. Holland and Switzerland said Chris rescued their economies.

Iowan Christian Nelson changed the way the world screamed for ice cream when he cooked up the world's most popular confection, the Eskimo Pie®.

INVENTED numerous machines to improve and speed the manufacturing process of frozen desserts, the dry ice preservation of dairy products, and the extrusion process of producing ice cream confections.

Born: Grumstrup, Denmark, March 12, 1893. *Educated:* Dana College, Blair, Nebraska; B.A. University of Nebraska in elementary education. *Family:* Myrtle Rhoda, wife; four adopted sons. *Iowa Connection:* lived and invented in Iowa.

David C.
NICHOLAS (1944–)
Speeded up the fax

Modern digital facsimile (fax) machines did not exist when Dave Nicholas invented a filler and synchronization scheme for Huffman codes that today is required for all fax machines.

In the late 1960s Dave was a doctoral student at ISU attempting to develop a technique to statistically compress voice. At that time, there were perhaps nine computers at the university. By careful planning and plaintive pleading, Dave found one where he could share some computer time to work his data.

By 1973 two patents based upon his research had been issued. Although not an ISU employee, Dave had voluntarily assigned the patents to the ISU Research Foundation (ISURF) in return for the Foundation's help in filing the patents. According to University protocol, the inventor receives one-third of the royalties, if any, after expenses. In ordinary commerce, in the United States, patent rights are signed away to the employer as a condition of employment. No payment, or nominal payment, is made to the inventor if patents are developed during his employment.

In 1971 Dave graduated from ISU and returned to Cedar Rapids to work for Rockwell International, formerly Collins Radio, where Dave has received 10 more patents to date.

When Dave began to gather data for a paper on his ISU research in 1986, he uncovered an amazing finding. Buried in the foot-thick books of the CCITT international telecommunications standards was the requirement that newer facsimile machines, using Huffman code compression and developed since Dave's patents were filed, could not be built unless they employed his invention.

These new digital machines speeded up the process of data transmission, so that faxes that had taken three to six minutes in the past now took 30 seconds.

When Dave informed the ISURF of the new fax standard, ISU officials went to the courts to require those who profited from Dave's invention to reimburse the Foundation for use of the patent process.

To date, the Foundation has profited to the tune of many millions of dollars in royalties, the highest amount for a single invention in ISU history. These earnings have made ISURF nationally one of the top five research organizations for royalties and top eight for receipts from patents.

The modern digital facsimile machine, with Huffman code compression and Dave's filler and synchronization technique, plays a crucial role in the information age. The royalties from Dave's invention now provide an endowment so that ISURF can continue to provide research money and patent protection for future ISU inventors.

In all honesty, to completely understand an invention as technical as Dave's requires a level of knowledge beyond the average. That's perfectly all right. We don't have to know how a computer stores data to understand the wonders of its application. The good news about Dave's ideas is that, since his invention, the fax works more usefully, with improved speed and accuracy. In these times, where rapid data transfer crucially impacts government, business and private lives, the magnitude of this invention is difficult to overstate.

On a personal note, the research for this book commanded hundreds of faxed documents. Extra hours of data transmission could have delayed progress and might have caused the effort to be scrapped.

HOLDS 12 patents in communications-related areas.

Born: July 14, 1944, Cedar Rapids, Iowa. *Educated:* Iowa State University, B.S., 1967; M.S., 1968; Ph.D., 1971. *Family:* Kathleen (divorced), wife; Christopher, son; Sarah, Jane, daughters. *Iowa Connection:* born, raised, educated, invents and works in Iowa.

Honors: Achievement Citation in Engineering, ISU. Iowa Inventors Hall of Fame. Elected to membership in these honorary societies: Phi Kappa Psi, Tau Beta Pi, Eta Kappa Nu, Sigma Xi.

George P.
NISSEN (1914–)
Invented the trampoline

Abner Doubleday did it. James Naismith did it. Iowa's George Nissen did it, too. What did they do? They each invented a sport, something few people even dream of doing.

Doubleday is credited with inventing baseball. Naismith invented basketball. Nissen invented the trampoline and the sport of trampolining. Doubleday and Naismith probably wouldn't recognize their sports today, but George's sport is practiced virtually the way he planned. Modern trampolining is enjoyed in over 60 countries, surpassing both baseball and basketball.

As a youngster Nissen carried water for the circus elephants to earn free admission to watch in awe as aerialists ended their act with a dive into a huge net. By the time he was in high school he had fashioned a rudimentary net to practice dives into, and to rebound from. The rebound captured George's imagination, for, if a person rebounded high enough, he could perform acrobatic stunts in midair during the rebound.

After high school George attended UI, where he excelled in gymnastics, specializing in tumbling. During his sophomore, junior and senior years he won the National Tumbling Championship, an unbelievable feat.

During his senior year, he learned that the Iowa swimming team needed a diver. Despite not having dived competitively for three years, George joined the diving team, too. When the season was over, George won the National Tumbling Championship and was named All-American in diving!

114

"Each night at UI, when we finished our workouts—even in the dead of winter with snow covering the ground—I would go to the football field and do a row of back handsprings the length of the field," he says.

After college George went to Mexico, where he put on acrobatic and diving exhibitions and dived for the Mexican government in what was the forerunner of the Pan-American Games. He then returned to the United States and continued his performing career.

By the time World War II broke out, George had put on over 2,000 exhibitions across the country. He also had perfected his rebounding apparatus, naming it the *trampoline,* from the Spanish word *trampolina,* which means diving board. For more than 15 years, *trampoline* was his registered trademark, until he finally allowed it to become generic and go into the public domain.

Joining the Navy, he served first aboard a destroyer; then he was assigned to be a preflight instructor, teaching navigation, gymnastics and trampolining, the latter being used to develop timing and coordination in naval aviators.

At the end of the war George formed the Nissen Trampoline Co., ultimately installing trampolines in 10,000 schools and camps and taking the sport worldwide. His name became so interwoven with the sport that in many countries a trampoline is simply known as a "Nissen."

In 1947 competitive trampolining was first introduced at the National AAU meet in Dallas. The following year the first national intercollegiate trampoline champion was crowned.

During his many activities, he found time to help form and be a major owner and director of the Senoh Gymnastic Equipment Company in Japan—now the most important company of its kind in the Orient.

During the 1960s Nissen's company expanded both its markets and its product line. The line included parallel bars, horses, balance beams, tumbling and wrestling mats, electric scoreboards, basketball backstops and table tennis tables. At the end of that decade, the Nissen company was the world's largest manufacturer of gymnastic equipment.

George says, "There are three things that make people

happy: love, work and creating." George Nissen, the inventor of a sport, can't stop doing any of those activities. The King of Bounce just can't stop bouncing.

⎯⎯⎯⎯⎯⎯⎯⎯⎯⎯⎯⎯⎯⎯⎯⎯⎯⎯⎯⎯⎯⎯⎯⎯⎯⎯⎯⎯⎯⎯⎯⎯⎯⎯⎯⎯

ORIGINATED the sport of trampolining. Created and built the world's largest manufacturing company of gymnastic equipment. Invented the sport of Double Mini-tramp, which became an international competitive event in 1975. Invented the sports of Spaceball, Rebound Track, Barsumo. Invented stadium and gymnasium Seatmasters®, Bunsavers® and holds over 40 other patents on sports-related inventions. Created the Nissen Award, given annually to the outstanding collegiate male gymnast.

Born: February 3, 1914, Blairstown, Iowa. *Educated:* Cedar Rapids Business College; B.S., UI; graduate work in naval engineering, Cornell University, New York. *Family:* Annie, wife; Dagmar and Dian, daughters. *Iowa Connection:* born, raised, educated, invents in Iowa.

Honors: National Tumbling Champion, 1935, 1936, 1937. Big Ten Award for Scholarship and Athletics, 1937. All-American, springboard diving, 1937. Hall of Fame, Helms Foundation, for noteworthy contributions to the sport of gymnastics. Hall of Fame, Trampoline Association. Distinguished Service Award, President's Council on Physical Fitness, 1973. Honorary President, International Federation of Trampoline (FIT). Member of the Executive Committee of the International Federation of Sports Acrobatics, 20 years.

Austin N.
PALMER (1859–1927)
Invented the Palmer Method of writing

Austin N. Palmer knew how to write right. Photo courtesy of the Cedar Rapids Gazette.

Palmer method

The Palmer Method of writing. Courtesy of the Cedar Rapids Gazette.

Austin Palmer always did things with a flourish.

But the flourishes of his pen were why insurance companies hired him. Before the turn of the twentieth century, people were wary of buying a chancy new thing called insurance. To convince their customers of their soundness, insurance companies made up beautiful certificates, decorated with fancy scrolls much like an old-fashioned valentine. That's where Austin came in.

When Austin was 20 years old, he made the three-week trip

117

from New York State to Cedar Rapids, Iowa, to visit his sister. He liked the city and found a job as penman for an insurance company. Austin hated the system of writing in use. He believed that writing should flow with arm movements and be simple to learn—none of which was true of the Spencerian system.

In the Spencerian style, students first copied a perfect letter, then copied it over and over again. "No one ever learned to write from a copybook," Austin proclaimed.

Austin thought the Spencerian method was pure bunk, so he opened a business college to teach a method he had invented, the Palmer Method of writing. Slowly the college grew, teaching more and more students, many of whom were writing teachers. Teachers liked the new method because students learned it more quickly and developed a better style of writing.

To further promote the Palmer Method, Austin established the *Western Penman* magazine which quickly gained a readership of 25,000. Still, his method hadn't received the national acceptance he felt was its due. It wasn't until a parochial school system in Monroe, Michigan, invited Austin to give a summer's course of training in his system that his technique took hold with teachers. Parochial school officials soon adopted the Palmer Method in schools around the nation.

The St. Louis World's Fair in 1904 offered Palmer an excellent showcase which he seized. Taking several instructors and making a large sign that showed before-and-after writing styles, Austin bought exhibit space at the fair and swirled his stuff.

Some school officials from New York State saw his exhibit and decided it was worth a try. Their proposition was a tough one, though. They gave Austin a test school in the Bowery of New York City. It was a school attended by some of the most deprived and incorrigible students in New York City.

Austin eagerly accepted the challenge. He and his team of instructors showed up at the school and taught the students to make ovaled and angled strokes first, then flow them into letters, using muscular arm movements, without wrist action. The results were eye-opening, as the students quickly mastered the new style to astound their New York teachers.

In quick succession, first New York City, then New York

State, then New England adopted the Palmer Method, which then swept the country. By 1920 the majority of the public schools in America had adopted the Palmer Method.

The *Western Penman* became the *American Penman*; publishing houses were set up in Chicago, New York and Portland, Oregon, to produce Palmer inks, Palmer pens, Palmer penholders, Palmer posters, Palmer instruction books, Palmer practice paper and all manner of writing materials.

Correspondence courses were established and taught 50,000 people; Austin's business college graduated 30,000 teachers of penmanship who spread out across the land carrying Austin Palmer's good news about writing. A young man with a better idea had taught the world how to write.

If you wanted to write to Austin Palmer and thank him for saving you the grief of the Spencerian method, and to express your appreciation of your ability to write free-flowing script, you'd use his own creation to pen your letter. That's because the Palmer Method is the method that you learned. That holds true for your penmanship teacher, too.

Two basic credos of Austin Palmer were the foundation upon which he built his success. They were

• A teacher cannot teach what she does not know. For this reason he refused to allow his method to be taught in schools where the teachers had not first been schooled by himself or by his teaching staff. And,

• A teacher has not taught until the pupils have learned.

INTRODUCED, taught and installed his system of writing in virtually every school in the land. Founded the Cedar Rapids Business College that taught thousands of teachers his writing method. Founded the Cedar Rapids Chamber of Commerce.

Born: December 22, 1859, Fort Jackson, New York. *Educated:* New York grade schools; largely self-taught. *Family:* Sadie, wife. *Iowa Connection:* invented, worked and lived in Iowa.

D.D.

PALMER (1845–1913)

Discovered the science of chiropractic

D.D. Palmer, "Old Dad Chiro." Photo courtesy Palmer College of Chiropractic.

An amazing one-third of the first class in Dr. D.D. Palmer's new college of chiropractic was composed of medical doctors. And D.D.'s doctorate was self-anointed.

Before that momentous day, the science had an interesting and tumultuous birth. It started with D.D., who never had a problem earning a living. Once he raised bees, then carted gallons of honey to East Coast markets and pocketed an unheard-of thousands of dollars' profit.

D.D. read every book he could find. He especially liked books about the body and healing. His search for knowledge led him to a man who cured by magnetic healing. D.D. learned the art, opened his own office and soon attracted a large clientele.

One afternoon in 1895 D.D. asked his black janitor, Harvey Lillard, how he had become deaf. Harvey told him that 17 years before, he turned his neck just so and became suddenly deaf. D.D. thought about that for a time, then persuaded Harvey he could cure his deafness by righting his vertebrae.

A few evenings later, during one of D.D.'s treatment ses-

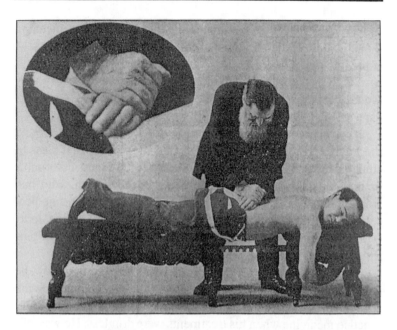

D.D. Palmer demonstrates an early chiropractic adjustment.
Photo courtesy Palmer College of Chiropractic and Douglas
Dvorak, Cedar Rapids Gazette.

sions, Harvey's neck popped and suddenly he could hear. The man who a moment before could hear almost nothing could now hear even the wagons in the street below!

D.D. went to his anatomy books and searched for the answer. He reasoned that somehow a nerve had become pinched between poorly aligned vertebrae. Correcting the malpositioned vertebrae then allowed the nerves to function normally again. That concept became the bastion of the science of chiropractic.

For the first few months D.D. practiced on patients whom he felt qualified for the treatment by having what he determined to be subluxations of the vertebral column. Early adjustments reportedly took place on a pad on his floor, for he had not yet perfected the chiropractic treatment bench. It was reported that patients often left bruised and bleeding from his manipulations.

To name his new science D.D. turned to the Reverend Samuel Weed, a preacher friend who spoke fluent Greek. The Reverend Mr. Weed thought at length, then proposed an amalgam

121

of the Greek words *cheir,* meaning hand, and *praktikos,* meaning done. D.D. loved it, and the name chiropractic—done by hand—came into being.

D.D. was sure that if he let others in on his discovery they would steal the idea and compete with him for patients. A near escape from an accident changed his mind.

D.D. accepted his first student in 1897 and went on to found the Palmer School of Chiropractic. One-third of the first class of students already held medical degrees as physicians, osteopaths or homeopaths. One early student was Mabel Heath, who had studied some medicine. She took other courses in medical schools and for 40 years taught anatomy at Palmer College, married D.D.'s son B.J., and became known as the first lady of chiropractic.

As Palmer's practice, school and public recognition grew, he was charged by the medical community with practicing medicine without a license. He defended himself by stating he could hardly practice medicine when his treatments were drugless. He was still found "guilty" and served a short sentence.

D.D.'s son B.J. was as strong-willed as his father; eventually they parted with the son buying D.D. out. The rest of his days, D.D. established other chiropractic schools in Oregon and Oklahoma. Unfortunately, father and son never reunited.

Except in posthumous accolades, the founder of chiropractic never reaped his just rewards. His son B.J. became known as the developer of chiropractic. Under the leadership of B.J. and his wife Mabel Heath, chiropractic rose to the status of the second-largest health care discipline. Today it is recognized by most major scientific, governmental and insurance bodies.

The Palmers, father, son and daughter-in-law, made their marks on the history of chiropractic and on the health care system of the world. Another Palmer, Dr. Dave, who was D.D.'s grandson, and Mabel and B.J.'s son, worked diligently to upgrade the educational standards of the Palmer School and elevated its status to become the Palmer College of Chiropractic.

Chiropractic survived for one simple reason: It got sick people well.

FOUNDED the Palmer College of Chiropractic.

Born: March 7, 1845, Port Perry, Ontario, Canada. *Educated:* self-taught, eighth-grade education. *Family:* Abba, Louvenia, Martha, Villa, Mary, wives; May, Jessie, Bartlett Joshua (B.J.), children. *Iowa Connection:* lived, worked, studied and discovered in Iowa.

William D. "Shorty" _____
PAUL (1900–1977)

Developed Bufferin® and Rolaids®

Although "Shorty" Paul fixed a lot of headaches in his lifetime, one was to make him famous.

He was tough and irascible and beloved by by generations of UI athletes and coaches. Yet few who knew his attraction to athletics realized that Shorty Paul was a pioneering physician who packed a powerhouse punch in academia.

During a 40-year tenure at UI, Paul put his creative mind to finding new surgical avenues to alleviate pain and suffering. From his base as team physician to the UI Hawkeye football team, he pioneered in the budding field of sports medicine and, through his studies and research in rehabilitation and training regimes, he became a driving force in helping sports medicine achieve a respectable status.

Paul's specialty of rheumatology allowed him to treat many patients with daily rations of aspirin to ease their discomfort—all except those whose stomachs had an aversion to harsh aspirin acidity.

One day a colleague complained of a headache, but said she couldn't stomach an acid aspirin. Paul had just received a batch of an antacid he was using in experiments to combine with penicillin. On a hunch, he mixed the antacid with the aspirin and gave it to his friend, who reported her headache left and her calm stomach remained. After a two-year UI study, the popular product Bufferin® popped up on drug counters throughout the world.

Working with another colleague, Paul conceived an over-the-counter antacid product that became known as Rolaids®.

Dr. William D. "Shorty" Paul, in a career marked by singular accomplishments, proved that stature has nothing at all to do with size. At four feet, nine inches, Shorty Paul towered as a giant among men.

TEAM PHYSICIAN for UI athletes. Hundreds of published articles in his specialty area of rheumatology, sports medicine and other fields of interest. Developed numerous new medicines. Pioneer work in surgery, gastroenterology and diabetes therapy.

Born: January 31, 1900, Brooklyn, New York. *Educated:* biochemistry studies at New York's Polytechnic School; M.D., University of Cincinnati. *Family:* Louise Ebeling, wife. *Iowa Connection:* worked, lived, invented, created, and wrote technical papers in Iowa.

Carl Emil
SEASHORE (1866–1949)
*Invented speech pathology
and audiology*

The whole nature of a person, the true significance of the
person, is all in that physical record of the voice.
— C.E. SEASHORE

Carl Seashore heard more than words when people talked.

In 1887, there was no professorship of psychology in the world and few course titles in institutions of higher learning used that term. Yet, Professor G.T.W. Patrick at the UI already offered a course called Empirical Psychology. This began the Iowa Psychological Laboratory, one of the first three in the world.

In 1897 Patrick brought Carl Seashore back to Iowa to head the new lab. Carl was born in Sweden, raised in Iowa from age three and was then doing graduate work at Yale University. The two men shared an "enormous enthusiasm for the new psychology and had perhaps an even greater enthusiasm for instrumentation."

Seashore immediately plunged into developing measurements to give meaning to the applications of psychology. His first job was to construct the first sound-, light- and jar-proof room in existence. He also continued his research studies in music, voice and hearing, building instruments such as tonoscopes. For 15 years his audiometer was the only one available.

By 1905 Seashore had succeeded Patrick as the head of the

department of Philosophy and Psychology, where he was now positioned to make his move in developing the Iowa Program in Speech Pathology. In 1908 Seashore was also made Dean of the Graduate College. Here he was given broad sway to lead, inspire, support and augment new programs. His broad interests and wide base of knowledge made others seek his input for their projects.

Some of his jobs entailed studies of the psychology of music and of reading disabilities, the formation of the Child Welfare Research Station, the School of Religion and the Psychopathic Hospital, student placement examinations, speech pathology and what he called the psychology of otology. By Seashore's expansion into applied fields—hygiene, child development, otology and speech—the die was cast for the development of the discipline of speech pathology.

At this time he appointed a staff member in the department of Speech with a special agenda, which was to explore the speech arts, to study variations from the normal and perhaps find methods of correcting them. At that time the department of Speech was concerned only with what was then referred to as artistic speech, or dramatic speech.

A graduate student in psychology, Glenn Merry, was hired and given rein to study every aspect of speech possible, from the anatomy of vocal cords to the physics of sound and resonance, including acoustical analysis and even X-ray experiments.

In 1921 Seashore led the committee for the establishment of a speech clinic. It was awarded $8,000 to organize a clinic which "would be so organized as to conserve the chief interests of the Departments of Psychiatry, Speech, Laryngology, and Psychology as the chief contributors of scientific work in this field."

As the fledgling discipline found its legs, Dr. Samuel Orton, director of Iowa's Psychopathic Hospital, presented a case of a child who had a serious reading and speech disorder. Dr. Orton thought it wise to find someone trained in psychiatry and psychology to deal with the child's problem.

A search of the country turned up no one, so a program was begun to train such a student in those two disciplines. The one selected was Lee Edward Travis, who went on to become the first student to be trained by design at the doctoral level for the spe-

Iowa Pride

cific objective of working experimentally and clinically with speech and hearing disorders.

Travis was placed in the Seashore Plan, or Gifted Student Plan, where he was given a card that admitted him into any classroom on campus. These students received small stipends and were examined often by heads of the various departments.

From Travis' ultimate research, cooperatively undertaken with Orton's deep involvement, came the hypothesis that so-called stutterers are different from so-called normal speakers in the dominance pattern of the brain's hemispheres. Studies related to this hypothesis eventually led to the *dominance theory,* as Travis and Orton named it.

The University of Iowa's Department of Speech Pathology and Audiology, and the world, are richer for these and many other Iowans who dared to think in new directions.

It is interesting to note that the child that prompted this search was well-known to both researchers. She was Dr. Orton's daughter.

INVENTED the Iowa Pitch Range Audiometer. Established the Iowa Psychological Clinic, a first in studying abnormal psychology. Established the Iowa Child Welfare Research Station, the first institution to be concerned scientifically and systematically with the behavior and development of the well, normal child. Developed pioneer interdisciplinary approaches to problem solving in education.

Born: January 28, 1866, Sweden, moved to Iowa at age three. *Educated:* Yale University. *Family:* Mary, wife; Robert, Carl, Sigfrid, Marion, sons. *Iowa Connection:* taught, invented and created in Iowa.

Jessie Field
SHAMBAUGH (1881–1971)
Founded 4-H Clubs International

Jessie Field Shambaugh, mother of 4-H. Photo courtesy of Nodaway Valley Historical Society.

Little Jessie Field was born with questions on her lips.

Which corn kernels will grow the best corn? How do you know if a cow is producing good milk? How come farmers rotate crops? Her sagely named father, Solomon Field, wisely answered Jessie's questions and instilled pride in her being a farm girl.

After high school she attended Western Normal College in Shenandoah. During the middle of her sophomore year she was asked to fill a teaching vacancy in a small country school. She accepted, thrilled with a chance to teach farm children her brand of Iowa pride.

Her excitement was challenged when she learned that her boy students didn't know about dragging roads, judging livestock, and seed selection, and her girl students didn't know the

129

basics of sewing, gardening and baking. Jessie promptly formed a Boys' Corn Club to teach the boys successful farming things and a Girls' Home Club to teach the girls domestic duties.

The clubs met with enthusiastic response from the children and their "(at first) wary" parents. Jessie turned their drab lives into sparkling moments and they began to feel good about being farm youth.

Soon Jessie quit teaching to return to college for a Bachelor of Arts degree. Armed with this important document, she accepted a principal's job in Montana before being asked to return to Page County as superintendent of 130 country schools.

Immediately Jessie inspired her teachers to establish Boys' Corn Clubs and Girls' Home Clubs for their students. She established competitions for project work and brought in professors from ISU, to teach short courses in livestock judging and seed corn judging.

The program prospered and resulted in her students competing with adults and carrying off prizes in baking, sewing, and corn and livestock judging. After one remarkable win in Omaha, visitors came to Page County from all over America, to observe her youth clubs and to leave amazed at what they saw. Even The New York Times praised her.

As a tangible symbol to reward her children's achievements, she designed a three-leaf clover pin. On each leaf the letter "H" was printed, standing for Head, Heart and Hands. The next year she added another H for Home, a designation later changed to stand for Health.

Jessie's 4-H movement has benefited untold millions of farm youth and their families. But Miss Jessie would have never doubted that outcome.

AUTHORED and coauthored books relevant to teaching and inspiring farm youngsters.

Born: Celestia Josephine Field, June 26, 1881, Shenandoah, Iowa. *Educated:* Western Normal College, Shenandoah, one and one-half years; Tabor College, B.A. *Family:* Ira W. Shambaugh, husband; William, son; Phyllis Ruth, daughter. *Iowa Connection:* born, raised, educated, and made her mark in Iowa.
Honor: Doctor of Humane Letters, Doane College, Crete, Nebraska.

Walter A.

SHEAFFER (1867–1946)

*Invented the first practical
self-filling fountain pen*

*Walter A. Sheaffer, his
ideas never ran dry. Photo
courtesy of Sheaffer Inc.*

Walter Sheaffer was so afraid
he couldn't protect his patent against the big pen
companies that he almost decided against going
into the pen business even though he knew that
he had invented the world's greatest pen.

Walter grew up in the jewelry business, first in his father's
Bloomfield jewelry store and later in an uncle's jewelry store in
Unionville, Missouri. As later events would prove, Walter received a thorough grounding in the jewelry trade at the elbows of
his father and uncle.

After working for several years with his uncle in Unionville,
Walter returned to Bloomfield and became a partner with his father in his then-struggling jewelry business. Profits had disappeared as the Sears and Wards catalogs were advertising cheap
watches, silverplate and other jewelry items at the same prices
the Sheaffer's could buy them for. To counter this the Sheaffer's
took on some fine jewelry products not being sold through the
catalogs, including a new line of Hamilton watches. They then
advertised the cheap watches at less than the catalog prices.

When customers asked to see a cheap watch, Walter brought
out a velvet-lined tray of 10 expensive watches and two cheap

131

ones. The prospect invariably asked about the expensive watches, and many times bought one after Walter had demonstrated and explained the advantages of the Hamilton over the cheap watch and convinced the prospect that "Quality is always cheaper in the long run."

When Walter married, he and his father added pianos and organs to their line to give more financial support for the two families. They placed their musical instruments in the center of the shop so that people couldn't help but see the fine pianos.

Salesclerks were instructed to write down which piano seemed to please the family; then Walter would load it in a wagon and haul it out to their home. There he would trade the farmer a couple of hours of work in the field for the same amount of time to show off the piano he had now put in the farmer's living room. The farmers bought the fairness of that and their wives bought the pianos.

One day a store-for-sale ad in a jeweler's magazine caught Walter's eye and he soon exchanged a farm he owned for the store. Established in business now for himself, he happened on an ad showing a pen that had a bulge in the side for filling. He thought it looked terrible and thought about how to improve on it.

By morning he had the answer, and within a year he had patented the world's first practical "self-filling, self-cleaning" fountain pen. He improved his invention with another patent, but he was afraid to market his pen because he didn't have the money to fight court battles he knew giant penmakers would wage against him.

Shortly after getting the patent on his improvement, two former Conklin pen salesmen who called on Walter said that they could sell all the pens he could make.

Based on this assurance, Walter somewhat reluctantly decided to go into the pen business. He hired seven men, put them in a 10-foot-by-14-foot room in the back of his jewelry store and began making Sheaffer pens. True to their word, the two salesmen sold more pens than Walter could make.

In the first year the company showed a 50 percent profit on

invested capital and captured 3 percent of the entire fountain pen market, which was an incredible success. Through a series of shrewd marketing tactics—such as the idea of combining a pen and a pencil into a gift set, something no one had thought of before—the Sheaffer Pen Company wrote writing instrument history.

In a few years the LIFETIME® Sheaffer pen was the No. 1 seller in the world, selling at a price three times that of most competitors' pens. Walter never lost faith in his belief that quality is cheaper in the long run.

True to Walter's predictions, major penmakers came gunning for this upstart company in Fort Madison, Iowa. Through a harrowing series of near-misses, Walter outplayed, outwitted, and outgunned his scheming competition. The company grew to be one of the leading writing instrument manufacturers in the world, adding inks and other office accessories to round out its line.

Two years after making his first pens, Walter placed a full-page ad in *The Saturday Evening Post,* an unheard-of expense for such a new company. The ad claimed that a Sheaffer pen put "Brains in your hand!"

Walter's brains were always in his head, as his story of jewels to riches proves.

ESTABLISHED Sheaffer Pen Company. Invented a machine to make a clutch for a lead pencil. Introduced: Skrip® ink. The Top-Well® ink bottle. The White Dot logo on Sheaffer pens. Break-resistant Rodite plastic. The spiral-type, propel-repel-expel pencil mechanism. The desk set concept. The blance or streamline shape. The Touchdown and Snorkel filling systems. A visible ink supply on a pen barrel. The inner spring pocket clip. Pen and pencil gift set concept. The inlaid pen point. Created scores of inventions and improvements in writing instruments, desk sets and related accessories.

Born: July 27, 1867, Bloomfield, Iowa. *Educated:* did not finish high school. *Family:* Nellie, wife; Clementine, daughter; Craig, son. *Iowa Connection:* born, raised, educated, worked, invented, and lived in Iowa.

Honor: 1945 Army-Navy E Award for contribution to the World War II effort.

Jane
SMILEY (1949–)
Pulitzer Prize-winning author

Jane Smiley spilled the beans in her newest novel *Moo.*

She claims Moo U. isn't really ISU. Maybe not. But her Moo U. just happens to be in Iowa (ISU is located at Ames), features an agricultural curriculum and staff (ISU is one of America's premier agricultural schools), is a land-grant institution (ISU was America's first land-grant college—see Iowa Firsts chapter) and is near Des Moines (Ames is a half-hour north of Des Moines.) No, Moo isn't really ISU, despite the fact that generations of ISU students have fondly referred to their alma mater as Moo U. Sure, Jane.

Smiley was born in Los Angeles and moved to St. Louis as a youngster. There her mother was editor of the women's pages of the *St. Louis Globe-Democrat.* She became an avid horseback rider and developed a fondness for the farm. Smiley went on to Vassar for her baccalaureate degree, then joined the Iowa Writers' Workshop where she earned two masters degrees and a Ph.D. in literature.

After success with early novels, Smiley based her two most recent novels in the Midwest: *A Thousand Acres,* a gripping tragedy that some have called King Lear in the farmyard, and which gained her a Pulitzer Prize and many other awards; and *Moo,* a ribald poke in academic spareribs and a genuinely fun read.

In teaching writing at ISU, Smiley utilizes a technique where the words "good" and "bad" are not employed. Rather, she

134

focuses on why a piece of writing either works or doesn't. Her students could hardly find a better teacher, for Jane's writing works.

PULITZER PRIZE-WINNING novelist of the Iowa scene.

Born: September 26, 1949, Los Angeles, California. *Education:* Vassar College, B.A., 1971; University of Iowa, M.A., 1975, M.F.A., 1976, Ph.D., 1978. *Family:* John Whiston (divorced); William Silag (divorced); Stephen Mortensen; Phoebe Graves Silag, Lucy Gallagher Silag, daughters; a son. *Iowa Connection:* educated, writes and teaches in Iowa.

Honors: Fulbright fellowship, 1976–77; Breadloaf Scholar, Breadloaf Writers' conference, 1977; grant from National Endowment for the Arts, 1978, and 1987; Friends of American Writers Prize, 1981, for *At Paradise Gate;* O. Henry Award, 1982, 1985, and 1988, *The Age of Grief* was nominated for the National Book Critics Circle Award, 1987, 1992 Pulitzer Prize for *A Thousand Acres,* National Book Critics Circle Award, 1992, Heartland Prize, 1992, Midland Authors Award, 1992.

Writings: Barn Blind, At Paradise Gate, Duplicate Keys, The Age of Grief (story collection), *Catskill Crafts: Artisans of the Catskill Mountains, The Greenlanders, Ordinary Love and Good Will* (two novellas), *Life of the Body (Deluxe), Moo, A Thousand Acres.* Work has appeared in such anthologies as *The Pushcart Anthology, Best American Short Stories, Best of the Eighties.* Has contributed stories to *Redbook, Atlantic, Mademoiselle, Fiction, TriQuarterly,* and *Playgirl.*

Cloid H. _____
SMITH (1871–1939)
*Built the world's largest
pop corn business*

*Cloid H. Smith made the movies
more fun. Photo courtesy The
American Pop Corn Company.*

How long would it take for you to eat 71 quarts of pop corn?

You did it last year, or at least the average American did, according to statistics. And that fact largely came about be cause of an Iowan named Cloid Smith, a man who bagged his destiny when it popped up before him.

In his early 20s, C.H. managed his own drugstore, where he invented and manufactured several veterinary medicines and his own hand lotion, which he distributed widely under the label "Huskers Lotion." He learned early the value of promotion, marketing, packaging, and distribution, talents that later would stand him in good stead.

After a brief oil well fiasco, C.H. established a telephone exchange in Odebolt, Iowa, merged it with others, then sold it to

The Bell Telephone Company. With some of his profits, C.H. bought some land on which his tenant grew a few acres of pop corn.

When the tenant sold his crop for less than C.H. thought he should have received, he questioned the pop corn buyer on the price. The resulting argument ended with the pop corn buyer telling C.H. that if he didn't like the way he did business, he should go into the pop corn business himself.

C.H.'s first-year crop of 75,000 pounds of pop corn was sold under the first brand name ever applied to a pop corn, Jolly Time®.

During the following years of phenomenal growth, Jolly Time® was the first to advertise in national magazines, taking the first pop corn ad in *Good Housekeeping* magazine in 1925. After *Good Housekeeping* tested Jolly Time®, they promptly awarded the prestigious *Good Housekeeping* Seal of Approval to the product, a designation it has held since 1925.

The American Pop Corn Company was also the first to advertise on radio and television. Two of its marketing plusses were the "Volumized" process of increasing the popped size of pop corn, a process the company patented, and packaging pop corn in a metal can.

Realizing that pop corn kernels need to contain a set amount of moisture to pop properly, C.H. went to the American Can Company with a request for an airtight can that would keep his pop corn in perfect condition until it was used. The can American Can came up with was the precursor to the first beer can (see First Can of Beer).

When C.H. Smith hosted the company's 25th Anniversary in 1934, he told the audience that they were privileged to be shown the company's first cornshelling equipment. C.H. held up his own two hands. Those hands built quite a company out of pop corn.

CREATED the first brand-name pop corn as Jolly Time®. Created the first metal pop corn container. Marketed the first pop corn "Guaranteed to Pop." First pop corn to be advertised on radio and television. Patented the "Volumized" pop corn process.

Iowa Pride

Born: February 14, 1871, Pennsylvania. *Educated:* Sac County public schools. *Family:* Elizabeth, wife; Howard, son. *Iowa Connection:* born, raised, educated, worked, and founded his pop corn business in Iowa.

Note: We are pleased to comply with the wishes of the Iowans who run the American Pop Corn Company—and who edited this article—in their request for the split spelling of "pop corn."

Frank H.

SPEDDING (1902–1984)

Co-invented the production process of pure uranium

Frank H. Spedding speeded the end of World War II. Photo provided by Iowa State University.

The atomic age might still be in the test tubes if Frank Spedding had not decided to be an Iowan.

Spedding accepted a position on the faculty at Iowa State University in 1937. It was there that he joined his departmental cohort, Harley Wilhelm, to produce the means of creating pure uranium, cheaply and quickly.

To begin the large-scale nuclear chain reaction, hundreds of tons of uranium were required. Until 1941, top U.S. physical chemists had only been able to produce a few pounds of uranium, and even that amount was flawed by impurities. A few pounds is an enormous distance from a few hundred-thousand pounds, and a nuclear reaction seemed to be hopelessly out of reach.

Spedding and Wilhelm had been given the job of finding a substitute material to use in trying to initiate sustained nuclear fission. President Franklin D. Roosevelt had defined the project's goal: Be first to create an atomic bomb. If enemy Axis powers had beaten the Allies in this atomic race, every person alive today living in formerly Allied countries could well be enslaved.

Instead of finding a substitute for uranium's role in the reaction, Spedding and Wilhelm conceived a method of extracting pure uranium. When they placed an 11-pound ingot of uranium on the project director's desk, it became only a matter of time until a nuclear chain reaction was accomplished, the bomb was created, and the explosion blew World War II away.

Following their discovery, the Ames Laboratory which they directed produced over two million pounds of high-grade uranium.

The terrible price of peace was paid largely through the vision of two intrepid Iowa scientists, Drs. Spedding and Wilhelm.

PUBLISHED over 260 articles in professional journals.

Born: October 22, 1902, in Canada to American parents. *Educated:* Bachelor of Chemical Engineering, University of Michigan, 1925; Master of Science, University of Michigan, 1926; Ph.D., University of California at Berkeley, 1929. *Family:* Ethel, wife; Mary Ann Elizabeth, daughter. *Iowa Connection:* lived, taught, and invented in Iowa.

Honors: Winner of the Langmuir Award, Nichols Medal, Douglas Medal, Clamer Medal and a Guggenheim Fellowship. Nominated for the Nobel Prize. Honorary degrees from: University of Michigan, Case Institute of Technology, and Drake University.

Phil

STONG (1899–1957)

Wrote State Fair

Few Iowans could claim roots that were stronger or longer than Iowa author Phil Stong. It was appropriate, therefore, for this Iowan to introduce a tongue-in-cheek Iowa to the nation. Until his time, Iowans were generally depicted as being rather somber and humorless.

Stong's great grandfather settled in Iowa in 1837, making Phil a fourth generation Iowan. He was born near Keosauqua and graduated from Drake University in 1919. Stong taught high school English for a year in Minnesota, then spent a year on graduate studies at Columbia University. Next he taught for over two years in Kansas, before returning to Drake to teach debate and journalism.

While teaching at Drake, Stong also moonlighted for *The Des Moines Register.* He claimed that his newspaper experience honed his skills, an observation many authors have affirmed. By 1926 the excitement of newspaper journalism took him to New York City where he worked for several publications. From New York he went north to Connecticut to launch his career in free-lance writing.

Several early novels failed to get off the ground but, when he returned to his Iowa roots and wrote *State Fair,* a national audience followed him. Will Rogers starred in an early screen version (1932) and Rodgers and Hammerstein wrote a screen musical for *State Fair* (1944). In 1961 another screen version starred Pat Boone, and in 1995 a stage musical was produced using the

Iowa Pride

original Rodgers and Hammerstein scores and adding works of theirs from lesser-known productions.

Stong continued writing until his death in 1957, but *State Fair* will live on, and always be Iowa.

WROTE: *State Fair* and somewhere between 42 and 60 books. Reports vary.

Born: January 27, 1899, Pittsburgh, Iowa. *Education:* graduated from Drake in 1930 with a B.A. in English. Received Master's Degree from Columbia University. *Family:* Virginia, wife. *Iowa Connection:* born, educated, began writing career in Iowa.

Orland R.
SWEENEY (1882–1958)

Created useful products from agricultural waste

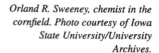

Orland R. Sweeney, chemist in the cornfield. Photo courtesy of Iowa State University/University Archives.

Orland Sweeney's first real job was to figure out how to kill soldiers with war gas. He spent the rest of his life improving the lives of the survivors.

During the World War of 1914–1918, American Doughboys were decimated and maimed by killing clouds of poison gas. Sweeney was given the job of taking raw chemicals and making counterwarfare effective.

Eventually the war ended, and with it Sweeney's job. The department of physical chemistry at ISU beckoned and he accepted the leadership role. A chemist at ISU could no more avoid farm chemical applications than soldiers could avoid wars.

Soon Sweeney found himself immersed in bringing the benefits of physical chemistry into the farmyard. The common corn-

Iowa Pride

cob became one of his early targets. His research created ways to cook the cobs down to become a rugged paper that worked well as a binder to hold construction wallboard together. A plant for this manufacture came into being and what was once a throwaway was no longer. Giant gypsum mills in Fort Dodge became eager users of Sweeney's corncob wallboard paper.

Quaker Oats saw his success and laid a new problem in his lap. Their question: How do we dispose of the useless oat hulls that we create when we make America's breakfast?

In the production of oatmeal countless tons of oat hulls were left over, seemingly of no value, and posing a costly disposal problem. Sweeney soon developed the chemical equations to turn oat hulls into valuable *furfural*. To most people furfural is a weird and meaningless name. But manufacturers seized on this new source of what they knew to be a highly valuable chemical.

Furfural has more creative uses than hamburger has in creating different kinds of meals. Furfural has use as a substitute for plastics, to preserve milk, embalm dead animals, cure athlete's foot, improve the bouquet of wines, manufacture golf tees, as a paint remover ... and on and on.

As if those accomplishments were not enough, Dr. Sweeney devised methods to soften water with the zeolite process, again opening new avenues of use for chemistry to enhance human lives.

Iowa and the world have benefited enormously from Dr. Sweeney's agrivision in a test tube. And Quaker Oats hasn't thrown an oat hull away since.

WAS AN AUTHORITY on the manufacture of paper from corncobs resulting in a wallboard manufacturing business. Designed a furfural extraction process so that Quaker Oats (and others) could extract value from waste oat hulls. Developed a manufacturing facility for the manufacture of Chloropicrin, a deadly war gas, for the U.S. Army. Discovered methods to produce economically the antiseptic known as Dakin's solution. Devised new methods of softening water by the zeolite process. Headed the Department of Physical Chemistry, ISU.

Born: Martin's Ferry, Ohio, March 27, 1882. *Educated:* 1909–10, B.S. and

M.S. in chemical engineering, Ohio State University; 1914, Ph.D. in chemical engineering, University of Pennsylvania. *Family:* Louella, wife; Elizabeth, Jacqueline, daughters. *Iowa Connection:* lived, invented, created, and taught in Iowa.

Honor: Sweeney Hall, the building now housing the Department of Chemical Engineering at ISU, was named for him.

William P.
SWITZER (1927–)

Created the vaccine for atrophic rhinitis in swine

William P. Switzer cut the cost of the Iowa chop. Photo courtesy Iowa State University photo service.

Bill Switzer didn't set his cap on being world-famous.

His original plan wasn't to be acclaimed as the man who rescued the pork industry from a devastating disease. His goal wasn't fixed on being hailed as one of the world's greatest investigators of animal disease. He just wanted to work with animals and solve some of those pesky problems plaguing his friends who raised animals.

Bill had grown up on a farm in southwest Kansas, and he liked animals and things of the soil. He wanted to attend Texas A&M, one of the Southwest's most prestigious schools. However, a school policy would only allow good ol' boys from Texas into the veterinary medical school. Undeterred, Bill entered Texas A&M as an engineering student, then got a job cleaning out the horse barns.

The dean of the vet school happened to frequent the horse barns to admire the stallions and Bill would bring out a stallion whenever the dean wanted. One day, the dean asked Bill why he wasn't in vet school. Bill told him that out-of-state guys didn't qualify.

The dean admitted that enrollment was down due to World

War II. The next year Bill was one of the first non-Texans to attend the veterinary college at Texas A&M. After he graduated, the ISU vet school advertised for a diagnostic laboratory vet, which was exactly what Bill wanted to be.

As Bill worked with meat producers, helping them solve the vexing disease problems they encountered, he realized that atrophic rhinitis (AR) caused serious health repercussions in hogs. First, the hog's eyes watered, then the hog would sneeze and cough, the bone in the nostrils would deteriorate, until finally, from some unknown cause, the hog died or its growth was stunted.

The disease spread through herds of hogs and was thought to be infectious. But nobody knew for sure. AR became Bill's thesis for his master's degree. No one knew which of millions of organisms in a hog's system was accountable. But Bill's master's thesis shed some light on the disease.

The light grew brighter during his Ph.D. thesis, which opened up the whole field of swine mycoplasmas. By now, he had found new tools, and developed better techniques for his sleuthing. Filtering a broth of ground-up nasal tissue from an infected hog through a new porcelain filter he had seen advertised, he was rewarded with another broth. This one held only one organism, which when inoculated in swine produced AR!

But what exactly was the bacterium that filtered through the new porcelain filter? Bill noted that the bacterium reconstituted in culture, going back to its original bacterial shape. He had identified *Bordetella bronchiseptica* as the culprit. Now he had to figure out how to control it, and the disease. But at least he knew which bug to go after.

The organism from AR is much like the one from whooping cough in humans, and pork producers quickly learned from Bill's work that they could get modest relief from AR by inoculating their swine with human whooping cough vaccine. That move caused serious shortages in human whooping cough vaccine.

Two decades after he discovered this cause, this persistent sleuth created a vaccine that solved the problem. Finding that the cause of this disease in hogs is similar to the cause of "kennel cough" in dogs, he was able to develop a vaccine for that disease, too.

The next time you enjoy an Iowa chop—the other white meat—thank Dr. Bill Switzer for hanging in there and saving the industry from this costly swine disease. It's certain the pets of the world, saved from kennel cough, are equally thankful.

Bill Switzer has been praised for his research discoveries by millions of people around the world. But he counts something else to be his most important contribution to society.

"Teaching students so that they can go on to become a cadre of capable hands, training the next generation, and on and on," he says. Bill Switzer wears his Iowa modesty well.

DEVELOPED treatments for bordetellosis of swine. Developed immunizing product for control of "kennel cough" in dogs. Discovered the first known mycoplasma from swine and characterized the polyseositis disease it causes. Discovered the cause of mycoplasmal arthritis of swine. Discovered the cause of mycaplasmal pneumonia of swine, considered to be the disease causing the greatest economic loss to the worlds' swine population. Participant in numerous international conferences dealing with issues related to his research and area of expertise. Inventor and co-inventor of patents for immunizing swine and dogs.

Born: April 9, 1927, Dodge City, Kansas. *Educated:* 1948, D.V.M., Texas A&M University; M.S., 1951, ISU; 1954, Ph.D., ISU. *Family:* Irene, wife; Bonnie and Robin, children. *Iowa Connection:* educated, taught, researched and lived in Iowa.

Honors: 1964, Honorary Master Swine Producer. 1970, ISU Faculty Citation. 1977, Distinguished Professor, ISU. 1977, American Feed Manufacturer's Association Veterinary Medical Research Award. 1978, National Hog Farmer Award for Outstanding Service to the Pork Industry. 1979, Dr. h.c., University of Vienna. 1979, Iowa Inventors Hall of Fame. 1980, Award of Merit, Gamma Sigma Delta. 1981, Gamma Sigma Delta International Award for Distinguished Service to Agriculture. 1981, Howard W. Dunne Memorial Award for Outstanding Service to the AASP and the Swine Industry. 1988, Iowa Veterinarian of the Year, Iowa Veterinary Medical Association.

John J.
TOKHEIM (1871–1941)

Invented the gasoline pump

Iowan John Tokheim hated smelly hands, especially when they were his. And every time he filled a can with kerosene, he hated the smell even worse. He vowed to find a better way to serve his customers.

In the late 1880s a bold and daring 16-year-old Norwegian lad left the comforts of his familiar Norwegian family, friends and school, language and culture, and sailed to America.

John's brother in Iowa advanced him the money for the trip and three years of labor on his brother's farm near Thor squared the debt. By then John had learned enough English to enroll in a Des Moines business college for a short term of study. From there he went to Chicago, spending three years learning the sheet metal trade, studying sheet metal drafting at night.

With a small sum he had saved, John returned to Thor and opened a combination hardware store, machine shop and water pump service. He put everything he owned into his little shop.

He worked long days making his investment in his business grow, but one special problem in his store caused his Norwegian hackles to rise. Each time a customer bought some lamp kerosene, John got some of the kerosene on his hands, and kerosene simply stinks. John remembered a toy pump he had as a child in Norway.

He thought, What if I put the kerosene tank in the cellar beneath the shop, then pump the kerosene up and into the customer's pail? He reasoned that several problems would be solved

149

with his solution: (1) the kerosene would be stored safely away from fire hazard; (2) kerosene would not smell up his store; and (3) delivering kerosene to a customer now would be a clean process, getting none on his hands.

John's invention worked exactly as planned, so John hunted out a lawyer in nearby Humboldt and applied for a patent on the world's first hand-operated, self-priming, visible measuring pump for kerosene.

Others who saw John's pump agreed that it was an idea whose time had come. They wanted one, too. So John moved to Cedar Rapids to find labor, materials and markets large enough to support the Tokheim Manufacturing Company, which now offered these wondrous patented pumps.

At that time, the Standard Oil Company was stumped on how to deliver gasoline to newfangled critters called automobiles. Company executives asked John if his pump might help solve their problem. They liked John's novel idea of hiding the storage tank underground. No one else had thought of that simple concept.

Not only did John's pump create the first "filling station," but his other inventions—such as the gas gauge—were used in the first cars to indicate gasoline and oil levels to the driver. Until that time people drove their cars until they ran out of gas or oil, then scouted about for refills. The simple gauge John invented let drivers know when they were running low on gasoline. Gas pumps sprang up everywhere people went. Drivers drove assured of the fuel needed to arrive at their destination.

Dry cleaners saw John's pump and wondered if it could solve their problems in dealing with their volatile products. It could, would and did.

In those days, gasoline from pumps often contained water. John developed devices to extract the unwanted water, clean up the gasoline delivered, and ultimately improve the performance of the engines the gasoline fired.

John went on to solve problem after problem with inventions that poured from his mind as cleanly as kerosene and gasoline poured from his pumps. He figured out the system that solved how to dispense vinegar and cider in grocery stores, created the world's first electric pump, devised measuring devices for tanks, produced predetermined product delivery instruments, and during one of his brightest inspirations, invented flame arrestors, to prevent dangerous tank storage fires.

His automatic liquid primer, to prevent drainback in suction pumps, was recognized by insurance companies as the required standard for the industry.

Soon, John's gasoline pumps and curb service stations dotted the world, and the auto age was born, largely delivered by one Norwegian immigrant Iowan who hated having kerosene-soaked hands. There was only one difference between John J. Tokheim and tens of thousands of others in those days who sold kerosene and got smelly hands.

Ja, Norwegian-Iowan John J. Tokheim did something about it.

RECEIVED over 29 patents including the following: Invented the first electric-operated power pump. Invented a predetermined stop measurement attachment for pumps. Invented a vacuum system for vinegar and cider. Invented a liquid level tank gauge for automobiles. Invented public garage pumps. Invented power pumps for dry cleaners. Invented agitator tanks and renovators to reclaim gasoline and naphtha for dry cleaners. Invented breather vents for gasoline storage tanks. Invented tank vapor control and condensing valves. Invented tank flame arrestors. Invented tank gauges. Invented tank temperature and test units. Invented "Vac" vinegar and cider measuring equipment. Invented generating gear grinders. Invented the first Curb Service pump for autos. Invented the Triune, three-cylinder piston pump.

Born: May 17, 1871, Odda, Norway. Educated: elementary schools, Odda, Norway; Capital City Business College, Des Moines. Family: Senva, wife; Agnes, daughter. Iowa Connection: studied, invented, lived and worked in Iowa.

Ray

TOWNSEND (1913–)

Invented new ways
to process meat

Ray T. Townsend, meat magnate. Photo courtesy of Ray Townsend.

Ninety-nine percent of my ideas are bad, but I can't give up until I know why they're bad.

—RAY TOWNSEND

As the saying goes, there's more than one way to skin a cat. Iowan Ray Townsend could probably think of several. That's because Ray revolutionized the meat industry, first in 1946 when he solved a problem that had repeatedly stumped the experts. Ray invented mechanized skinning of beef, pork, fish and fowl.

He grew up tinkering in his father's blacksmith shop, tearing things apart and occasionally reassembling them. As a young boy, he invented a machine to plant tomatoes. In the midst of his creative pride, he did not foresee that it would take at least two people to carry the thing!

Ray attended Iowa State University in Mechanical Engineering, but financial realities forced a return to the shop. One day his father sent him to repair machinery in a meat packing plant. There he first observed the dangerous, laborious process of removing ham from the bone. Believing he could find a better way, Ray set out to first remove the skin. As yet he did not realize that meat packers had been trying desperately for years to solve this problem. "Since I was new to the challenge, my mind could try a new approach." Rather than try to force a knife to follow the uneven contours of animal skin, he found a way to force the meat to lay flat along a straight, stationary blade.

After months of trial and error, he took a prototype to Chicago, looked up the first meat packer in the phone book (Armour), and asked them to try his machine. Several weeks later, he returned to find his invention left in a salt cellar to rust. This time he went to the other end of the phone book. It didn't take the people at Wilson long to realize that this young man from Iowa had delivered to them a revolution. Two years later Ray's machine was recognized by the American Meat Institute as the best technological advancement in a decade. Townsend Engineering Company of Des Moines was born.

In 1964, Ray and his team of engineers introduced another revolution, the Frank-a-Matic, a machine to create frankfurters of uniform size and weight at the astonishing rate of 30,000 per hour. Again the world meat industry raced to buy this Iowan's latest creation.

Ten years after that, it happened again. This time it was a machine to inject a wide variety of meats with cure and flavor. Within two years, 80 percent of the nation's bacon was processed after being injected by a Townsend Injector.

"My favorite recreation is to think, analyze and create," says Townsend. Today, a wide range of meat products consumed around the world have been treated with the genius of Ray Townsend. Those meals are less expensive, healthier and taste better because Iowan, Ray Townsend, found a better way.

INVENTED a meat injection machine. Invented a wiener-making machine. Invented a handheld fish-skinner. Holds over 100 patents in meat processing applications. Created a heralded model of employer-employee relations.

Iowa Pride

Born: May 27, 1913, Des Moines, Iowa. *Educated:* Bachelor of Mechanical Engineering, ISU, 1934. *Family:* Cleda Roberts, wife; Ted, son; Sheryl, daughter. *Iowa Connection:* born, raised, educated, invented in Iowa.

Honors: 1947, most outstanding contribution to the meat processing industry in a decade, American Meat Institute. 1978, Iowa Inventors Hall of Fame. 1982, Professional Achievement Award in Engineering, ISU. Library of Congress, repository of films of the Frank-A-Matic® frankfurter-making process.

James

VAN ALLEN (1914–)

Astrophysicist, discovered earth-encircling radiation belts

James Van Allen, world-renowned astrophysicist.

Iowan James Van Allen's belt is world-famous. Not the one he wears, the one that scientists named after him.

After receiving his doctorate in physics at the UI, Van Allen served as a research fellow at eastern schools until he was commissioned an officer in the United States Navy. He was directed to develop a proximity fuze for projectiles—a discovery that helped assure victory in the war with Japan. Upon completing this assignment, he returned to UI to chair the physics department, where he has remained ever since.

An expert on space radiation, he has led expeditions to Peru, Alaska, Greenland, and Antarctica to study the effects of cosmic rays, much of this work coming about because of an interesting idea he and a group of his colleagues had at his home one evening. They decided to sponsor a world-wide International Geophysical Year (IGY). During that year more data about space was gathered than had been accumulated since the beginning of time.

His international reputation in space exploration has brought him a wealth of opportunities to employ his brilliance in fields such as the exploration of cosmic rays, the earth's magnetic field,

155

balloon-launched rockets, aurorae, controlled thermonuclear reactions, rocket and satellite research, global atmospheric research, planetary and lunar exploration and space physics.

In 1958 instruments which he placed aboard America's first earth satellites, Explorers I and III, led him to discover bands of extremely high-intensity radiation particles circling the earth. These bands were named the "Van Allen Radiation Belts" in his honor.

Dr. Van Allen has done research work for the National Defense Research Council, NASA and every reputable space organization in the world. He has written several books and authored incredibly numerous articles on physics, rockets, and satellites. Dr. Van Allen's curriculum vitae, a partial listing of his many accomplishments, covers 12 typewritten pages, a tribute to a life lived as fully as the heavens are starred.

One thing is certain: People going into space, or sending objects there, do so more knowledgeably because of a small-town boy from Iowa, whose vision went there first.

And no one is going in orbit today without taking a product of Iowan James Van Allen along. All that space is no place for amateurs.

GRANTED five patents of space exploration hardware. One of America's authorities on cosmic rays, rockets, and outer space. He is a pioneer in high altitude research. Discoverer of Ring G around Saturn. Outfitted over 50 space flight missions. Principal investigator on 24 of those missions. All four planetary probes carry equipment from his teams of researchers. Discovered radiation belts on Saturn. Confirmed radiation belts on Jupiter. Designed the Aerobee sounding rocket. Devised a method to measure the absolute intensity of gamma rays. Designed vacuum tubes capable of withstanding the 20,000g shock of discharge from high velocity guns. Studied the fusion of atomic nuclei at high temperatures. Created the International Geophysical Year (IGY). Discovered the 11th moon of Saturn. Discovered lightning on Jupiter. Perfected a target-sensitive proximity fuze for use in projectiles. Coinvented the vacuum tube in this fuze. As leader of the UI space program, he made it possible for the University to claim: more contributions to space flight, more space-related discoveries, more work done in the sky than any other school in the world.

Born: September 7, 1914, Mt. Pleasant, Iowa. *Educated:* 1935, Iowa Wesleyan, B.S. summa cum laude; UI, Master of Science, 1936; UI, Ph.D., 1939. *Family:* Abigail, wife; Cynthia, Margot, Sarah, Thomas and Peter, children. *Iowa Connection:* born, raised, educated, teaches and researches in Iowa.

Honors: Doctor of Science Degrees: 1951 Iowa Weslyan College. 1957 Grinnell College. 1958 Coe College. 1959 Cornell College. 1960 University of Dubuque. 1961 University of Michigan; Northwestern University. 1963 Illinois College. 1966 Butler College; Boston College. 1967 Southampton College. 1969 Augustana College. 1982 St. Ambrose College. 1987 University of Bridgeport. 1949 C.N. Hickman medal of the American Rocket Society; Physics Award of Washington Academy of Science. 1958 Space Flight Award, American Astronautical Society. 1959 Distinguished Civilian Service medal (U.S. Army.) 1960 Louis W. Hill 1959 Space Transportation Award; Richtmyer Memorial Lecture. 1961 First Iowa Award in Science; First Annual Research Award, American Rocket Society; Elliot Cresson medal, Franklin Institute. 1962 David and Florence Guggenheim International Astronautics Award. 1963 John A. Fleming Award, American Geophysical Union. 1963 Golden Omega Award, Electrical Insulation Conference. 1964 Commander of the Order du Merite pour la Recherche et l'Invention; Iowa Broadcasters Association Award. 1972–1985 Carver Distinguished Professor, UI. 1974 NASA Medal for Exceptional Scientific Achievement. 1975 Distinguished Fellow Iowa Academy of Science. 1976 Navy's Distinguished Public Service Award. 1977 William Bowie Medal. 1978 Gold Medal, Royal Astronomical Society; Award of Merit, American Consulting Engineers Council. 1982 Space Science Award, American Institute of Aeronautics and Astronautics; Governor's Science Medal. 1984 COSPAR Award; International Space Hall of Fame. 1986 Distinguished Alumni Award, UI. 1986 Gold and Silver Salute, The Franklin Institute; First AAAS-Philip Hauge Abelson Prize. 1987 National Medal of Science; Hall of Fame, Society of Satellite Professionals; William Proctor Prize, Sigma Xi; UI Centennial Alumnus. 1989 Crafoord Prize, Royal Swedish Academy of Sciences. 1990 Nevada Medal; Hancher-Finkbine Medallion, UI; Cosmos Club Award; Nansen Medal and Prize Award, The Norwegian Academy of Science and Letters. 1991 National Space Club Science Award, National Science Board Vannevar Bush Award; James Harlan Award for Exemplary Service to the Nation; UI Presidential Award.

Gary J.
VERMEER (1918–)

Agri-industrialist, invented the large round hay bale

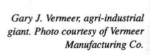ary Vermeer only wanted to empty a wagon full of corn.

He did it the easy way by inventing a hoist that lifted up one end of the wagon, letting the corn spill out. It sure beat shoveling the corn, the way everyone had done until that time.

When his neighbors saw how neatly his wagon hoist worked, they asked him to make one for them, too. A local machine shop was told how to make the hoist. But the demand that grew, as soon as several hoists were in use, told Gary he could produce a product that had consumer appeal.

Gary started building his own wagon hoists, and they sold well. But when competitive hoists came on the market, he realized he must come up with another product, if his company was to survive.

In those days some farm equipment was run off the flywheel on a tractor, but, unless conditions were ideal, the belt would slip off and the operation would halt. Gary looked at that problem as another opportunity for his creativity.

He designed a right-angle power takeoff drive—the Pow-R-Drive—that met with immediate success. When he took out a small ad in a farm publication, he was deluged with orders, and the one-year-old Vermeer Manufacturing Company took off.

Turning his attention to the problem farmers experienced when they placed drainage tile, Gary invented the right solution. His device again saved aching backs and high tile-installation costs and was popular from the start. Since then, the Vermeer line of trenchers has expanded to include crawler units and many associated pieces of earthmoving equipment.

In 1956 Gary tackled a different kind of problem, the job of cleaning out and cutting up stumps of trees that had been downed. His solution took the shape of a stump cutter that removed stumps easily and affordably. Brisk sales proved he was again focused on a target market.

One of the buyers of his stump cutters suggested to Gary that he design a solution to transplanting large trees. That's exactly what he did, by introducing the first machine that could mechanically cut a seven-foot ball of earth around the base of the tree, then transport and replant the tree and ball.

But in 1971, with a prosperous, busy manufacturing plant behind him and patents piling up in his pocket, Gary's biggest victory lay before him.

It started when a friend told him he was getting out of the cattle feeding business because it was just too much work putting up the small hay bales for winter feed.

Gary mulled that problem over and came up with a one-man hay system. The idea was to make huge, round, wrapped bales that a farmer could assemble simply while seated on his tractor. The large round bale retained its shape better, protected the hay from deterioration and held more of the nutrients than any prior form of handling hay. Gary's invention instantly revolutionized hay baling.

Gary's company came out with heavy-duty brush trimmers

in 1978 that were useful in clearing land, cleaning up storm damage, pruning operations and Christmas-tree disposal. In the 1990s Vermeer Manufacturing has introduced a line of trenchless technology, allowing horizontal holes to be bored in the earth without destroying the topography.

As many of these first-time products came into the market, the Vermeer Manufacturing Company grew to astonishing proportions, with over 2,000 employees and a worldwide dealer network.

The company has maintained the old Dutch philosophy that Gary Vermeer instilled in his family and his family of workers, which was simply: Build the Best.

It's a philosophy that still works for Vermeer Manufacturing.

INVENTED a hydraulic wagon hoist. Introduced the first stump cutter. Introduced the first large-tree spade. Introduced the first track-mounted trencher. Founded the Vermeer Manufacturing Co.

Born: September 29, 1918, Pella, Iowa. *Educated:* Pella High School graduate. *Family:* Matilda, wife; Stan and Robert, sons; Mary, daughter. *Iowa Connection:* born, raised, educated, worked, invented, farmed and founded his business in Iowa.

Honors: 1977 Community Service Award of Pella. 1984 Inventor of the Year (Iowa). 1986 Iowa Business Hall of Fame. 1992 Junior Achievement Business Hall of Fame.

Henry A.
WALLACE (1888–1965)
*Vice President of the United States,
pioneered hybrid seed corn*

A pig doesn't care what an ear of corn looks like.
—H. A. WALLACE

A 16-year-old boy, Henry A. Wallace, wondered why the 10 prettiest ears of corn won the blue ribbon in the corn judging contest.

The contest judge, Professor P.G. Holden, explained that pretty ears of corn would yield the best corn if used as seed the following year. Henry doubted that and said so.

His father patiently explained that professors always know best, but, just to prove the point, he would give Henry a plot of ground on which to grow corn from the best ears and the sorriest-looking ears to prove to himself that Professor Holden knew what he was talking about.

When the crops were harvested that fall, the results amazed Henry, his father and Professor Holden. The worst ears outproduced the best ears by a wide margin. This experiment launched a career in agriculture that carried a doubting Henry to the highest levels of politics and service to farmers.

Henry A. Wallace was born into a family of two other Henry Wallaces, his father Henry C., and his grandfather Henry Wallace, known widely as "Uncle Henry." Uncle Henry began the family's ventures into agriculture and politics. He had been a pioneer United Presbyterian minister in Iowa, who gave up the pulpit for reasons of health and began farming.

Iowa Pride

In 1908 President Theodore Roosevelt appointed Uncle Henry to the Country Life Commission, a group challenged with finding ways to improve the life of the nation's farmers. In his role on that commission, Uncle Henry helped expand the work of another Iowan, Jessie Field Shambaugh, founder of the 4-H movement through her work with farm youngsters.

Under President Warren G. Harding, Uncle Henry's son Henry C. was appointed Secretary of Agriculture, a job he held while acting as editor of the family publication called *Wallaces' Farmer.*

Henry A.'s discovery formed the basis for his lifetime rebuke of the "pretty ears" corn judging contests. In time, his opinions became those of agriculture and corn was judged on a system he devised called the Iowa Corn Yield Test. In this test, corn was planted and measured at harvest against other test plots.

As Henry A. finished high school, then college at ISU—where he graduated top in his agriculture class—he continued his corn-growing experiments. Borrowing both seed and ideas from the nationally known hybrid corn research center known as Connecticut Station, Henry continued developing new strains of corn that grew hardier, were more disease-resistant and produced higher yields.

After college, Henry accepted the editorship of the family magazine known as *Wallaces' Farmer.* In its pages he extolled the merits of growing hybrid corn.

As Henry's corn-breeding experiments grew he entered his strains in the Iowa Corn Yield Test, and finally in 1924 Henry captured the coveted Gold Medal. He had finally shown that inbred and hybrid corn would outproduce open-pollinated field brands. It was to become a revolutionary finding.

Seed from his winning Copper Cross strain became the first hybrid seed corn ever commercially sold. In the spring of 1924, Henry advertised his Copper Cross hybrid, under the banner headline, **"An Astonishing Corn Yields Astonishing Results!"**

By 1926, aided by corn-growing friends and business partners, Henry formed the first company exclusively to develop strains of hybrid corn and to produce and distribute hybrid seed.

Originally, the company was called simply the Hibred Corn Company, but in the mid-thirties the name was changed to the Pioneer Hi-bred Corn Company because the words *Hi-bred* and *hybrid* sounded confusingly similar. By this time, the word *hybrid* had been accepted into the common vernacular.

In the following years Wallace and his associates—Simon Casady, Jay Newlin, Ray Baker, Wayne Skidmore, Jim Wallace, Nelson Urban and Fred Lehman—designed buildings that enabled the efficient processing of hybrid seed corn. They built the first forced hot-air corn dryer for hybrid seed corn, and constructed the first modern hybrid seed corn drying and processing plant.

In 1933 President Franklin Roosevelt asked Henry to fill the same shoes Henry's father had once filled as Secretary of Agriculture. Prior to running for his third term, President Roosevelt asked Henry to be his vice presidential running mate.

Henry A. Wallace was elected to the nation's second-highest position and served for four years with President Roosevelt. It all began because a 16-year-old youngster questioned whether pretty ears of corn produced the fullest bins.

DEVELOPED the first hybrid corn seed sold. Was first to advertise hybrid seed corn for sale. As a corn breeder he developed many strains of hybrid seed corn. Organized the first company ever to be formed exclusively devoted to developing, producing and distributing hybrid seed corn. With his associates, developed the first forced hot-air corn dryer and built the first modern hybrid seed corn drying and processing plant. Conceived the Iowa Corn Yield Test, the oldest corn research program of its kind. Secretary of Agriculture, 1933–1940. Vice President of the United States, 1941–1945. Secretary of Commerce 1945–1946. Editor of *Wallaces' Farmer.*

Born: October 7, 1888, Adair County, Iowa. *Educated:* B.S. in agriculture, 1910, ISU. *Family:* Ilo, wife. Henry B. and Robert B., sons; and Jean B., daughter. *Iowa Connection:* born, raised, educated, created in Iowa.

Honors: Numerous.

Harley A. _____
WILHELM (1900–1995)

Co-invented the pure uranium
production process

Wilhelm showed up like a diamond in an ashpile.
—TINGLEY *VINDICATOR*

One of the world's top nuclear scientists treasures the above quote more than any other of the dozens of honors that have been heaped on his shoulders over the years. It was printed in the local paper after his starring role in a ninth grade basketball game. Iowan Dr. Harley Wilhelm liked sports almost as much as science.

Harley, a tenant farmer's son, used his athletic talents in basketball and baseball to win a scholarship to Drake University. As the team's captain, he led the Drake basketball squad to a winning series record that went unbroken for 45 years.

Following a brief stint in semipro baseball and coaching, Wilhelm accepted a graduate assistantship at ISU, going on to earn a doctorate in physical chemistry. Following graduation, Wilhelm stayed on at ISU where he established courses for ceramic engineering and spectro-chemistry students and did industrial consulting.

In February of 1942 as the world came awake to the unspeakable horrors of World War II, President Franklin D. Roosevelt gave the go-ahead to study ways to harness the atom and produce a nuclear bomb. He created a secret group bearing the name Manhattan Project. Tons and tons of high-purity uranium metal were required to initiate this research, yet no process had been discovered which would yield that much pure metal.

For years, several firms produced uranium, but their entire

production totaled less than 10 pounds and the product was impure, at that. Because scientists at Westinghouse, MIT and Princeton had failed to discover a feasible method of creating pure uranium, Wilhelm and his colleague, Iowan Frank H. Spedding, were appointed to develop an alternate material.

For a few months they worked on this problem with two graduate students without luck. Finally, they decided to go back to Square One. "Since we're getting nowhere with our search for a substitute for uranium, why not solve the original problem and figure out how to make pure uranium? It can't be any harder than what we are trying to do now," they reasoned.

On August 5, Harley's birthday, he received an incredible present. Just six months after starting, the team discovered a method of producing pure uranium. In a few weeks the crew of scientists formed an 11-pound ingot of metal which was carried to the project director in Chicago and placed on his desk.

Never had the director seen more than a few ounces of precious uranium. He was so suspicious that this Iowa-made ingot was a fraud that he had it sliced into small pieces to see if there was lead inside it. Of course there wasn't.

By December 2, the team had refined two tons of pure uranium. That was the day the world's first self-sustaining chain reaction went critical. Atomic scientists believed the nuclear pile was a vital first step in bomb production.

From late 1942 until the dropping of the bomb on Hiroshima, two million pounds of high-grade uranium were produced at the ISU laboratory which Wilhelm headed. On August 6, 1945, the first atomic bomb was dropped signifying the end of a killing war. Peace settled out of the ashes.

Wilhelm showed up like a diamond in a nuclear pile.

MADE inventions in the field of nuclear energy for which he holds 40 patents. Discussed and presented his special processes and methods at the International Conference on the Peaceful Uses of Atomic Energy, Geneva, Switzerland, 1955. Star basketball player, Drake University.

Born: August 5, 1900, near Ellston, Iowa. Educated: B.A. degree in mathematics, Drake University, 1923. Ph.D. in physical chemistry, ISU, 1931. Fam-

Iowa Pride

ily: Orpha, wife; Lorna, Max, Myrna and Gretchen, children. *Iowa Connection:* born, raised, educated and worked in Iowa.

Honors: Phi Beta Kappa, Scholastic Honorary Society, Drake University. Sigma Xi, Honorary Society, 1932. ISU Alumni Merit Award, 1949. Gold Medal of the Iowa Section of the American Chemical Society Award, 1954. Represented the United States at the International Conference on the Peaceful Uses of Atomic Energy, 1955. Distinguished Service Award, Drake University Alumni, 1959. Honorary LL.D., Drake University, 1961. Service Certificate, State of Iowa, 1961. Eisenman Award, American Society of Metals, 1962. Faculty Citation, ISU Alumni Association, 1967. "Double D" Award, Drake University, 1968. Centennial Citation, Iowa Academy of Science, 1975. Centennial Award, Drake University, 1981. Harley A. Wilhelm Hall, the Atomic Energy Commission's metallurgy building at ISU, 1986. Hall of Fame, Iowa high school basketball, 1988. Gold Medal of American Society of Mechanical Engineers, for "eminently distinguished engineering achievement," 1990.

Annie
WITTENMYER (1827–1900)
Founded diet kitchen
management

From the start Iowans knew you had to earn your bread by the sweat of your own brow. They didn't understand enslaving another person to perform their work for them. So it was natural that Iowans believed in wiping the scourge of enslavement from America. But, as bitter as the thought was to bear, Iowa women knew their men would lose limbs and lives in erasing slavery through the Civil War. Getting medical support to their men in the battlefield became their No. 1 priority.

Keokuk, strategically located on the Mississippi River, was Iowa's jumping-off point into the Civil War. Here, Iowa volunteers converged before they rushed off to crush the Rebel Grey.

Within hours after Fort Sumter was fired upon, launching the Civil War, a group of Keokuk women—headed by Annie Wittenmyer—formed the Keokuk Ladies Soldiers' Aid Society, later shortened to the Keokuk Society (KS). Their purpose was to gather medical supplies, and see that those vital needs got to the battle sites where Iowan regiments fought.

Annie had already established a local reputation for leadership by founding schools for the needy, long before Iowa public schools began. Born, raised and educated in Ohio, Annie was widowed early in her Keokuk life, where she was the wife of a prosperous merchant.

A few months after the formation of the KS, the United States Sanitary Commission was formed in New York City. Iowa

Iowa Pride _____

Governor Samuel J. Kirkwood duly followed the national pattern by appointing 13 "honorable Iowa men" to create an Iowa State Sanitary Commission (ISSC). If Governor Kirkwood thought the Civil War was bad, he hadn't reckoned on the enraged ladies of the Keokuk Society.

They told the governor that men were insensitive to the soldiers' medical needs, all the men wanted was glory and salaries, the women had already conscripted other women's groups throughout Iowa and in the few months of their existence their success was gaining a fine reputation.

In a fiery newspaper letter the women scathed the men who had once taken over Annie's school program: "The gentlemen (of Keokuk) ... blowed and gassed generally ... and then led it to chaos, neglect and ultimate ruin." The women concluded that Iowa "Honorables," who were on the ISSC, had better either roll up their sleeves and do some work or get out of the way so the Keokuk Society women could get the job done.

Recognizing he had insulted the women, Governor Kirkwood added injury to it by asking the KS to join the ISSC, implying that they were unorganized and would do better to let calmer male heads systematize their operations. Oops. Second mistake. Iowa women generally ignored the governor and went on with their operations, doing exactly, through the KS, what the ISSC was unable to accomplish. Annie forged ahead, making deals with the military for most supplies from Iowa to go through the KS. She obtained free transportation for her goods and got a free pass on all rail and boat transportation, signed by President Abraham Lincoln, to personally deliver her supplies to battlegrounds.

The next year Governor Kirkwood joined Annie by appointing her to the ISSC, and within a year, the KS and ISSC merged. In 1864, Annie resigned and proposed a plan for asylums to be dedicated to Civil War orphans.

Throughout the year she used her (by now considerable) political skills to launch her orphanage plans, through the Orphan Asylum Association (OAA). She shrewdly asked newly elected Iowa Governor William Stone to preside over the OAA, and soon asylums opened in Farmington and Davenport.

In 1864 Annie had come up with the idea that was to catapult her to national prominence. During her battlefield experience she had seen unacceptable food served to the wounded, on rusted utensils. A cup of wretched coffee—colored from logwood, rather than coffee grounds—with a plate of greasy fried meat and a chunk of poorly baked bread was not food to get well on.

She lobbied the United States Christian Commission (USCC) to underwrite diet kitchen projects and appoint her as supervisor. Both events promptly happened.

Within 18 months 200 diet kitchen managers worked directly under Annie in every U.S. military hospital. Thousands of soldiers labored under her women managers to deliver tasty, nutritious food to injured and sick soldiers. National publicity credited Annie Wittenmyer with saving thousands of soldiers' lives through the more than one million meals her crews fed to troops each month.

Annie Wittenmyer saved thousands of soldiers' lives through healthful diets. She established asylums for Civil War orphans. She set up medical supply lines to aid soldiers on the line.

She founded the profession of diet kitchen managers. She helped organize the Woman's Christian Temperance Union (WCTU) and was its first president.

Iowan Annie Wittenmyer simply broke the mold.

FOUNDED one of the first nontuition grade schools in Iowa. Founded the Keokuk Service, supplying bandages and support services to Iowans serving in the Union army. Headed the Iowa State Sanitary Commission. A co-founder of the Woman's Christian Temperance Union.

Born: 1827 in Ohio. *Educated:* at an Ohio women's school. *Family:* William, husband; Charles, son. *Iowa Connection:* worked and created in Iowa. *Honors:* Iowa Women's Hall of Fame.

F.A. WITTERN (1900–)

Invented the change-giving vending machine

I've made mistakes; but whenever I did, I put it behind me,
corrected it and went on to do it right the next time.

—F.A. WITTERN

F. A. Wittern thought that achieving fame and fortune was peanuts. And that's exactly how he started, with peanuts. But that's getting ahead of the story.

F.A. was a creative kid. During World War I he sent President Woodrow Wilson a design for an underwater magnet bomb that would attach to and destroy enemy submarines. Government officials were so impressed they immediately wired F.A. a job offer in the War Department but wanted to know which college he had gotten his engineering degree from. It was a difficult question to answer, considering that F.A. was a sophomore in high school at the time.

The job could wait because at the time F.A. and his dad were carefully disassembling a Ford auto, then as carefully reassembling it. F.A.'s mother thought the two were crazy for taking apart a perfectly good automobile, but F.A.'s father said, "Now we will know how to fix it when things go wrong." F.A. learned about more than cars from that early lesson.

As a young man F.A. invented a coin-operated table baseball game. He constructed a beautiful working model which he took from store to store, selling thousands of the models with only that one game. Returning to his shop, F.A. first made games and then made good on his orders.

170

By his early thirties F.A. had made his first million dollars. When he told his father he was now a millionaire, his father hugged him and wept on his shoulders. Within a few years F.A. lost his million and took his last $12.50 to buy some used tools to open Fawn Engineering, taking the name from his initials.

In those days, peanut machines dispensed a scoop of peanuts for a penny. It was a simple deal but F.A. saw a better way. His peanut machine rang a loud bell as it gave a bonus scoop of peanuts to the ninth customer. People loved the element of chance he put into peanut vending, for often the winning customer had to buy a round of drinks for having won the free peanuts. "Russian Roulette," F.A. called it.

F.A. took his machine into bars and stores, telling the owners if they didn't sell more peanuts than ever before he would take back the machines. He never took one back and soon a half-million of his machines were ringing profits for owners and F.A. alike.

F.A. looked for another problem to solve in vending. The problem he found dealt with oddly priced items. Vending machines could only take single coins. If a product cost 20 cents, and the machine only took a quarter, the vendor slit the side of each package and inserted a nickel change, which the customer got along with the product. The transaction was clumsy, awkward and costly. F.A. knew there must be a better way.

In 1945, as World War II ground to a halt, F.A. hand-tooled the world's first change-returning vending machine. He immediately cornered the vending market, building Fawn Engineering in Des Moines into the leading vending manufacturer, turning out vending machines almost as fast as dealers clamored for them.

The sales of his machines showed another facet of F.A.'s genius. Prior to his entry into the market, vending companies owned many machines, placing them strategically in stores. The store owner was paid a mere 5 percent of the machine's profits, while the vending company reaped 95 percent of the profit.

Again, F.A. found a better way. He suggested to the owner that he buy his own machine and earn 100 percent of the profit. Soon stories of happy business owners enjoying a rich new source of revenue made the rounds. F.A. again was chased by people begging for his goods. F.A.'s success has proven that his business philosophy works perfectly. The philosophy is simple: "When you take care of the customer, you take care of yourself."

RECEIVED a patent on an oil gauge when he was only 16. Over 40 patents, mostly on vending-related machinery. Created the world's most popular peanut vending machine. Founded Fawn Engineering Corporation, one of the world's largest manufacturers of vending equipment.

Born: October 19, 1900, Cushing, Iowa. *Educated:* high school Flandreau, South Dakota; a short while at the University of Minnesota, although no formal engineering training. *Family:* Viola, wife; F.A., Jr., son. *Iowa Connection:* born, raised, invents and works in Iowa.

Honors: Who's Who in American Business: limited to those individuals who have demonstrated true leadership and achievement in their occupation and have contributed significantly to the betterment of society. Governor's Award: by Iowa Governor Robert Ray, recognizing excellence in creating opportunity to improve the quality of life. 1976, Presidential E Award, for outstanding export trade. 1977, Iowan of the Month, *Iowa Business and Industry Magazine.* Wittern Street, Flandreau, South Dakota. Iowa Inventors Hall of Fame, 1989.

Grant
WOOD (1892–1942)
America's painter laureate

All I contend for is the sincere use of native material by the
artist who has command of it.

— GRANT WOOD

The joke is on the cultural snobs
who don't really get it.

Grant Wood's *American Gothic* is arguably
the most-copied painting in the world and probably the most parodied. Those who parody do so as a putdown of
bucolic America, us Iowans to be specific.

Grant understood cultural elitism far better than those who
mimic him fathom regionalism in art. He clearly noted his per-
ception when he wrote: "Culturally our Eastern states are still
colonies of Europe." Grant Wood was speaking in his profound
essay, "Revolt Against the City."

Grant believed that American art, like American drama, music, and even literature, had too long been dominated by cultural
chauvinists in the East. He referred to those who so all-know-
ingly wink among themselves about the Midwest hicks in "fly-
over America," and snicker about our pitchforks and overalls, un-
aware of the broad culture that springs from these prairies in the
form of art, theater, dance, literature and music.

Grant Wood took the artist's then-obligatory trip to France,
to mimic French impressionism. He was painting uninspired canvases, trying to find himself, when he ran into an old Cedar
Rapids pal, William Shirer. Shirer was then a foreign correspondent assigned to Paris.

Iowa Pride _____

The two met one day for a lunch at Les Escargots, a delightful street cafe on the Rive Gauche, or Left Bank. Their lunch lingered for several hours through several carafes of white wine, as the two Iowa-bred geniuses discussed life and directions they should take with their lives.

As Shirer later wrote of the event in his autobiography, "Grant was that day discovering what was wrong with his painting and why he had to return to Iowa to paint the regional things he knew best—the honest faces of people of the soil, the barns and hills and crops and things rural, bucolic." As Grant said, "Your true regionalist is not a mere eulogist; he may even be a severe critic."

Grant left Paris, scrapped impressionism, and returned to Iowa to paint what he knew best. The first person he saw on his return was his mother, whom he now saw in a new and lovely light. The resulting canvas, *Woman with Plant,* is hailed by many artists as his finest work.

Finding this perspective was no easy struggle for Grant. His sketchy education had been mostly art courses, here and there. But reading his "Revolt" essay shows a man with a brilliant command of language, the ability to think and express his thoughts, and importantly, a man with something to say: "There is, of course, no ownership in artistic subject matter except that which is validated by the artist's own complete apprehension and understanding of the materials."

Like any great artist, Wood had command of many media in which he interpreted his feelings. He became an expert in stained glass painting and created a treasured window in the Cedar Rapids city hall. The window's theme pays tribute to the American military forces.

The man who painted the most-known American painting—*American Gothic*—led the way for regionalism to supplant the facade of Europeanism that until then had frozen the fine arts in a pretentious posture. He wrote,

> Let me try to state the basic idea of the regional movement. Each section (of the country) has a personality of its own, in physiography, industry, psychology. Thinking painters and writers who have passed

their formative years in these regions will, by care-taking analysis, work out and interpret in their productions these varying personalities.

Cultural snobbishness has no more place in art than a parody poking fun at the *American Gothic* has a place on the cover of *Time* magazine. The effete elite still don't get it.

CREATED a legacy of Americanism in art.

Born: February 13, 1892, Anamosa, Iowa. *Educated:* Handicraft Guild, Minneapolis, 18 months; UI, one art course; Chicago Art Institute, one course; Academy Julien, Paris, several months. *Family:* Sara Sherman, wife. *Iowa Connection:* born, raised, studied, taught, painted in Iowa.

IOWANS
who made it elsewhere

Bess Streeter
ALDRICH (1881–1954)
Widely-read author

Her husband never got to know how famous his writer wife was to become, for his 1925 untimely death while in a church service occurred just before his wife's work achieved national fame.

Born in Cedar Falls, Bess graduated from UNI then taught in schools in Utah and Iowa until she met Captain Charles S. Aldrich, a Tipton lawyer and banker. In 1907 they married and moved to Nebraska where the couple's four children were born.

Her work concerned family life among the pioneers who settled Iowa and Nebraska. Two of her novels, *Miss Bishop* (1933) and *Song of Years* (1939), were set in Cedar Falls, with the latter also revealing early Sioux City history.

Bess's fifth novel, *A Lantern in Her Hand*, was translated into over 20 languages. Her novel *Miss Bishop* was made into the motion picture *Cheers for Miss Bishop* and was adapted for the screen by Stephen Vincent Benet. In addition to her novels she wrote over 160 short stories.

POPULAR WRITER.

Born: February 17, 1881, Cedar Falls, Iowa. *Education:* Cedar Falls public schools, graduating in 1898. In 1901, received her degree from Iowa State Normal School (now University of Northern Iowa). *Family:* Charles Sweltzer Aldrich, husband; James, Charles, Robert, sons; Mary Eleanor, daughter. *Iowa Connection:* born, raised and educated in Iowa.

Iowa Pride

Honors: Awarded the Johnson Brigham Award in 1949 from the Iowa Library Association. Was named to the Nebraska Hall of Fame in 1973. Inducted into the Iowa Women's Hall of Fame in 1995.

Bix

BEIDERBECKE (1903–1931)
Renowned cornet jazz stylist

All I've ever called the dear boy was Bix ... just that name
alone will make one stand up.

—Jazz great LOUIS ARMSTRONG

When he was two years old, Bix
stunned his parents by toddling up to the piano
and picking out a tune. Few diaper-clad babies
have ever wowed their parents more than this
Davenport baby did that day. In a few years he could play any
song he heard. So perfect was his ear that he even played the
same mistakes that were in the piece he copied.

Bix (Leon) Beiderbecke (By-der-beck) later was to become
an American musical genius—and an American tragedy. Along
with Louis Armstrong, he towered over jazz in the twenties. His
life loosely inspired Dorothy Baker's celebrated thirties novel,
Young Man With A Horn, a book that later became a film.

When he was a young teen, a friend gave him a cornet,
which he quickly mastered, and Bix was never the same. As a
youngster he got jobs playing in the riverboat bands that plied the
Mississippi River past his Davenport home.

He also joined band after band, perfecting a technique that
changed the entire cornet-playing musical world. As his fame
grew, fellow musicians became his most rabid fans, listening
with awe as he played his new and exciting style.

Bix had two problems. One, with a sheet of music which he
couldn't read; the other, with a bottle of gin which he couldn't
control. Gradually Bix learned to read enough music to hold
down jobs with the leading orchestras of the time, most notably

181

Iowa Pride

the world-renowned Paul Whiteman orchestra where he played lead cornet. Bix never did conquer booze.

When he was 28, the music stopped. Bix, numbed and debilitated by alcoholic excess, died without wife or child, and with only a few solos recorded on popular songs of the day. But this Iowa legend left a legacy in his unique style of jazz that today has been copied by virtually every jazz cornetist, from Louis Armstrong to the present.

> And when he played—why, the ears did the same thing.
>
> —LOUIS ARMSTRONG, 1954

CREATED a unique cornet jazz style.

Born: March 10, 1903, Davenport, Iowa. *Educated:* Davenport public schools, Lake Forest Academy. *Iowa Connection:* born, raised, educated in Iowa.

Mildred Wirt
BENSON (1900?–)
Prolific and acclaimed author

Alice B. Emerson wrote the Ruth Fielding books, Julia K. Duncan penned the Doris Force stories, Joan Clark turned out the Penny Nichols mysteries, Carolyn Keene bound her readers in spells with the Nancy Drew books and Mildred Wirt Benson created other works involving the characters of Doris Force, the Brownie Scouts, Dan Carter—Cub Scout, and the Girl Scouts.

All in all, well over a hundred book titles from these authors—mostly teen-age mysteries—sold millions of copies from the 1930s to the present, with sales still going strong. Nancy Drew alone accounted for 80 million books sold. You would think it would take even more than Emerson, Fielding, Duncan, Clark, and Benson to produce all these books. If you thought that you would be wrong.

All of this literary activity came from just one person, Iowa-born (Ladora) Mildred Wirt Benson whose pen names included all the above.

As the twentieth century draws to a close, Benson—who is well into her advanced years—works as a reporter for the *Toledo* (Ohio) *Blade*, flies her own plane, cranks out teen mysteries, and writes stories on archeology and sports. This ageless author wields a mighty pen.

The Nancy Drew series may be Benson's best-known books. Many parents (this one included) recall reading several chapters of Nancy Drew every night to their daughters for a bedtime treat.

Iowa Pride _____

(My daughter Cathy and I still kid about the time that Nancy Drew was mistaken for Nanny Doo!)

Demographic studies show that children generally start reading Nancy Drew at about 8–10 years of age and stop around 10–13 years, with youngsters today reading her at an earlier age.

A 1993 conference on Nancy Drew, sponsored by the UI, drew hundreds of people anxious to meet the author and renew their friendship with their old pals Nancy Drew and her handsome friend and football star, Ned Nickerson.

Returning to Iowa for the conference, Mildred Wirt Benson felt right at home, for in 1927 she became the first woman recipient of a master's degree from the University of Iowa School of Journalism and Mass Communication.

WROTE NANCY DREW and other adventure stories.

Born: July 10, 1905, in Ladora, Iowa. *Education:* Graduated from Ladora High School in 1922; one of four students. Earned a bachelor's degree from the University of Iowa and in 1927 was the first woman to earn a master's degree in journalism from the university. *Iowa Connection:* born, raised and educated in Iowa.

Honors: Recognized with numerous writing awards and received the University of Iowa Distinguished Alumni Achievement Award in 1994. Member of Iowa School of Journalism and Mass Communication Hall of Fame. Member of Ohio Women's Hall of Fame. Inducted into Iowa Women's Hall of Fame in 1994.

Works: Wrote 23 Nancy Drew mysteries under the pseudonym Carolyn Keene; has written more than 120 children's books under her own name and pen names.

Norman

BORLAUG (1914–)

Nobel laureate

If an Iowan hitches himself to a plow, you have to wonder which doctor to call to care for the poor soul.

You really don't think of offering him a Nobel Prize, unless the man before the plow is Iowan Norman Borlaug. For Iowa-born and raised Norman Borlaug pulled that plow through his many test plots. And because he did, millions of people who might otherwise have starved, with or without a plow, could grow the staff of life, wheat.

Raised on a 160-acre Iowa farm, Norm always competed toughly, whether as captain of his football team or winning a wrestling match. But athletics was not his calling. After graduating from the University of Minnesota, he accepted various jobs dealing with genetics testing and research.

In 1944, he was appointed to head the International Maize and Wheat Improvement Center in Mexico City. It was here he was to fulfill his need to compete.

The competitor? Starvation. For, in the forties, existing strains of wheat produced poorly. Since they grew erratically and produced small crops, those wheat varieties failed to provide the food required to serve the needs of Third World countries overrun with populations dependent on wheat.

Borlaug's success in his search for wheat that would better respond to fertilizer and prompt larger yields was recognized throughout the world. Cliff Hardin, secretary of agriculture under President Richard Nixon, called Borlaug "one of the foremost hunger fighters of our generation."

185

Iowa Pride———————————

The Nobel committee, in awarding Borlaug the coveted Nobel Prize, said about his work, "If ... we could match Borlaug's ... food production ... for development of the Third World, we should look for greater optimism concerning ... global peace." To which Borlaug responded, "I'm just a farm boy from Iowa. If anything, I have only provided the spark."

DEVELOPED new strains of cereal grains to increase the food-producing capacities of Third World countries.

Born: March 25, 1915, Cresco, Iowa. *Education:* B.S. in forestry, M.S. in plant pathology and Ph.D. in plant pathology from University of Minnesota. *Family:* Margaret, wife; Norma Jean, daughter; William, son. *Iowa Connection:* born and raised in Iowa.

Honors: 1970 Nobel Peace Prize for development of new cereal and grain varieties for developing countries; received the American Citizenship Award at Graduation, 31 honorary degrees; buildings named after him at University of Minnesota, and research centers, streets and schools in Bolivia and Mexico.

Johnny
CARSON (1925–)
Noted talk show host

Johnny Carson, his kind of talk wasn't cheap.

"**The Great Carsoni will entertain one and all next Saturday!**" the sign announced. The Great Carsoni was 14-year-old Johnny Carson, who staked out an early claim to entertain.

Johnny first vocalized in Corning, Iowa (October 23, 1925), then moved to Omaha where he began his career in acting and comedy.

Johnny's magic act was the beginning of a career in entertainment that grew to astonishing proportions. Certainly, the magic continued in his professional life, even though it left his act.

Few entertainers have achieved the acclaim that Johnny Carson did. NBC Research has estimated that 12 million viewers nightly enjoyed his stand-up comedy and the talk show he hosted.

During a thirty-year stint as host of *The Tonight Show Starring Johnny Carson,* he introduced 22,000 guests in over 7,500 hours of shows.

Johnny Carson taught Americans to stay up late, and like it.

Born: October 23, 1925, Corning, Iowa. *Family:* Alexis, wife; Chris, Cory, Ricky (deceased), sons from previous marriages. *Iowa Connection:* born in Iowa.

187

Iowa Pride

Honors: Six Emmy Awards, Academy of Television Arts and Sciences' Governors' Award in 1980, George Foster Peabody Award in 1986, inducted into the ATAS Hall of Fame in 1987, Scopus Award by the American Friends of Hebrew University, Man of the Year in May 1985 by the Variety Club, Iris Award of the Year from the National Association of Television Program Executives in 1984, Harvard University's Hasty Pudding Award in 1977, Entertainer of the Year Award from the American Guild of Variety Artists (AGVA) in 1978, Friars Club Man of the Year Award in 1979.

George Washington
CARVER (1864–1943)

Acclaimed botanist, humanitarian

George Washington Carver, botanist, inventor, humanitarian. Photo provided by Iowa State University.

It's possible that George Washington Carver's artwork might have excelled his scientific exploits.

Carver was born into slavery in southern Missouri. His family were the only slaves of Moses Carver. George and his brother Jim were orphaned, and after the Civil War Moses Carver allowed the boys to live as if they were his foster sons in the cabin he built for his family. It was a humble beginning for a man who would make such an important impact on black freedoms.

As a youngster, after various odd jobs—including working in the homes of some affluent people—Carver entered Simpson College in Indianola and immediately excelled in science and art courses. But science, not painting, ultimately won his heart. Soon, he left Simpson to attend Iowa State University, where he obtained a Master of Agriculture degree.

Upon graduation, Carver refused a teaching position at ISU for a job at Tuskegee University, in Alabama. Since Tuskegee was a school for African-Americans, with an all-black faculty, the rest of his life he lived and worked with those whom he called "his people."

Carver established the agriculture department at Tuskegee as an important part of the University. Through the next 47 years

Iowa Pride ──────────────────────

of his life he earned a salary of $1,000 per year and achieved international fame. He also became known as the "Sweet Potato Man" and the "Peanut Man," nicknames awarded him for the ways he sought to champion new crops for poor blacks.

With great foresight, Carver foresaw the emergence of the *chemurgic* movement, which is the blending of the disciplines of agriculture and chemistry. He espoused the concept that there is no waste in nature. His work with fungi, especially the peanut fungus that decimated Southern crops during one time in his career, was one of his finest accomplishments. And is virtually unknown.

There is no question that Iowa-educated George Washington Carver had an enormous impact on poverty in the post–Civil War South, on the perceptions of blacks by whites, and on inspiring thousands of African-Americans to reach within themselves to find a higher purpose.

───────────────────────

KNOWN AS the "Sweet Potato Man" and the "Peanut Man." Devised many uses for the peanut crop and discovered methods to combat the peanut fungus, considered by many to be his finest achievement.

Born: 1864 (exact date unknown), near Diamond Grove, Missouri. *Education:* Simpson College, Indianola; Bachelor of Agriculture, ISU 1894; ISU master's degree in agriculture 1896. *Iowa Connection:* educated in Iowa.

Honors: Fellow of the Royal Society for the Encouragement of Arts, Manufacturers, and Commerce (London, England, 1916). Spingarm Medal by the National Association for the Advancement of Colored People (1923). Iowa State College Alumni Merit Award (1938). Roosevelt Medal (1939). Thomas A. Edison Foundation Award (1943). Honorary Doctor of Science degrees from Simpson College (1928), University of Rochester (1941), Selma University (1942). Feature film of his life was made in 1938. Birthplace was designated the George Washington Carver National Monument in 1943. In 1944 the governors of Connecticut, Illinois, Indiana, New Jersey, New York, Pennsylvania and West Virginia issued proclamations designating the first week in January 1945 as Carver Week. President Harry S Truman designated January 5, 1946, as George Washington Carver Day. January 5, 1948, the 3-cent Carver Commemorative stamp was sold. Carver Science Hall, Simpson College, was named for him. George Washington Carver Hall, Iowa State University, was dedicated on September 27, 1970.

William F. Cody
"BUFFALO BILL"
(1846–1917)
Frontier plainsman

Buffalo Bill Cody. Photo by Eugene Pirou, 1896, courtesy of Denver Public Library, Western History Department.

The boy was seconds away from losing his life.

His adversary peered over the ridge, axe poised. The next target was the fair head of an 11-year-old boy, a lad who should have been safely home.

But this boy was Iowa-born and -raised Bill Cody who, before he was 10, was at home on a horse and knew how to shoot, lasso a calf and drive a team of horses. When his daddy was killed for speaking out against slavery, Cody took a man's job and became a teamster on a wagon train going West.

During the trip, an Indian attack chased the frightened teamsters down a riverbed. Young Cody's legs were short and he lagged behind. But the boy already knew the Code of the West. It was called *survive.* Calmly he raised his rifle and aimed at the enemy. Later, when a reporter wrote praise of Cody's feat, Bill Cody's reputation began.

At age 14, when most boys are thinking of Boy Scouting, Cody hired on with Pony Express, riding into history during the few months this company existed. Once he rode 328 miles in less than 23 hours, a feat never duplicated. Cody's exploits fed the campfire tales of rough-hewn men who loved his daring and dash.

191

Iowa Pride

In his twenties he killed buffalo for the railroads, providing them with their required 5-pound ration of fresh meat for each man per day. Later he entered a buffalo-killing contest, and his one-day total of 69 vanquished the other hunter's mere 46. From that day on he bore the moniker "Buffalo Bill."

Cody's career covered every aspect of the life of a plainsman: cattle herder, wagon teamster, scout, guide, and soldier. He was named a justice of the peace, elected to the Nebraska legislature, became a cattle baron on his own ranch, and was appointed an Indian agent to negotiate with the Indians he employed in his Wild West shows.

A novelist glamorized the young Buffalo Bill in dozens of novels making him a national celebrity. Friends sponsored him in stage shows which brought the excitement of the Old West to the cities of America. Iowan Buffalo Bill personified the West.

AMERICA'S premier plainsman, hunter, scout and western guide. Helped found the rodeo.

Born: February 26, 1846, LeClaire, Iowa. *Educated:* on the prairie. *Family:* Louisa, wife; a daughter and a son. *Iowa Connection:* born, spent the formative first seven years of his life in Iowa.

Lee
DE**F**OREST (1873–1961)

Father of the wireless, commercial radio, and talking pictures

Lee deForest, pioneer radio engineer, invented the talkies. Photo courtesy of Liveright Publishing Corporation.

As a lad, Lee deForest had three goals in life. He wanted to (1) invent lots of things, (2) become rich, and (3) became famous.

He succeeded in two out of three, which isn't all that bad. Here's how he did it.

Despite his father's wish that Lee join him in the Congregational ministry, Lee announced that he would go to Yale and get the education he needed to achieve his very clear goals.

By the time he left Yale University, at the age of 22, he had invented an electrolytic decoder, a device to accept wireless transmissions. His unique invention worked better than the one Marconi, the Italian inventor of the wireless, had put together.

During the next five years, deForest invented a method of using a telephone receiver for the reception of wireless signals,

193

an alternating current method of transmitting wireless signals, 2- and 3-coil slide tuners for improved reception of signals, a loop antenna, and a beam transmitter, and filed 34 other important patents. These discoveries ushered in the age of communications, and earned him the title of the "Wizard of Wireless."

When he was 34 years of age he suddenly quit working with wireless to perfect the audion, a 3-electrode thermionic vacuum tube, commonly known as the radio tube. This tube magnified sound, and was useful in relaying telephone sounds over long distances.

The two patents covering this invention have been called two of the most important patents ever developed. In a few years he became known as the "Father of Radio," having invented substantially all of the key elements to bring this industry into existence.

Once again, he quit the field completely and turned his attention to another field that required his inventive genius, motion pictures. DeForest quickly invented a method of adding the soundtrack to film, creating an entity known as talking pictures.

Iowa-born Lee deForest achieved world acclaim for his inventive brilliance. He missed only one of his goals. At his death, it was reported that he had little over $2,000 in his bank account.

HOLDER of over 300 invention patents.

Born: August 26, 1873, Council Bluffs, Iowa. *Education:* graduated from Yale. *Family:* Nora, Mary, Marie, wives; Harriet, daughter. *Iowa Connection:* born in Iowa.

Honors: Elliott Cressam Medal of the Franklin. Hohn Scott Medal, City of Philadelphia Institute. Medals of Honor of the Institute of Radio Engineers. Gold Medals of St. Louis & San Francisco World Fairs. Honorary Doctor of Science from Yale and Syracuse Universities. Sigma Xi, Aurelian Honorary Society of Yale. Cross of the Legion of Honor, French government. Fellow, Institute of Electrical Engineers. Fellow and President, Institute of Radio Engineers.

Wyatt

E ARP (1848–1929)
Frontier marshal

Not many frontier marshals lived past their 30th birthday. Wyatt Earp beat all odds.

Wyatt died peacefully at 80 years of age, wealthy, respected and esteemed as a role model for youngsters. Few lawmen of the Old West had it so good.

Wyatt's parents moved to Pella, Iowa, when he was two years old. There he and his brothers, Virgil, Morgan and Jim, mastered the skills of riding and shooting that would eventually lead rough and tough men of the Old West to call them "The Fearless Earps."

At age 16, Wyatt drove a team of horses during his family's move to California, where his father Nicholas prospected for gold. Wyatt proved his worth as a man on this trip, handling himself with calm deliberation, even during attacks by Indians.

In California, Wyatt for a while studied law, but a restless spirit drove him at age 17 to accept a job driving a stagecoach over a route that had repeatedly been robbed by thieves. During three months of driving, he was never late and never lost a cent. For the next few years Wyatt drove stagecoaches that carried large amounts of cash. He never lost a cargo, and his legend grew.

At age 21, Wyatt hired out to provide fresh meat for a group of surveyors, then followed the railroads, providing meat for railroad gangs. A shrewd Wyatt was soon a wealthy man. As the buffalo hunting business became tougher, due to dwindling herds and railroad completions, Wyatt settled in Wichita, Kansas, where he became as skilled at gambling as he was at hunting.

195

Iowa Pride

The towns were generally peaceful until cowboys brought cattle to market. The cowboys were flush with money in their pockets, thirst for strong drink on their lips and trouble on their minds. Since Wyatt was known as a sober and honest man, the townsmen pleaded with him to be their marshal and control the drunken and dangerous outlaw cowboys that took over the town.

Wyatt tamed the mobs, facing posses of armed and ruthless men, hungry to kill him. He always survived. Several outlaws who fired on Wyatt learned too late that it would be their last shot in life. Never once did Wyatt Earp lose a fight.

The next few years, Wyatt was marshal in Wichita, then Dodge City, Kansas, finally Tombstone, Arizona. It was during these years that awesome episodes gave Wyatt's legend fodder to grow on. Even the stories fell short of the truth of the incidents. Iowa-raised Wyatt Earp was a man for all people, a man larger than his legend.

U.S. MARSHAL who lived a legendary life.

Born: March 19, 1848, Monmouth, Illinois. *Educated:* Pella, Iowa, public school. *Family:* Josephine, wife. *Iowa Connection:* raised and educated in Pella where he learned to ride and shoot.

Honor: Considered to be one of the finest lawmen to have lived.

Mamie Doud
E ISENHOWER (1896–1979)
First Lady

Mamie Doud Eisenhower, first lady. Photo courtesy Mamie Doud Eisenhower Birthplace, Boone, Iowa.

Mamie always claimed a lot more Iowa than was bred into her. She liked Iowa and Iowans that much.

Born in Boone, Mamie Doud was the daughter of a successful meat packer. When she was nine months old, the family moved to Cedar Rapids where her father was associated with T.M. Sinclair Packing Company, later to become Wilson Packing Co.

Before she was 10 the family moved to Colorado Springs, then to Denver, Colorado. As a young lady, on a visit to a winter home in San Antonio, Mamie met 2d Lt. Dwight D. Eisenhower, who was stationed at nearby Ft. Sam Houston. They fell immediately in love, married in 1916 in Denver, and went on to write history. Eisenhower became a five-star general, Supreme Commander of All Allied Forces during World War II, and served as President of the United States from 1953–1961.

When General Eisenhower was inaugurated, he stepped from the podium and kissed his wife, becoming the first President to kiss his wife in public.

Mamie received the coveted Iowa Award in 1970, in Boone, the first woman to receive that award. In 1993 she was inducted into the Iowa Women's Hall of Fame. She was on the Gallup Poll's list of most admired women in the world for a number of

Iowa Pride

years, and received many other awards and honors during her lifetime.

She spent her retirement years at their farm in Gettysburg, Pennsylvania, the only home she and the General ever owned. Ike died in 1969, and Mamie died in 1979. Mamie visited Boone many times over the years to visit her relatives and friends. Her birthplace, located at 709 Carroll Street in Boone, has been restored with many items of family furniture and was dedicated in 1980. It includes a museum and library of the Eisenhower era.

Born: November 14, 1896, Boone, Iowa. *Education:* Jackson School, Cedar Rapids, Iowa; graduated from Corona, Denver, Colorado; attended Mulholland School, Denver, Colorado. *Family:* Dwight "Ike," husband; Doud Dwight, John, sons. *Iowa Connection:* born in Iowa.

Honor: The first "First Lady" to be included by fashion designers among the "Ten Best Dressed Women in the U.S."

Simon
E*STES* (1938–)
Renowned bass-baritone

Simon Estes, Iowa's opera star.

All winter, Simon Estes and his father went to the coal mine and picked up coal that had dropped off at the entrance of the coal mine.

But while that home may not have been filled with material comforts, it overflowed with the greater wealth of love. "Never for a single night do I remember not having mommy and daddy at home, loving and caring for us," Simon Estes says.

After Estes finished a year in Centerville's junior college, he enrolled at the University of Iowa because, as he says, "There's a wonderful friendliness in Iowa. There is something natural and earthy there," Simon says.

Denied admittance to the UI 300-voice choir, he joined the Old Gold Singers, a campus pop singing group. But when Charles Kellis, a voice teacher in the university's music department, heard Estes sing, he asked him if he was interested in opera.

"What's opera?" Estes asked. When Kellis played some records of Jerome Hines, Leontyne Price, and Maria Callas, Estes was hooked and Kellis became his first and only voice teacher.

Under Kellis's tutelage and aegis, he studied for a year and a half at the famed Juilliard School of Music in New York City, then made a career move to Germany. There, he won a role in the

Deutsche Oper, and also won the Munich Vocal Competition, a prize that launched his career. He capped that win by taking the silver medal in the first international Tchaikovsky music competition in Moscow.

Estes has performed with virtually all of the major opera companies of the world and appears regularly with the world's leading orchestras. Several performances have been marked as historic milestones in Estes's career, such as his triumphant debut as the Flying Dutchman at the Bayreuth Festival.

In 1982, Simon made his long-delayed debut at the Metropolitan Opera, some 16 years after his Tchaikovsky competition triumph. It was long overdue. For no bass-baritone in the world is considered better than Simon Estes. "In music, the only color should be the voice," Simon says.

———————————————————————————————

THE WORLD'S FOREMOST BASS-BARITONE. The first African-American man to sing at the Bayreuth Festival. Has sung with virtually all of the major opera companies in Europe and the United States and with the world's leading orchestras. Has established Simon Estes scholarship funds at the University of Iowa and at Centerville Community College, a Simon Estes Educational Foundation in Tulsa, and the Iowa Arts Scholarship Fund, and the Simon Estes International Foundation for Children in Zurich, Switzerland.

Born: March 2, 1938, Centerville, Iowa. *Educated:* junior college, Centerville; Bachelor of Music, UI, 1956; attended the Juilliard School of Music. *Family:* Yvonne, wife; Jennifer Barbara, Lynne Ashley, Tiffany Joy, daughters. *Iowa Connection:* born, raised, educated in Iowa; maintains close ties with family living in Cedar Rapids, Iowa.

Honors: Munich International Vocal Competition, 1965. Tchaikovsky Competition, Silver Medalist, Moscow 1966. Honorary degree, Siena College in New York. Honorary degree, Luther College in Iowa. Distinguished Faculty Member, Juilliard School of Music. Honorary degrees, The University of Tulsa, Oklahoma, and Drake University in Iowa. Honorary Colonel of the Iowa National Guard. Iowa Award, 1996.

Bob

FELLER (1918–)

Hall of Fame baseball player

Bob Feller couldn't finish his first season in the major leagues. He had to hurry home to Van Meter to finish high school.

Few youngsters pitch in the baseball major leagues before they graduate from high school. Bob Feller did it. But then, Bob was no ordinary Iowa feller.

As a 17-year-old high-school junior, Bob was invited by the Cleveland Indians baseball team to show his stuff against big league players, seasoned vets with years of baseball savvy. Baseball scouts had seen him pitch as a high-school standout, but the big leagues in baseball are as different from high-school baseball as Van Meter, Iowa, is from Cleveland, Ohio.

In three innings, he struck out eight of the nine players he faced. One of the things Bob did best was to propel that small stitched orb with amazing speed. Bob's fastball was clocked at 98.6 mph.

After his first season with the Cleveland Indians, Bob went home to finish high school. He then returned to the Indians. In 1939, while Iowan Nile Kinnick was winning the Heisman trophy, Bob posted his first 20-win season (24-9). The next year he opened the season with a no-hitter and finished 27-11, with an impressive earned run average of 2.62.

At the height of his baseball success, World War II changed Bob's life, as it did so many others. After service in the U.S. Navy, Bob returned to baseball to set the then single season strikeout record of 348 batters. He also won 27 games, captured a no-hitter, and acquired an incredible 2.18 earned run average.

During his career, Bob was voted to the American League All-Star game eight times. And, in 1957, Bob was the first professional athlete to incorporate himself, allowing him to enjoy the fruits of his skills and paving the way for modern-day sports finance.

During Bob's career he established many records that have been an inspiration to ballplayers everywhere. But perhaps one of his greater accomplishments was to become known as a role model for youngsters, showing that high principles and fine character are worthy goals.

When Bob Feller hung up his glove, the Cleveland Indians retired jersey number 19, for they believed that no one could possibly fill those awesome sleeves again like a small-town guy from Iowa did.

———————————————————————————

CONSIDERED to be one of the 100 greatest athletes of all time. Three no-hitters, twelve one-hitters, pitched a fastball clocked at 98.6 miles per hour.

Born: November 3, 1918, Van Meter, Iowa. *Educated:* Van Meter High School. *Iowa Connection:* born, raised, learned to play baseball in Iowa.
Honor: 1961, elected to the Baseball Hall of Fame.

Esther P. and Pauline E. _____

FRIEDMAN (1918–)

The world's most-read women

Esther P. (Ann Landers) [left] and Pauline E. (Abigail Van Buren) Friedman, the world's most-read women. Photos courtesy of Creators Syndicate (Ann Landers) and of Abigail Van Buren (Dear Abby).

They give free advice to millions of readers across the globe and have become the most-read women in world history.

Ann Landers and Abigail Van Buren, pen names for Esther P. and Pauline E. Friedman, respectively, are Iowa-raised twins who virtually own the advice column business. Together, their columns appear in nearly 2,500 newspapers worldwide.

As youngsters growing up in Sioux City, the girls were inseparable friends and constant companions. Friends and family nicknamed them Eppie and Popo. Following high school, both girls attended nearby Morningside College and then, in a move in sync with their psyches, married in a dual wedding ceremony.

In the late 1950s Eppie moved to Chicago. Looking for an outlet for her considerable energies, she contacted the editor of the *Sun-Times,* offering to write some answers to questions submitted to a lovelorn column titled "Ann Landers," syndicated in 40 papers. As it happened, the column's author had just died. To find a replacement for "Ann Landers," the newspaper held a contest. Eppie entered, won, and rewrote advice column history. As her readership soared, additional newspapers signed on.

Meanwhile, Popo had moved to San Francisco where she talked the editor of the *San Francisco Chronicle* into trying a sample advice column. Soon her readership also mushroomed.

Iowa Pride _____

Despite individual differences, the success and renown of each grew, because both provided honest expertise of value to their readers. As a consequence of their success at sorting out readers' problems and their activities on behalf of many charitable organizations, numerous honors have come their way.

World Almanac polls have named them as the Most Influential Women in the United States, quite a recognition for these daughters of Iowa. In addition, the American Medical Association chose Ann Landers to be the recipient of the Citation for Distinguished Service, the highest honor given to a lay person.

Truly homespun, Iowa-rooted philosophy can be taken to heart. And that's exactly what American newspaper readers have done with Ann and Abigail, taken them into their hearts.

THE WORLD'S most-read advice columnists: Esther as Ann Landers, "Ask Ann," Pauline as Abigail Van Buren, "Dear Abby."

Born: the twins were born July 4, 1918, Sioux City, Iowa. *Educated:* Morningside College, Sioux City. *Family:* Abigail Van Buren: Morton Phillips, husband; Edward, son; Jeanne, daughter. Ann Landers: Jules Lederer, husband (divorced); Margo, daughter. *Iowa Connection:* born, raised, and educated in Iowa. *Honors:* incredibly numerous.

Hamlin

GARLAND (1860–1940)

Dean of American letters

He was to the printed page what Grant Wood
was to an artist's canvas.

—D.A.S.

Hamlin Garland never made a lot
of money. Yet, he spent his life pursuing the only
passion that gripped him: putting words on a
page for the pleasure of his peers.

Hamlin came to Iowa with pioneer parents who had broken
prairie sod before, and would again. For a dozen of his most formative years Hamlin waxed strong in Iowa, developing a pioneer
spirit to match his parents'.

After attending a seminary in Osage, Hamlin went on to
Chicago and New York City, to slowly build his expertise with
his writing craft. He became a friend and companion of many sig-
nificant people of the day, including the future President of the
United States Theodore Roosevelt, and authors George Bernard
Shaw and Mark Twain.

During these years he traveled to the untamed western
United States, becoming knowledgeable in Indian ways. His was
one of few voices writing about civilizing the West through the
eyes of the Indian. It was a view that few turn-of-the-century
readers had considered.

An incredibly difficult, 1,000-mile horseback trek to the
Yukon gold strike, during the late 1890s, fueled his imagination
to capture in striking prose the struggles that men would endure
to seek the elusive yellow metal, gold.

Following his days as a "Trailer" (which is what campers

Iowa Pride

were then called), he settled down to write his *Middle Border* books, which referred to the rugged early days in the Midwest.

At age 40, Hamlin married the heroine in his book, *A Daughter of the Middle Border,* and fathered two girls whom he immortalized in this Pulitzer Prize-winning, semi-autobiographical novel.

As Grant Wood taught eastern and European artists that regionalism was honestly American—and worthy of the talent—so Iowan Hamlin Garland taught eastern and European writers the same message about regionalism in writing.

CONSIDERED by the literati of his day to be the Dean of American Letters. Established and/or made a lasting impact on the genre of cultural realism, i.e., regionalism. Principal works: *Main-Travelled Roads; A Spoil of Office; Crumbling Idols; Rose of Dutcher's Coolly; Life of Ulysses S. Grant; The Trail of the Gold-Seekers; Boy Life on the Prairie; The Captain of the Gray Horse Troop; A Son of the Middle Border; A Daughter of the Middle Border; Trail-Makers of the Middle Border.* Co-founded the International Academy of Arts and Letters and the American Academy of Arts and Letters.

Born: September 14, 1860, West Salem, Wisconsin. *Educated:* studied at the Cedar Valley Seminary in Osage without a degree. *Family:* Zulime, wife; Mary Isabel, Connie, daughters. *Iowa Connection:* raised from age eight and educated in Iowa.

Honors: Pulitzer Prize for *A Daughter of the Middle Border.* Gold medal from the Theodore Roosevelt Society. Honorary Doctorates of Literature from the University of Wisconsin, Northwestern University, Beloit College and the University of Southern California.

Herbert
HOOVER (1874–1964)
President of the United States

Boys are very durable. A boy, if not washed too often and if kept in a cool dry place after each accident, will survive broken bones, hornets' nests, swimming holes and five helpings of pie.

—HERBERT HOOVER

The eight-year-old future President of the United States lay lifeless.

Dimes were placed on his motionless eyelids, as the family sobbed in wrenching grief. Suddenly, the doctor burst into the room, grabbed the lad's body and blew into his mouth. "Praise Thee Lord!" rang out as the boy coughed alive.

Before the Civil War, Quakers had settled in West Branch, Iowa. Two of them produced a famous son, Herbert (or Bertie) Hoover. Jesse and Hulda Hoover instilled stern disciplines in their prized boy.

A year after his parents' death, 10-year-old Bertie went to live with an uncle in Oregon. He soon showed that he was a hard worker, with a head for figures. At 17, he was admitted to the first class at Stanford University where he studied geology, became a mining engineer and met fellow Iowan Lou Henry, from Waterloo.

Upon his appointment in 1899 as chief mining engineer for the Chinese government, Hoover married Lou and they at once accepted global responsibilities. Fifteen years later, World War I then engulfed Europe, and 10 million Belgians were starving, trapped between the Germans and the British. Hoover badgered nations, corporations and Americans to deliver $1 billion worth of food for beleaguered Belgians. Grateful Belgian children soon called a bowl of soup and a piece of bread a "Hoover lunch."

When America entered the war, President Woodrow Wilson asked Hoover to head the U.S. Food Administration. Hoover accepted, asking only *total control* and *no pay*. At war's end, famine stalked the Continent and "The Great Humanitarian" again brought relief.

In 1921, Hoover was appointed Secretary of Commerce by President Warren G. Harding. Eight years later he became the President of the United States. His vast popularity was to be short-lived, for a crushing financial collapse engulfed the nation soon after his inauguration. In 1932 he was defeated for re-election by Franklin Delano Roosevelt.

Later, when World War II finally ended, President Harry S. Truman asked for Hoover's help. Called back into service "like a trusted family doctor," Hoover headed global relief for the United States.

There are 12 presidential libraries in the United States. One of them, in West Branch, is dedicated to the 31st President of the United States, Iowa-born Herbert Hoover: the last great humanitarian.

SUCCESSFULLY LED efforts to feed Europeans ravaged by World War I and again following World War II. Secretary of Commerce; but, because of his energetic work for the government, was known as the "Secretary of Everything."

Born: August 10, 1874, West Branch, Iowa. *Education:* B.A. in Geology, Stanford University (1st class). *Family:* Lou Henry, wife; Herbert Jr., Allan, sons. *Iowa Connection:* born in Iowa.

Honors: French Legion of Honor. Honorary Citizen and Friend of the Belgian Nation. 90 honorary degrees.

Laurence C. _____
JONES (1884–1975)
Established the Piney Woods Country Life School

The turning point of the nine-teenth to the twentieth century was a turning point for a young man from Marshalltown. Laurence Jones graduated from high school and decided to attend the University of Iowa, a courageous step for an African-American in those days.

Like many students, Jones worked his way through school then debated his future. His choice to go into business for himself became sidetracked when he discovered a mission of teaching poor blacks in the South.

Moving to rural Mississippi, Jones found work to finance the purchase of a few acres of ground surrounding an abandoned log cabin. In these humble beginnings he established the Piney Woods Country Life School.

Here his students were taught to grow and can vegetables, learn carpentry, dairy farming and other skills, and cooked their own meals. Slowly the sparse livelihood and meager conditions began to improve as a few acres at a time were added to the compound.

When Jones went on a Ralph Edwards national television broadcast, Edwards suggested that his listeners each send one dollar bill to help the struggling school. Within 48 hours nearly $250,000 were received, a sum that eventually grew to nearly $750,000.

Within several decades, the school had a multi-million dol-

Iowa Pride

lar endowment, owned 1,600 acres of land, and had helped hundreds of black youngsters become self-sufficient and able to lead rewarding lives.

The school continues on a mission that came about because a young Iowan gave up thoughts of how he could help himself to find ways to help his fellow men and women.

Born: November 21, 1882, 83, or 84? Raised in St. Joseph, Missouri. *Education:* graduated from Marshalltown, Iowa, High School in 1903. Received B.Ph. (Bachelor of Philosophy) UI, 1907. *Family:* Grace Morris Allen, wife; Turner, Laurence, sons. *Iowa Connection:* educated in Iowa.

Honors: Featured on Ralph Edwards' television program, "This Is Your Life," December 1954. Cited by the University of Iowa Alumni Association, 1957. Honorary doctorates from Buckness University, Clarke College, Cornell College, University of Dubuque and Otterbein College. Also M.A. (Honorary), Tuskegee University.

Cloris
LEACHMAN (1930–)
Oscar-winning actress

*Cloris Leachman,
actress architect.*

Cloris Leachman almost lost the Miss Chicago contest by laughing so hard at being selected the winner. She eventually ended up in the Miss America Pageant where she impressed judges enough to win a $1,000 talent scholarship.

Born in Des Moines, her family occupied a small house on the outskirts of town that had no running water. She later recalled that because water had to be hauled to the house from a well two city blocks away her mother "would wash the asparagus in the water, then wash Cloris in the same water, then use the water to scrub the kitchen and the floors and throw what was left on the flowers."

As a five-year-old Cloris began music and dancing lessons, practicing the piano on a cardboard keyboard, since the family did not own a piano. After graduating from high school—having obtained some acting experience through the Des Moines Little

211

Iowa Pride

Theatre—she went to Northwestern University in Chicago on an Edgar Bergen scholarship. She lasted a year and dropped out, going first to Atlantic City for the Miss America Pageant and then directly to New York City.

Within a few days of her arrival, Cloris was working as an extra in a movie. There followed a succession of jobs in the theater, interspersed with studies at the Actors Studio. In the mid-fifties she deserted the safety of the stage for the new medium called television, where she played a variety of roles.

In 1970 she landed a key role in the *Mary Tyler Moore Show* as Phyllis Lindstrom, Mary Richard's obnoxious landlady. Her four Emmies were earned for best supporting actress in a comedy series, in this hallmark role.

Leachman's TV role gave her freedom to follow a movie career at the same time and in 1972 she was awarded an Oscar for best supporting actress of 1971 for her portrayal of Ruth Popper, the unattractive wife of the football coach in *The Last Picture Show.*

One of the busiest actresses, Cloris has captivated critics and audiences alike and, during her 40-year acting career, has been applauded in 30 motion pictures, 75 television series, 30 films for television, a dozen TV specials and two dozen theatrical roles. Most recently she has played an outstanding role in the astounding revival of the traveling musical known as *Showboat.* Also, her role in *Grandma Moses* garnered her extraordinary reviews that left critics spellbound.

"I am not an actress," she smiles, "I am an architect. Architecture has to do with ideas more than anything. The context behind what we do gives rise to the expression of ourselves—the way we come into the world."

OSCAR-WINNING actress.

Born: June 30, 1930, Des Moines, Iowa. *Education:* Attended Northwestern University. *Family:* George England, husband (divorced); Adam, Bryan, George, Morgan, sons; Dinah, daughter. *Iowa Connection:* born in Iowa.

Honors: Academy Award, Best Supporting Actress, 1971, *The Last Picture Show;* 6 Emmy Awards.

John L.

L EWIS (1880–1969)

Foremost union organizer

An Iowa coal mine is about the last place you'd look for someone to change the lives of millions of workers.

But such a person came out of an Iowa mine, and both battered and bettered the world.

John L. Lewis grew up in an Iowa mine, working alongside his father and brothers, sweating in the inky darkness below ground and fighting the black dust that choked the souls of miners. In his late twenties, he married the doctor's daughter in Lucas and moved from the coal fields of southern Iowa to the mines of Illinois.

In Illinois, John L. decided he could represent miners' interests better than anyone else. He quickly rose from secretary of his union local of the United Mine Workers (UMW) to district jobs. He finally landed a job with the American Federation of Labor (AFL) where he traveled the country acting as a liaison between the AFL and the UMW, and building a following within the UMW for his ultimate capture of its presidency.

When the UMW presidency came, John L., through a series of strikes, catapulted into national prominence, his bushy-browed face glowering from the front pages of every newspaper. President Franklin Delano Roosevelt (FDR) appointed him to a national board to design how the National Recovery Act (NRA) should deal with labor. In this role, John L. fathered Section 7A, which said that unions could collectively bargain with groups of employers.

Iowa Pride

The AFL was a *craft* union, banding carpenters, say, with carpenters into a union local. John L., however, believed that workers should unite by industry, in *trade* unions. Where the AFL might organize a factory into many locals—one for carpenters and one for electricians, for example—a trade union lumped all workers in the industry into one giant, and more powerful, union.

Failing to convince the AFL to become a federation of trade unions, John L. pulled the UMW from the AFL and formed the Committee for Industrial Organization, known as the CIO (1935–38). In 1938, this union was renamed the Congress of Industrial Organizations, lasting until December 1955, when John L.'s longtime dream came true and the CIO and AFL merged. As head of these unions, he was now considered the most powerful man in America, behind FDR.

Iowan John L. Lewis was the commander-in-chief of a revolution that created an entity setting America apart from many other countries—a powerful middle class.

RESPONSIBLE for industrial unionism. President of the United Mine Workers and AFL-CIO.

Born: February 12, 1880, near Lucas, Iowa. *Education:* finished three-and-one-half years of high school in Des Moines. *Family:* Myrta Edith, wife; John, Jr., son; Kathryn, Mary, daughters. *Iowa Connection:* born, raised, educated and began his mining and union careers in Iowa.

Honors: Honorary LL.D. University of West Virginia, 1957. Doctor of Humane Letters, Georgetown University, 1960. President Lyndon Johnson presented the Freedom Medal, 1964. Eugene Debs Award, 1965.

Glenn
MILLER (1904–1944)
Invented the big band sound

Alton Glenn Miller, big bandleader, wrote "America's Other National Anthem."

Adjusting for inflation, it's claimed that no entertainer in history ever made more money than Iowa-born bandleader Glenn Miller.

As a youngster, Glenn Miller milked cows to earn his first musical instrument, a trombone. He spent the rest of his life milking that trombone to become America's premier bandleader, a title undimmed a half-century after his death.

Miller was born in Iowa (1904); his parents soon left for first Nebraska, then Missouri (where Glenn acquired his first trombone), then to Fort Morgan, Colorado. After two years at the University of Colorado, Glenn headed for the West Coast where he joined a small band and taught himself how to arrange music. Soon Glenn moved to New York City where he arranged for numerous orchestras.

After one disastrous attempt to form a band, Glenn reorga-

215

nized a new one which, after a year of one-night stands, soared to become the most popular band in America.

The sound Glenn sought was an ensemble effect, where the band, as one music critic put it, soloed more often than any of its soloists. Tonal balance was dominant in the Miller band, the strongest feature being harmony created from a skillful blend of clarinets and saxophones. This blend created a distinctively new and different style.

At the height of its popularity as the No. 1 band in the world, the clouds of World War II raced across the sky. Glenn let his band go and accepted a position in the Army Air Force. At the time he was the highest-paid bandleader America had ever known, and adjusting for inflation and taxes, probably the highest-paid entertainer of all time.

Glenn's army band duplicated the sound GIs had grown up with and they cheered themselves hoarse to hear him again in countless army outposts. He then went to England to bring a touch of America to lonely GIs readying to sacrifice their lives for world freedom.

On December 15, 1944, Glenn Miller took off in a small plane, heading for Paris to make arrangements for his band to entertain troops embattled on the European continent. The plane was never heard from again. America's premier musical trendsetter disappeared without a trace.

Iowa-born Glenn Miller wrote the popular song *Moonlight Serenade.* During his lifetime, the dancing public (nearly everyone) referred to this beautiful "sweet" song as "America's Other National Anthem."

WROTE: *Moonlight Serenade,* which was considered by the public to be "America's Other National Anthem."

Born: March 1, 1904, Clarinda, Iowa. *Education:* high school at Fort Morgan, Colorado; University of Colorado. *Family:* Helen, wife; Steven, son; Jonnie Dee, daughter. *Iowa Connection:* born in Iowa.

Honors: Unofficially known as the "King of the Rug-Cutters." Bronze Star for service during World War II.

John R.

M OTT (1865–1955)
Nobel laureate

There is something like the mountains and the sea
in John R. Mott.

—HENRY NELSON WIEMAN, *University of Chicago*

A lot of young people join the
YMCA. The YMCA joined John Mott.

When John signed up for a Y membership
he enlisted tens of thousands of other young
people to join, as well. Then he developed programs to make a Y
membership more meaningful. He wrote books to enrich people's
lives, and headed the international YMCA program. An adoring
world gave Iowa-raised John Mott many awards, including the
Nobel Peace Prize.

John Mott grew up in Iowa and dedicated his life to Christ
while yet a lad. It was claimed that he influenced the lives of
more young people than any evangelist of the day. Interestingly,
the values John learned on the landlocked Iowa plains would
later lead people to refer to John in terms of the sea and mountains.

When John was two years old, he moved to Postville, Iowa,
from New York State. In Iowa, his father entered the lumber business and soon prospered as the leading dealer in town. John
might well have followed his father's footsteps and never been
heard from again.

But, when he was 13, John and both his father and his sister
attended a meeting held by Iowa evangelist J.W. Dean and fell
under his spell. It was an influence that would spell great things
for generations of young people the world over, for John went on

217

to eventually become the president of the World's Alliance of Young Men's Christian Associations, also known as the YMCA.

In his capacity as world leader of the YMCA, Iowan John Mott has been credited with being "the chief instrument in modernizing missionary work," and was regarded by the National Cyclopedia of American Biography as "one of the most constructive religious geniuses since John Wesley."

Starting as a student secretary for the International Committee of the YMCA, immediately after graduation from Cornell University, John traveled the country advising college student groups on how to create useful programs for students. By 1925, he was credited with having personally recruited over 10,000 student volunteers.

During his life, which took him around the world many times, he found time to author 16 popular books. He also received hosts of awards from various institutions, culminating in what may be the most prestigious award possible, the Nobel Peace Prize, which he shared with Emily Balch, who founded the Women's International League for Peace and Freedom.

EXPANDED the YMCA into a worldwide force among young people. Organized, inspired and founded Christian college-student organizations throughout the world.

Born: May 25, 1865, Livingston Manor, New York. *Education:* at 16 enrolled at Upper Iowa University, graduated from Cornell University, New York, 1888. *Family:* Leila, wife; John Livingston, son; Irene, Eleanor, daughters. *Iowa Connection:* raised and educated in Iowa.

Honors: Phi Beta Kappa, Cornell University. Distinguished Service Medal for work on a special Diplomatic Mission to Russia during World War I. Seven honorary degrees. Decorated by 15 governments. Prince Carl Medal. 1942 Honorary life member, Foreign Missions Conference of North America. 1946 Nobel Peace Prize Co-winner. 1948 World Council of Churches, First Assembly, Amsterdam; elected Honorary President 1948–1955.

Robert N.
NOYCE (1927–1993)
Invented the computer chip

When was the last time that you heard of a mother who thought her son was not getting *enough* homework?

Robert Noyce's mother didn't think the schools were challenging her son the way they should. So, when Bob became restless, she gave him something to take apart to learn how it ticked. Soon, Bob had taken apart everything in the house. What do you do with a lad that inquisitive?

Robert Noyce's mother knew what to do. She went to Grinnell College Professor Grant Gale and told him the problem. Could Robert take an introductory physics course at the college level, even though he was still a senior in high school? Professor Gale was intrigued by the notion and allowed Robert to enroll in his class.

In the summer of 1948, Bell Laboratories developed the first transistor, a device that replaced vacuum tubes, because it took no warmup time, created no heat and could act either as an amplifier or an oscillator. More work in less space was a feature that inspired Professor Gale to acquire two of the valued items and begin *the first solid-state electronics course in America.*

Of course Noyce took the course and modern electronic technology took a turn for the better. Upon graduating, Noyce went to Silicon Valley in California and, together with several other inventors, founded Fairchild Semiconductor Company.

There he discovered how to connect thousands of transistors on a silicon chip without using any wiring to create the integrated circuit. Jack Kilby, another inventive genius, who worked for Texas Instruments in Dallas, Texas, made the same discovery, separately.

Computers, which Iowan John Atanasoff invented, never worked better than when their vacuum tubes were replaced with high-speed transistor circuits on silicon chips.

Next time you're watching instantaneous computer screens, thank Iowan Robert Noyce. Luckily for us, Robert had a mother who knew exactly what to do when her son said, "What can I do now, Mom?"

_____

CREATED the integrated circuit on a single silicon chip. Founded Fairchild Semiconductor Company.

Born: December 12, 1927, Burlington, Iowa. *Educated:* Grinnell College. Phi Beta Kappa in 1949. Doctoral degree in physics from MIT in 1953. *Family:* Ann, wife; four children. *Iowa Connection:* born, raised and educated in Iowa.

Honor: Received the first Charles Stark Draper Award for engineering achievement from President George Bush in 1993.

Donna
REED (1921–1986)
Academy Award-winning actress

Donna Reed, Oscar winner.
Photo courtesy The Donna
Reed Foundation.

It's a safe bet that not many movie actresses know how to milk a cow, bake biscuits and drive a tractor.

But Iowa-born and -raised Donna Reed (born: Donna Mullenger) is one actress who could perform those chores ... and she could act. Donna never liked her stage name, but still it served her well, as did her assets of petite (5'3") beauty, and a smile that would have melted a truckload of Iowan Chris Nelson's Eskimo Pies®.

Donna grew up on a farm south of Denison, where she learned what every 4-H girl learns, to bake, sew, cook, darn, grow good things to eat and generally manage a household, just like 4-H–founder Iowan Jessie Field Shambaugh planned.

Donna made many of her own clothes and was good enough at baking biscuits to win a blue ribbon at the Iowa State Fair. She was pretty enough to be Queen of the Crawford County 4-H Victory Fair as well as Homecoming Queen at Denison High.

After high school, Donna lived with her aunt in Los Angeles and attended nearby Los Angeles City College. She embarked on a secretarial course and worked in the library. But her break came when she entered a beauty contest and won, beating out 35 other contestants.

221

Iowa Pride

With the beauty title came a photo opportunity which appeared on the front page of the *Los Angeles Times*. Agents promptly beat down her door to help her launch a movie career. After roles in a dozen mediocre films, she was cast opposite Jimmy Stewart in *It's a Wonderful Life*. *LOOK* magazine immediately selected her as an actress who couldn't miss stardom.

In 1953, Donna received an Academy Award Oscar for Best Supporting Actress in the film *From Here to Eternity*. She followed that victory with a strategic move to television, where at age 35 she became the nation's symbol of model wife and mother, acting on ABC television's *The Donna Reed Show*.

During her television years she received many Emmy nominations and several nominations for *TV Guide*'s Most Popular Television Actress, and won the Golden Globe Best Television Actress award in 1963.

During her life she contributed to many worthy causes in and around Denison and participated in community affairs, just as all good citizens do. But isn't that what you'd expect from an Iowa girl-next-door?

Born: January 27, 1921, Denison, Iowa. (Real name Donna Belle Mullenger). *Educated:* Crawford County school in Nishnabotna Township. Graduated from Denison High School. Attended Los Angeles City College. *Family:* Grover W. Asmus, husband; Penny Owen Stigers, Mary Anne Owen, daughters; Tony Owen, Jr., Timothy Owen, sons. *Iowa Connection:* born and raised in Iowa.

Honors: Academy Award Oscar, 1953; Golden Globe Best Television Actress 1963; numerous Emmy nominations and several nominations for *TV Guide's* Best Television Actress.

Beardsley

RUML (1894–1960)

Developed the pay-as-you-go tax plan

One Cedar Rapids kid was always a step ahead of his classmates and look what it did for your taxes. His name was Beardsley Ruml, "Bee" his mother called him. When his teachers decided that Bee could skip grades on his route through school, Bee's mother decided otherwise. She said Bee needed time to grow up normally. She was about the only person who ever held this achiever back.

The kid from Cedar Rapids—who claimed he hated exercise—rose to exercise enormous influence on the economy of America. He was chairman of Hansen's Labs and of the American National Theater and Academy, trustee of the Spellman Fund of New York, and director of the Laura S. Rockefeller Memorial, the Museum of Modern Art in New York City, Dartmouth College and Fisk University.

Bee was trustee of the National Planning Association and the Committee for Economic Development, and board member of the national Bureau of Economic Research, Encyclopaedia Britannica, General American Investors Co., Muzak Corp., and Enterprise Paint Manufacturing Co.

He was secretary of The Scott Company, assistant to the president of the Carnegie Corporation, and director of the National Securities and Research Corporation and Peerless Casualty Company. He was economic advisor to the Puerto Rican govern-

Iowa Pride

ment and was both treasurer and chairman of R.H. Macy and Co., the giant New York retailer.

Dean and professor of education at Chicago University were two more of his jobs, and he served under another Iowan, President Herbert Hoover, on the committee on unemployment relief. For a man who hated exercise he seemed to have found plenty just scuttling to and from meetings.

Bee was also Chairman of the Board of the Federal Reserve Bank of New York, in which position he created the idea of people paying taxes out of each paycheck, rather than lump sums at year-end. Gallup polls showed that 83 percent of the rich and 85 percent of the poor favored his plan. Eighty percent of the population is an unheard-of level of agreement.

Despite popular acceptance, Bee's pay-as-you-go tax plan met opposition in Congress, due, it was claimed, to being so simple that congressmen were having a difficult time understanding it. The plan was adopted in 1943 as the law of the land and has never varied since. An Iowa boy found a better way.

Born: November 5, 1894, Cedar Rapids, Iowa. *Education:* Franklin High School, graduated from Washington High School. Graduated from Dartmouth. Doctor of Philosophy degree at University of Chicago. *Family:* Lois, wife; Treadwell, Alvin, sons; Ann, daughter. *Iowa Connection:* born and raised in Iowa.

Honor: Golden Key Award and numerous others.

William L. _____

SHIRER (1904–1993)

Renowned journalist, historian

When "Billy" Shirer was nine years old his world collapsed. His best friend, companion and idol—the person who was the center of his life—died. It was his dad.

Billy Shirer spent his life looking for the fulfillment that his father's arms had held for him. He searched for meaning to his life and some sense to the times that whirled around him. Then he shared that search with the world.

After his father's death, nine-year-old Billy, his mother and his sister immediately moved to Cedar Rapids, where his mother's family lived and where his new life began. After high school, Bill attended Coe College, where he vented his liberal tendencies as editor of the *Coe Cosmos*.

Upon graduation from Coe, he toured Europe, hoping to find a newspaper job to extend his stay. Just hours before his return from Paris, he was asked if he was still interested in a reporting job for the Paris edition of the *Chicago Tribune*. Though it paid less than he had earned as sports editor for the Cedar Rapids *Republican*—during his years at Coe—he snapped at the chance.

For the next 40 years, William Shirer covered the European scene, first from France, then Italy, and finally Germany where he became acquainted with a rising young politician and the men around him. The man he learned to know, and "was close enough to kill," was a man who inflicted a brilliant mind gone ruthless upon the world. He was Adolf Hitler.

During these years, Shirer's career encompassed not only newspaper journalism, but broadcast journalism as well, his being a familiar voice that brought home the developing world conflagration to Americans.

Following the war, Shirer's books told the story of a world gone mad. The titles of Shirer's major works read like best-sellers on *The New York Times* List: *The Rise and Fall of the Third Reich, The Collapse of the Third Republic, Berlin Diary* and *Gandhi,* each of which has enthralled millions of readers.

William Shirer, an Iowan who spoke many languages, spoke ours with eloquence. The message he gleaned from history was clear: Every man, woman and child is supremely important. Our every action must be weighed in the context of that belief.

WORLD-RENOWNED JOURNALIST and historian. Author of the acclaimed book *The Rise and Fall of the Third Reich.* Foreign correspondent, broadcast journalist, historical biographer. With Edward R. Murrow created the first world news roundup. Authored numerous noted historical books, including: *Berlin Diary, End of a Berlin Diary, The Traitor* (novel), *Midcentury Journey, Stranger Come Home* (novel), *The Challenge of Scandinavia, The Consul's Wife* (novel), *The Rise and Fall of the Third Reich, The Rise and Fall of Adolf Hitler, The Sinking of the Bismarck, The Collapse of the Third Republic, 20th Century Journey, A Memoir of a Life and the Times, Gandhi—A Memoir, 20th Century Journey* (Vol. 2), *The Nightmare Years, A Native's Return* and *20th Century Journey* (Vol. 3).

Born: February 23, 1904, Chicago, Illinois. *Educated:* Cedar Rapids, B.S. Coe College, 1925; College de France, two years. *Family:* Theresa, Irina, wives; Eileen, daughter. *Iowa Connection:* raised, attended high school and Coe College in Iowa.

Honors: Légion d'honneur. Peabody Award. President Authors' Guild. National Book Award.

Mona

VAN DUYN (1921–)

Pulitzer Prize-winning poet

Mona Van Duyn saw first light
in Waterloo and remained in Iowa to earn a
Bachelor of Arts degree from UNI and a Master
of Arts degree from UI, where she taught English
for a year. She then went on to win almost every poetry prize possible, capping those accomplishments with the Pulitzer Prize for
Poetry in 1991 for her book *Near Changes*.

Her extensive biography is peopled with poets who wax poetic on her unique talent, calling her variously a "domestic poet,"
a "love poet," a "poet of great wisdom," a "tough-minded poet,"
and a poet who has made great contributions to the "observation-and-description poem." Listen to her tell it.

Rarely, I think, has a poet been rewarded with more affectionate, appreciative praise or more prizes by her fellow poets. And yet
... and yet ... I have been waiting a long time for a critic who would
discern what has for thirty years seemed to me, and even to my non-literary friends, one obvious fact. Though I do write domestic poems of marriage, friendship, family, as does nearly every male and
female poet, *many* of my poems are extended domestic metaphors
which deal with a great many other concerns—death, the possibility of atomic destruction, the nature of the human imagination, unsettling scientific experiments, the nature of poetry, the limits of
aesthetics, and so on. Perhaps I have used the extended domestic
metaphor to explore the complexities of the world more consistently than any other poet presently writing. I don't know.

I do know that reading my poems, the most brilliant and perceptive critics seem to go blind to the subject of the poem. "Walking the Dog: A Diatribe" is not a descriptive poem about walking
the dog ("How do they know what is insufferable in their ignorant
gloss?") as a distinguished critic labeled it. ... When "I cupboard

these pickled peaches in time's despite" I am not talking about pickled peaches.

"The Fear of Flying" (the title preceding Jong's) is an analysis of my relationship to the world, written in the extended metaphor of a marriage and not a "confessional" poem about marriage. Both editors and my most brilliant poet friends have not hesitated to urge upon me their own re-writings of my poems, destroying the ideas, the subject, and the whole careful direction of the poem, reducing it to a mere description or a purely "domestic" attitude, embarrassing me into having to point out to them what the poem is doing.

When Van Duyn was in second grade she published a poem in a little newspaper. Since that auspicious beginning, the career of this Iowan has carried her to become Poet Laureate Consultant in Poetry to the Librarian of Congress and win every poetry prize in sight. Not bad for an Iowan—or anyone.

POET LAUREATE of the United States.

Born: May 9, 1921, Waterloo, Iowa. *Education:* Iowa State Teachers College (now University of Northern Iowa), B.A., 1942; State University of Iowa, M.A., 1943. *Family:* Jarvis A. Thurston, husband. *Iowa Connection:* born, raised and educated in Iowa.

Honors: Eunice Tietjens Memorial Prize, *Poetry,* 1956, for "Three Valentines to the Wide World"; Helen Bullis Prize, *Poetry Northwest,* 1964; National Endowment for the Arts grants, 1966–67 and 1985; Harriet Monroe Memorial Prize, *Poetry,* 1968; Hart Crane Memorial Award, American Weave Press, 1968; first prize, Borestone Mountain Awards, 1968; Bollingen Prize, Yale University Library, 1970; National Book Award for Poetry, 1971, for *To See, To Take;* John Simon Guggenheim Memorial fellowship, 1972–73; Loines Prize, National Institute of Arts and Letters, 1976; Academy of American Poets fellow, 1981; Sandburg Prize, Cornell College, 1982; Shelley Memorial Award, Poetry Society of America, 1987, for body of work; Ruth Lilly Poetry Prize, Modern Poetry Association, 1989; Pulitzer Prize, 1991, for *Near Changes,* D. Litt., Washington University, 1971, Cornell College, 1972, and University of Northern Iowa, 1991.

Van Duyn's writings have appeared in many anthologies including *The New Pocket Anthology of American Verse, Midland, The Honey and the Gall.* Regular contributor of reviews to *Poetry,* 1944-70. Founder and editor with husband of *Perspective: A Quarterly of Literature,* 1947-67, poetry advisor *College English,* 1955-57. Contributor of poems, short stories, critical articles and reviews to numerous periodicals, including *Kenyon Review, Critique, Western Review, Atlantic, New Republic, Yale Review,* and *New Yorker.*

John
WAYNE (1907–1979)
Academy Award-winning actor

John Wayne, Oscar-winning actor. Photo courtesy of John Wayne Birthplace, Winterset.

A man's gotta do what a man's gotta do.

—JOHN WAYNE

The day after Iowa-born (Winterset, 1907) John Wayne died, the Congress of the United States voted to award him its highest honor, the Congressional Gold Medal. John Wayne was by all standards the ultimate patriot.

A person like John Wayne wasn't born, he was created, and his creator adopted the stature of his creation. John Wayne began life as Marion Morrison, in Winterset, Iowa. During Marion's childhood, his pharmacist father developed heart trouble and a local physician suggested a drier climate, and the family headed for California where Marion grew to a 6'4", 225-pound captain of his high school football team and became known as "The Duke," after the name of his pet dog.

The Duke's neighbors were people in the movie business, so it was natural that one day on a lark, he and some teammates would audition for a football film. From there he graduated to bit roles and behind-the-scenes work, which eventually provided him a job when his college tuition money ran out.

229

Iowa Pride

One day the strapping Duke was spotted and awarded a starring role in a movie *The Big Trail*. The film flopped, but contributed one more important morsel to the Marion Morrison movie makeup: a new name, John Wayne. A name that filmmakers decided was tough enough to match its owner's looks.

Movie after movie followed. Most of them were of B quality, but they taught Wayne the business, gave him steady work, and provided screen exposure. Through these years, Wayne cultivated the person he became, adopting a certain swagger, tough demeanor and mannerisms of speech—both on screen and off—which ultimately propelled him to win an Oscar for his role in *True Grit*.

After winning a bout with what he called "The Big 'C'," cancer, and winning another battle with "The Big 'H'," heart disease, the Duke cashed in his chips and took his last journey to Boot Hill at age 72.

While the Duke, America's folk hero, never served in the Armed Forces, he personified the inscription Congress placed on his gold medal. It was:

JOHN WAYNE—AMERICAN

Born: May 26, 1907, Winterset, Iowa. (Real name Marion Robert Morrison. Changed to Marion Michael when brother died.) *Education:* University of Southern California. *Family:* Josephine (Josie), wife; Michael, Antonia, Patrick, Melinda, children; Esperanza, wife; Pilar, wife; Aissa, John Ethan, Marisa, children. *Iowa Connection:* born in Iowa.

Honors: 1969 Oscar for *True Grit*. Grand Marshal in 1973 Rose Bowl parade. *Photoplay* "Special Editors Award" in 1965. Named "Favorite Actor" in a *Photoplay* Award in 1969 (received four of these awards). Made Admiral in the "Texas Navy" on April 17, 1969. Became Dr. Wayne as an honorary Ph.D. by Pima College in Tucson, Arizona, on April 17, 1970. "The American Academy of Achievement Gold Plate" on June 24, 1970. "The U.S. Marine Corps Leagues 'Iron Mike Award'" on August 13, 1973. "The George Washington Award" on February 18, 1974. "All Time Favorite Star" by *Photoplay* in 1976. Presented a bronze plaque for the Boy Scouts from Ex-President Gerald Ford. *National Enquirer* voted Wayne one of "Hollywood's 10 Best Actors of All Time" in 1983.

Meredith
WILLSON (1902–1984)

"The Music Man"

Meredith Willson, music man. Photo courtesy of Mrs. Meredith Willson

It took him 38 rewrites before he got it right.

In Mason City high school, Meredith chose the flute and the piccolo as his boyhood instruments, tough instruments to master. After graduating from Mason City High School, Meredith struck out for New York City and the prestigious Juilliard (then Damrosch Institute of Musical Art).

After graduation, he first played with the concert bandmaster John Philip Sousa, then first chair in the New York Philharmonic. Meredith was now in his late twenties and eager to pen his own music. He turned to conducting and composing, becoming Musical Director of KFRC, San Francisco, and the National Broadcasting Company's Western Division until World War II broke out and he enlisted. When the war ended in 1945, Major Meredith Willson created, directed and entertained again on network radio.

This was a creative era for Meredith and the composing bug was in him. According to Meredith's book *But He Doesn't Know the Territory,* in 1951 it was suggested he write a musical. By this time he had written a couple of books, and music and lyrics for a number of songs. He decided to write it out and see if he could turn that theme into a musical production, but time after time his

231

idea was rejected. "How many people do you really think want to hear a story of a con-artist bandmaster in Iowa?" they asked.

Thirty-eight rewrites later, Meredith Willson brought *Meredith Willson's The Music Man* to Broadway. It became one of the five longest-running Broadway shows in history. *The Music Man* established a proud Iowan, Meredith Willson—who immortalized River City, aka Mason City, Iowa—as one of the all-time leading musical composers.

Meredith went on to compose other musical hits. His pre-1951 songs, such as "May the Good Lord Bless and Keep You" and "It's Beginning to Look (a lot) Like Christmas," remain favorites.

Every time the University of Iowa and the Iowa State University bands strike up their school songs they honor the Iowan who wrote them both, Iowa's own Music Man.

WROTE the book, music and lyrics to *Meredith Willson's The Music Man,* one of the five longest-playing musicals. Composer, conductor, author, lyricist, and performer.

Born: May 18, 1902, Mason City, Iowa. *Education:* Mason City High School; Damrosch Institute of Musical Art (now the Juilliard Institute of Musical Art). *Family:* Elizabeth and Rini, wives (deceased); Rosemary, wife. *Iowa Connection:* born and raised in Iowa.

Honors: Oscar for *Meredith Willson's The Music Man* were: Oscar from the Academy of Motion Picture Arts and Sciences for the music. Screenplay Award from the Writer's Guild. Honors for Meredith Willson: Drama Critics' Award for Best Musical, Best Music and Best Lyrics. Outer Circle Award. Five Tonys in the Antoinette Perry Annual Awards. Best Musical Award, *Variety* magazine. Best Musical Award, *Sign* magazine. *Parents Magazine* Award. Citations from various religious and educational groups and publications. Honorary Chairman, Library Week. Gold Library Card from the Librarians (Marians) of Los Angeles. Citation, Los Angeles City Council. Honorary Doctor of Music, Coe College. Honorary Doctor of Music, Parsons College. Honorary Doctor of Literature, Indiana Institute of Technology. Honorary Doctor of Fine Arts, Regis College. Honorary Doctor of Music, Wartburg College. 1958, The Distinguished Iowans Award. The First Annual Music Award of Texas. The First Grammy of the National Academy of Recording Arts and Sciences. Citations from various military organizations. Fellowship in the International Institute of

Arts and Letters. Annual Award of the Masquers (Hollywood's oldest show business club). Honorary Chairman of National Musical Week. Annual Award of the American Guild of Organists. National Big Brother Award, presented by President John F. Kennedy. Annual Humanitarian Award of the National Father's Day Committee. The Sally Award from the Salvation Army for his contributions to American music and human betterment. Edwin Franko Goldman Award, American Bandmasters Association. *The Music Man* was read into the Congressional Record on two occasions. Appointed to the Council on Arts and Humanities by President Lyndon B. Johnson. 1980, The Aggie Award from the American Guild of Authors and Composers. 1982, Induction into the Songwriters' Hall of Fame. 1987, The Presidential Medal of Freedom, bestowed posthumously by President Ronald Reagan, the highest civilian honor awarded by the President of the United States. 1988, The Iowa Award, awarded every four to five years to an outstanding Iowan, by the Iowa Centennial Memorial Committee. 1992, Meredith Willson Residence Hall was dedicated at the Juilliard, his alma mater.

IOWA
FIRSTS

IOWA'S natural resources pale when compared
to Colorado's Rockies, Arizona's Grand Canyon or Minnesota's
10,000 lakes. While to us Iowa scenery is magnificent, we really don't have the highest, flattest, wettest anything to brag
about like they do. But, then, those states, and most states—except maybe Illinois—don't have the fertile loam that turns this
rich region into America's breadbasket.

But peaks and canyons and lakes don't occur because a
Coloradian, Arizonian, or Minnesotan planned them. Come to
think of it, we've got some Big Sky country (north), the Loess
Hills (west), Little Appalachia (south), and West Okoboji is said
to be one of four blue-water lakes in the world. We can be
proud of those sights, even though Iowans didn't create them.

The Iowa firsts I now report are well-documented. Each
came from an Iowan rather than by a happenstance of nature.
Come share with me now the incredible firsts that sprang from
Iowans and ponder their impact.

First Agricultural Experimental Station: ISU

Until 1902 crops just grew and you hoped for the best.

Then, the Hatch Act was passed by Congress, and the Iowa legislature appropriated $10,000 for the Iowa Agricultural Experimental Station. This event marked the first time that a state had supported agricultural research, certainly one of agrarian Iowa's more appropriate firsts.

First Appendicitis Operation: Davenport

It was a tough choice: should he let the patient die of "natural causes," or chance killing her with an operation?

In 1883 few physicians possessed the bravery to correct an organic problem with an operation. In fact, outside of amputations, few operations of any sort were performed. There were some pretty good reasons for that. The germ theory was but a germ of an idea. There were no antibiotics, no electric lights, and anesthetics were crude. To top it off, by today's standards, scalpels were deadly dull.

237

Iowa Pride

But 22-year-old Mary Gartside of Davenport was deathly ill and Dr. William Grant had diagnosed acute appendicitis. That diagnosis was often a death warrant, for there was no treatment for an infected appendix.

On January 4, 1883, Dr. Grant administered anesthesia to Mary, then cut open her side and found a badly infected appendix. Whether he removed the appendix or merely drained and scraped away the infection from it isn't known. A newspaper account claimed removal, but newspapers also later reported that Mary had an appendectomy some years later.

First Baby Contest: Iowa State Fair

If we can improve cattle by breeding and feeding, why can't we improve our babies too?

In 1911 Mary Watts had an idea. At the Audubon County Fair, she noticed that the cattle, hogs, sheep and horses were groomed, sleek, and properly fed. Then she looked at the two-legged species standing outside the pens and decided they needed more help than the hogs.

She suggested to the Iowa State Fair board that Iowa's babies be judged like livestock. She believed this event would become a venue for teaching Iowa mothers how to raise better babies. She also harbored a hidden agenda, thinking that healthier babies would eventually mate and improve the human breed.

The board agreed, and pediatrician Margaret Clark of Waterloo made up a judging score sheet, patterned after ones used in the pens. The PTA sponsored the contest and called the program "The Iowa Idea."

The first year, 50 helpless babies and 100 hopeful parents crammed the judging arenas. The second year the word got out and 500 babies squalled through the event. By now, other states had heard of the contest and launched similar contests. And in 1912, the American Medical Association endorsed the project.

The contest served a 40-year purpose of dispensing healthy-baby advice to Iowa mothers. And then it folded its diapers and stole away.

A postscript: In 1934, the winner was a Des Moines baby named Roy Frowick. Later, when he was established as a major clothes designer, he was better known by his middle name: Halston.

First Band Law: Clarinda

Major George W. Landers loved to strike up the band. In the early 1900s, he was a professional bandmaster for the U.S. Army and had played in the Robinson Circus for three years. He now took his 51st Regimental Band into Clarinda to the delight of all Clarindans.

Major George Landers. Photo courtesy of Nodaway Valley Historical Society.

The town fathers huddled and soon dangled the promise of a new armory for use as a concert hall and practice arena if Major Landers would move to Clarinda. The lure worked and the Major and some of his band members moved to Clarinda. For many years Major Landers' Page County band was featured at the Iowa State Fair.

But there was a problem. A band needs music, instruments, uniforms and transportation. Who would finance these vital needs? Then the Major had a brilliant idea. Levy a small property tax and use the money for band betterment.

The townsfolk liked the idea, took it to the legislature for approval, and the Iowa Band Law was passed, allowing cities and towns to levy a small tax dedicated to cultural improvement. Soon, bands sprang up over the state, and when Iowa bandmasters trumpeted their new law outside Iowa borders, the law quickly spread to many other states.

Clarinda bandmaster Major George Landers raised the cultural level of the nation, the same way he led Clarinda to raise its cultural sights and sounds, through enactment of the Iowa Band Law.

First Basketball Game: UI (Intercollegiate)

At least, no one claimed, "We lost *another* one!"

In the fall of 1891, Henry Kallenberg, an Iowa City YMCA and University athletic instructor, received a letter from James Naismith, outlining instructions for playing a new game he had invented. The game was called basketball. The letter intrigued Kallenberg and so he set up a gym in which to play the game, teaching some athletic students the rules.

Iowa Pride

On January 16, 1893, the first basketball game between two college teams of five men on a side was played between the University of Iowa and the University of Chicago. Iowa lost the hotly fought contest 15–12. The game began at 8:30 p.m., with a gymnastic exhibition as the opener. Admission was 15 cents.

First Can of Beer: Cedar Rapids

Will people buy beer in cans? There's no question today.

In 1935 no one had sold canned beer and Pabst Brewery Company thought it might sell. Since many Cedar Rapidians held jobs in food plants in those Depression days, Pabst reasoned that perhaps they had the money to buy a can of beer. Pabst wanted to test this new idea.

Weaver Witwer, a beer wholesaler, asked prominent Cedar Rapids grocer Orrie Becker if he would try to peddle Pabst's new product: canned beer. Orrie told his son Hal to build the best-looking display he could. The store was located at 119 3rd Avenue SE, and known as Peoples Grocery & Market.

A month before, Krueger's, a small brewery in Newark, New Jersey, had introduced the first canned beer. But comparing a microbrewery with a major brewery—and the differing investments in the new product—is like comparing roller skates with an automobile.

Canned beer and iron interact to create a metallic taste. To neutralize this effect, the insides of the cans were coated with various substances, in an attempt to find a coating that kept beer and iron apart, yet didn't intrude on the flavor.

For several years, Pabst had worked with the American Can Company—both companies being located in Milwaukee—to find a liner that worked. In 1935, Pabst and American found a suitable heat-polymerized, synthetic resin that seemed to do the trick. Now came the huge task of educating the public to accept beer in a can.

Until then, beer was delivered to the consumer two ways: from a keg, which produced tap beer, or in a bottle. Since kegs are metallic, Pabst related the unknown new can to the known entity, the keg. American called this process "Keglined" and Pabst trademarked the can itself as "Tapacan.®"

To distance the company from the new product, should it fall flat (no pun intended), Pabst named the beer EXPORT, rather than Pabst Blue Ribbon®, which was the name of their standard product. To help stimulate impulse buying, the letters *BEER* were prominent on the can.

Several can openers were dropped in every case of beer. Since no one knew how to use a beverage can opener, instructions were printed on the can.

The test worked. People bought, and a scant two years later all major breweries sold their own canned beer.

It is small wonder that in a city known for strong German and Czech heritages, the national drink for both countries should be introduced in a new way.

First Cast Gold Dental Crown: Denison

In the 1890s a gold crown to restore a broken-down tooth cost only five dollars. There were two problems with that: it took hours and hours to earn five dollars, and the crowns—made by beating soft gold into a tooth shape—wore out in months.

Dr. B.F. Philbrook

Denison dentist B.F. Philbrook was concerned about that and hunted for a less costly way to build a crown that would last. When he learned how jewelry was cast out of an alloy of gold, which was far stronger than 24K gold, he reasoned a tooth crown also could be cast.

Dr. Philbrook reported how to cast gold crowns and inlays in a turn-of-the-century article in the *Iowa Dental Journal*. His report gathered dust for over a decade until other dentists discovered his finding and copied his process and results. Today, with minor variations, millions of tooth crowns are made each year the way Iowa dentist Dr. Philbrook invented.

First Chartered Land-Grant College: ISU

President Abraham Lincoln, as a farm state president, understood the key role agriculture must play in a huge and growing country.

And so, on July 2, 1862, President Lincoln inked into law a measure introduced by Justin Morrill of Vermont. The law gave each state federal lands to endow a college whose curriculum would include both the classics and agricultural development.

The speedy Iowa legislature took just weeks to leap into action. The following September 11, Iowa was first to accept the terms of the Morrill Land Grant Act. In 1864 Iowa solons designated the yet-to-be-opened Iowa Agricultural College and model farm, later called Iowa

Iowa Pride

State University, as the first official land-grant college in the United States. The college opened in 1868.

The Iowa legislature provided only $10,000 for the new college, but the residents of Story County were so eager to have the new school in their county they anted up an additional $21,355 for the ultimate birthplace of "Cy" Cyclone, the ISU mascot.

First Continuing Education Course for Herdsmen: ISU

Being first is a lot like eating one peanut; it's difficult to stop. ISU, being the first ag. college, continued with many other firsts in all phases of agricultural science.

In 1901 ISU offered a two-week short course for herdsmen, the first program of its kind in the nation.

First County Cooperative Extension Program: ISU

One ISU professor, Perry Holden, was so instrumental in plowing new ground for ag. science that he earned the title of "seed corn evangelist." In 1903 he did it again when he established the nation's first county cooperative extension plan.

First Dance Critic: Cedar Rapids

"A little too much is just enough for me," about summed up Cedar Rapidian Carl Van Vechten's philosophy. Carl chose Jean Cocteau's favorite saying to adorn his stationery and as his life's model. But the one thing Carl was never accused of doing "too much" of was work.

Carl Van Vechten grew up unremarkably in Cedar Rapids, attended Coe College for a semester, then studied English at the University of Chicago. After college, Carl landed a job with the Paris division of *The New York Times,* from which he eventually managed to get fired for play reviews that the editors' wives disliked.

Carl had a lifelong romance with the stage. He socialized with actors, actresses, and authors—including the noted author Gertrude Stein—and was a fixture in literary and artistic circles both in Paris and New York City. Because of this proximity to the arts, he eventually became America's first dance critic.

Carl eventually wrote a light novel called *The Tattooed Countess,* which he called a satire on provincial small towns and which Cedar Rapids residents hated, perceiving the book as ridicule of them. In a fit of high dudgeon, the Cedar Rapids library banned the book. When a fuller appreciation of Carl's literary talents later surfaced, the ban was lifted.

"I am the most completely prejudiced person alive," Carl Van Vechten claimed. "I am completely prejudiced against every form of prejudice."

Carl proved his words through his actions. In his latter years, he gave away numbers of his treasures to found collections of the arts, most notably the James Weldon Johnson Memorial Collection of Negro Arts and Letters, at Yale University.

First Dance-Fitness Franchise: Red Oak

Iowan Judi Sheppard Missett grew up dancing in Red Oak as therapy to help correct her pigeon-toes. The combination of Judi and dance was a natural and, after carrying off the local prizes, she carried her dance passion to Northwestern University in Chicago. Following a degree in theater and dance, she studied under the tutelage of jazz-dance choreographer Gus Giordano, then began teaching jazz dance.

In 1969 the term *aerobics* was just entering the vocabulary as people took off on a fitness kick. Yet the mindless repetitions of calisthenics soured attitudes toward those programs. That's when Judi's idea kicked in higher than she can kick her heels.

Judi Sheppard Missett. Photo courtesy of Jazzercise, Inc.

Judi turned her students away from the mirror—telling them they didn't have to model perfection in dance. They should merely try to mimic the teacher, and—above all else—have fun. People loved the jazz-exercise routines, and Judi took the idea with her to California where she and her husband Jack carried their own brand of sunshine.

In San Diego, Judi set up jazz-dance-fitness classes that soon burgeoned with more students than she could personally manage. To spread her idea, she trained some of her students to clone her style and concept. The name *Jazzercise* was coined to describe her program and, when the numbers of teachers went ballistic, she franchised the use of the name, style, and concept, and offered corporate support to her teachers.

Since then, aerobics pioneer Judi Sheppard Missett has developed thousands of dance-fitness routines, written fitness bestsellers, created

243

fitness videos, educated thousands of teachers and hundreds of thousands of students, and been one of the fitness industry's outstanding spokespersons. Presidents Reagan, Bush, and Clinton have praised her activities, and scores of awards have been heaped upon her trim shoulders.

Currently, over 4,700 franchised Jazzercise instructors teach 13,000 classes weekly to a half million people in the United States, Canada, Australia, Japan, and Europe. JM Television Productions, Jazzertogs—a mail-order clothing line—and Jazzercise Know More Diet nutrition education program round out corporate activity. Judi's philanthropic programs of charity fund-raisers and the KGF—Kids Get Fit—program keep her head as fit as her body.

The world is healthier and happier since Iowan Judi Sheppard Missett danced into people's lives. What nicer legacy could anyone leave?

First Educational Television: UI, and
First Educationally Owned Television Station: ISU

The first viewers of TV wanted entertainment. Educators saw this novel device as a teaching tool.

Commercial television easily developed the entertainment people bought. But it took the University of Iowa to first broadcast educational programming. In 1932 UI beamed 389 teaching programs over station W9XK, a schedule continued for seven years. While the equipment was crude by modern standards, the sound and picture matched perfectly.

Twenty years later Texas station KUIT in Houston broadcast the first educational TV with modern electronic equipment. It only took two decades for the world to catch up to Iowa.

In 1950 with some funds left over from the hush-hush Manhattan nuclear bomb project (see Harley Wilhelm and Frank Spedding), ISU President Charles Friley suggested that a commercial television station license be obtained.

Application was made and approved and on February 21, 1951, the nation's first educationally owned, commercial television station began broadcasting as WOI-TV.

On March 1, 1994, in a sale that generated considerable controversy, WOI-TV was sold to Capital Communications Company, Inc. of Bronxville, New York, for $14 million. The proceeds were used by ISU to endow various educational programs.

First Electronic Newsroom: Davenport

In the 1970s it was standing room only at the *Quad-City Times*.

Newsmen and newswomen arrived in droves, from over three dozen countries, to marvel at a technological triumph called the Electronic Newsroom.

Here, reporters wrote stories in word-processing files, editors called them up from the data bank to edit them, and composing room personnel put the finished stories together to make up the next day's newspaper. Not a single finger was smudged with ink in the process.

For the first time, classified ads were composed on video terminals during the customer's call-in. Computer software then automatically inserted the ad in its alphabetical order, under the appropriate heading, began and ended the publication on correct dates, and provided billing records. Display advertising was also composed and created on terminals with another part of the software package.

The electronic newsroom was a victory one might expect from big-city newspapers. But the entire journalistic world got scooped by a small-town Iowa newspaper. Within a few years, every newspaper worth its ink followed suit.

First Experimental Kitchen: ISU

In 1876, just five years after extension services started spreading technology to Iowans, Mary Beaumont Welch established the first experimental kitchen in a college. Mary's husband, Adonijah, was ISU's first president.

How to preserve nutrients, prepare tastier meals, and guide a family to health—farm or town—fueled the move to bring science into the nation's bellies, via the nation's breadbasket, Iowa.

First Extension Services: ISU

Farmers already know it. And city folks are beginning to learn.

If you've ever had a problem with food or fiber, either growing, harvesting, preparing or cooking, you probably know the valuable local resource called the Extension Service. Once you get some smart answers from them, it is hard to imagine a world without extension services.

But extension services didn't just happen. Someone planned them, and the first off-campus "Farmers' Institutes" appeared in 1870–71, just two years after ISU opened its doors. It didn't take the staff at ISU long to figure out people's needs and match them with smart services.

In 1906 the nation's first state-financed Agricultural and Home Economics Extension Service was established at ISU with the dynamic Professor Perry Holden at its helm.

Later, in 1914, the Smith-Lever Cooperative Extension Act provided federal support for extension work on a matching funds basis. Iowa was the first state fully organized under the Smith-Lever Act.

First Fast-Food Franchise: Muscatine

Fred Angell had a Muscatine butcher shop, but he wished it was a restaurant.

Unlike many idle dreamers, Fred took some action. He invented a new sandwich, and when his delivery man dropped by the shop one morning, Fred had one of his special sandwiches steaming hot for him. After a few bites the taster exclaimed, "Fred, you know this sandwich is made right!"

The Maid-Rite® was born on the spot. Fred immediately opened a shop to sell his new sandwich and soon others wanted to know the secret spices and ingredients that made it so special. To accommodate them, in 1926 Fred established America's first fast-food franchises, calling for each franchisee to sell the sandwiches at no less than 10 cents each.

In the mid-1920s, Fred established another first: drive-up, walk-up windows as a convenience to customers. In time, this novelty would be adopted by the fast-food industry.

Fred's sandwich contained 100 percent low-fat, lean beef, with no filler. It was trimmed to stringent specifications, and steamed in the unique Maid-Rite cooker, along with special seasoning. A spoon came with the sandwich, to pick up the spillover. Placed on a warm bun, with mustard, pickle and onions, the Maid-Rite® is all Iowan, and made right!

First Food Additive and More: Cedar Rapids

Who would guess that oatmeal let housewives sleep later in the morning? But once America's homemakers learned about this wonder breakfast they never let it go.

A hundred years ago housewives got up four hours before breakfast to prepare biscuits, breads and rolls, pancakes, eggs, hams and other meats that would "stick to a man's ribs."

Suddenly, oatmeal came on the scene. Oatmeal only took two hours to prepare. It was inexpensive and provided a good protein breakfast. Once housewives learned the way out of preparing killer breakfasts, there was no turning back.

John Stuart was a Canadian oatmeal miller who only wanted a few things. They were: a larger market, cheap oats, coal and electricity, access to metro markets, a stable work force and plenty of water. When John found Cedar Rapids he declared it had it all. So John and his family moved to the "perfect city."

Soon the mill was humming under the leadership of his son Robert. But Robert wanted more. So he moved to Chicago to found a new plant and find even larger markets for his oatmeal.

In the Windy City, Robert formed a liaison with Henry Parson Crowell, who had the Quaker Oats® logo and symbol established. This symbol seemed to portray honesty and virtue to the homemaker, and was her first glimpse of a national logo.

Prior to the advent of the Quaker Oats® brand, a housewife scooped oatmeal from barrels in grocery markets. But now, she bought the convenience of the two-pound boxes of Quaker oatmeal, free from crawling pests and predictably edible.

Over the next few years, a consortium of oatmeal manufacturers formed to limit oatmeal productive capacity, regulate quality, and operate uniformly under the Quaker label. In the process, the Cedar Rapids Quaker plant expanded until it became the world's largest cereal plant.

Quaker Oats—the first truly worldwide corporation—pioneered many firsts in the food industry. They were first in the development of irradiated foods for vitamin enrichment, first to develop a theory and practice of modern consumer advertising, first to approach packaging as a sales lure, first to make a national food label, and first to nationally market a breakfast cereal.

Quaker Oats was first to promote a food by national advertising, first to register a cereal trademark, first to manufacture ready-mix foods for the modern housewife, first to commercially develop furfural (See Orland Sweeney) and the first national manufacturer of feeds for cows, calves, hogs and poultry. And Quaker Oats led in the development of fast foods and let America's homemakers have a life, too.

First Home Microwave Oven: Amana

The world learned to "Nuke it!" because in August of 1967 a

strange new kitchen appliance was introduced by Amana Refrigeration, Inc.

The Radarange® was the first 115-volt countertop microwave unit for home use. Within 22 years, 80 percent of the homes in America had added a microwave oven to their kitchens. Since its invention, many additional features, especially dealing with transistor circuitry, have made the microwave a permanent fixture in modern kitchens of the world.

The first microwave oven was produced in 1945 in the laboratories of the Raytheon Company, Lexington, Massachusetts. Dr. Percy Spencer, while testing a radar vacuum tube for Raytheon, discovered that microwave energy produced heat. He thought that heat could be concentrated enough to cook food and, sources say, he then sent out for a chocolate bar which promptly melted in the heat from the vacuum tube.

The first marketable microwave ovens were large machines, designed for hospital and other mass-feeding uses. In 1965, when Amana Refrigeration became a subsidiary of Raytheon, engineers for both companies combined talents to produce the historic Radarange® microwave oven. The kitchens of the world have never been the same. And families have never had a better opportunity to eat nutritiously.

First Mosque and First Muslim Cemetery in North America: Cedar Rapids

Millions of Muslims in North America, and 7,000 Iowa Muslims, look to a little wooden building in Cedar Rapids and reverently call it their "Mother Mosque."

It began in the late 1800s when brothers Hajj Abbass Habhab and Moses Habhab immigrated to Iowa from Lebanon. As word went back to the Middle East, extolling the quality of life in Iowa, other Muslims shouldered their belongings and trekked into Iowa. In the mid-1920s, 20 Muslims gathered in Cedar Rapids to form the "Rose of Fraternity Lodge."

By 1929 the members had committed to build a mosque, the house of worship of the Islamic religion. Despite the Depression, these hardy sons and daughters of Syria pressed on and by 1934 had completed their small mosque, America's first.

In 1948 Cedar Rapidian Hajj William Aossey, Sr., gave over six acres of land to create the first Islamic cemetery in North America. All the plots face Qibla, or the direction of Mecca.

First State-Supported School of Religion: UI

Talk about separation of church and state!

You should have been in on the boiling discussions between UI officials and the Iowa Board of Regents when they argued over establishing a whole SCHOOL of religion.

Originally, the founders of Iowa educational institutions, being God-fearing people, naturally assumed it was perfectly proper to include religious worship in the curriculum of a tax-supported school. UI students in 1875 were required to attend daily chapel worship services. Then, in 1898, the Religious Education Committee relaxed the rules and began non-compulsory vesper service where religious leaders spoke in an atmosphere of worship.

In the mid-1920s educators developed a plan for a department of religious studies—as opposed to worship—jointly supported by representatives of the various religious traditions. By garnering national support from these faiths, the leaders overcame objections from the State Board of Education.

To obtain financing John D. Rockefeller, Jr., was approached and asked for help from his charitable foundation. Upon the demonstration of bilateral support from the several faiths, Mr. Rockefeller offered $35,000 to cover administrative expenses for the first three years of the school's existence.

Dr. M. Willard Lampe, University Secretary for the Presbyterian Board of Education, was appointed the first Director of the School of Religion. On August 27, 1927, the University announced, "The School of Religion represents a venture into a new territory ... an unusual recognition of the important place which the study and practice of religion must hold in the adequate system of education."

First Statistical Laboratory: ISU

If research is to have meaning, results from a small test must be related to a larger sample. The relationship of smoking to health defects was established this way, for one example among thousands.

Statisticians manipulate numbers to determine if there is meaning to scientific studies. An agricultural science school finds that it needs a great deal of statistical analysis. To meet this felt need, in 1933 ISU researchers gained a valuable adjunct when the nation's first statistical laboratory was established.

Iowa Pride

First Woman Chair of the Republican Party: Eagle Grove

In the early 1950s Mary Louise Smith accepted a neighbor's challenge to ring doorbells to get out the vote. Her Eagle Grove neighbor happened to be the wife of former Governor Robert D. Blue, who tutored Mary Louise on how she could contribute to the political system. For the next 40 years, Mary Louise vaulted through the political process, proving in countless ways that her ability to contribute and lead was matchless.

Mary Louise Smith. Photo by Maxheim, courtesy of Iowa Commission on the Status of Women.

In 1974 President Gerald R. Ford appointed Mary Louise first to cochair the Republican Party; then, a few months later, to act as sole chairperson—the first woman to chair the Republican Party. Few persons have been president of the United States, just as few have convened a national convention for the Republican Party. Mary Louise Smith rang a doorbell and the nation answered.

"The concept of 'giving back' to the community in return for the benefits received establishes a sound basis for public service," Mary said. Certainly some people are blessed with the ability and the willingness to give back far more than they could ever personally receive.

First Woman Dentist: McGregor

In the mid-1800s, dentists apprenticed just like a blacksmith or a barber. They looked over the shoulder of another dentist until they learned how to perform extractions and restorations.

Lucy Hobbs Taylor learned to be a dentist that way. But she was so good at it that her fellow Iowa dentists urged her to attend one of the then five dental colleges in the United States. She chose Ohio Dental College in Cincinnati.

Lucy Hobbs Taylor

In 1865 Lucy Hobbs graduated with the degree of Doctor of Dental Surgery, not only one of the first 65 graduate dentists but the first woman in history to wear that degree. Following graduation she moved to Kansas where she practiced for many years.

First Woman Electoral College Board President: Red Oak

As Dorothy Houghton (1890–1972) grew up in the early part of the twentieth century she cut her teeth on the burgeoning women's rights movement that swirled around Iowa. Principal among those battles was the one being waged by Carrie Lane Chapman Catt in her efforts to reshape national thought and get state legislatures to accept the Nineteenth Amendment to the U.S. Constitution.

Dorothy Houghton. Photo courtesy of Iowa Commission on the Status of Women.

Iowa had already become the gender-levelest prairie in the land, so it was logical that Dorothy Houghton would seize opportunities to assert her stand for equality. In 1949 she was designated Iowa's most distinguished citizen. In 1956 Dorothy became the first female president of the Electoral College Board. President Dwight D. Eisenhower thought so highly of her capacity to serve that he appointed her director of the Office of Refugees, Migratory and Voluntary Assistance, a post she held—serving 40 million refugees—from 1953 until 1958.

First Woman Engineering Teacher: ISU

Her college yearbook at ISU described Elmina T. Wilson (1870–1918) as a "Runaway in High Life," alluding to Elmina Wilson's running away from home at the age of seven. For the rest of her life she was on the go.

In engineering college at ISU, she rose to the rank of major in the ladies battalion and was active in the YWCA, and several other groups. After graduation with a degree in civil engineering, she studied at Cornell University in New York State, then returned to Ames where she was engaged as the first woman to teach engineering—possibly the world's first woman teacher of engineering.

The next year she earned a graduate degree—another first—and continued teaching at ISU until 1904, when she moved to New York City and worked in three architectural firms. She almost certainly met Carrie Lane Chapman Catt, who lived there at the time. Both women belonged to the same sorority Pi Beta Phi—Wilson was its local alumni secretary—and both were strongly involved in the suffrage movement.

251

Iowa Pride

Wilson's younger sister, Alda, was an ISU civil engineering graduate and worked as a superintendent in the Women's Drafting Department at the Iowa Highway Commission. Alda became a companion to Carrie Catt in 1928 and stayed with her until Catt died in 1947.

First Woman Notary: New Hampton

Emily Calkins Stebbins's biggest problem, when she took over as deputy county recorder and treasurer in New Hampton, was that people really didn't believe a woman could be good with numbers. Emily proved their doubts wrong and was an able replacement for the treasurer who had enlisted in the Civil War.

In 1861 Emily Calkins came to New Hampton, Iowa, from Longmeadow, Massachusetts, to live with her sister. She had been taught in the village school in her birthplace, and had supplemented her education with a course at the Peacham Academy in Vermont.

In 1865 Emily joined the law and abstract office of J.H. Powers, where she worked for many years as an abstracter, insurance agent, and pension attorney.

The next year, Iowa Governor William M. Stone appointed Emily to be the nation's first woman notary public, establishing another notable Iowa stride for women's rights.

The First Woman Professor of Journalism: Coe College

On the wall of her classroom a sign stated her absolute dictum: **ACCURACY ALWAYS.**

One of Ethel R. Outland's early students who became a famous international journalist credited that motto for much of his success. Iowan William Shirer (see Shirer entry) said Outland "was a stern teacher because her standards were high. And she helped stimulate a discipline of work, and of the mind, that we could only appreciate in later years when the need of it became so important."

Ethel Outland. 1887–1972. Photo courtesy of George T. Henry.

Graduating with highest honors—magna cum laude with a Bachelor of Science degree—from Coe in 1909, Outland did graduate work in English at Radcliffe, went to Bread Loaf, then earned an M.A. degree from Wisconsin. Her master's thesis was the first to be published by the university in its language and literature series in 1929.

Outland joined the Coe faculty in 1911 as an instructor in English. One of her duties was to oversee and censor the student publication *The Cosmos*. In 1913 her students petitioned the college to provide instruction in journalism and asked that Outland be assigned to teach the course.

For a woman in the early 1900s to be a professor of journalism was a distinctive event. When Outland occupied her chair, she became the world's first woman professor of journalism.

She went on to claim other gender firsts. Outland was the first woman to hold national office in Pi Delta Epsilon, an honorary collegiate journalism fraternity. The Iowa Press Association named her its first woman advisor, and she was listed in the first issue of "American Women."

If the measure of a teacher is seen in the careers of her students, then Ethel R. Outland played a role in journalism that few would match.

First Woman Professor of Physical Education: Centerville

The people around 12-year-old Mabel Lee of Centerville were annoyed by her persistent begging. Imagine a girl wanting to play basketball! Mabel could not only imagine the idea, she pestered her father, school officials, and friends so much they finally gave in and formed the first girls' basketball team in Iowa. On May 2, 1902, dressed in chemises and petticoats—rolled up at the waist to shorten them—Mabel and several friends played a game of basketball in an out-of-sight, outdoor court at the edge of Centerville.

Mabel's enthusiasm for athletics blossomed into the then unheard-of-for-women activity of running. In college, she further pursued athletic interests by studying gymnastics and dance. In 1910 the lithe lady from Centerville became the director of women's physical education at Coe College, Cedar Rapids. Eight years later (1918) Mabel was appointed the professor of physical education at Oregon Agricultural College. Accounts in *The Des Moines Register* indicate that she may have been the nation's first woman professor to hold this position.

A long and distinguished educational career saw her write the hallmark text on women's physical education, become a Fulbright professor in Iraq, and preside over the National American Alliance of Health, Physical Education and Recreation as its first woman president. Many deserved awards came Mabel's way, including induction into the Coe College Hall of Fame and the Iowa Women's Hall of Fame.

Iowa Pride

First Woman School Superintendent: Davenport

Phebe Sudlow had a radical idea. She believed a woman should get the same pay as a man.

Phebe held many positions where she could stand up for her belief. In 1874, she became the first woman superintendent of schools, a position she held for four years. Then she became the first female professor at UI, teaching English language and literature.

Not content with those firsts, Phebe beat two prominent male educators out of the presidency of the Iowa State Teachers Association to become the first woman elected to the honor.

Phebe Sudlow. Photo courtesy of the State Historical Society of Iowa.

First Women Lawyers: Tipton and Henry County

Arabella Mansfield became the first woman lawyer in the United States when she passed the bar examination in Henry County in 1869. She also pioneered the Iowa Suffrage movement by chairing the first Iowa Suffrage Association state convention in 1870.

Once the Iowa Code got the hang of dropping the word "white" from its requirements for admission to the bar (1873), it went ahead and did the right thing by dropping the word "male."

Two years later, in 1875, Tipton native Mary Humphrey Haddock not only graduated from the UI law school but topped her male colleagues by being named class valedictorian.

Mary then went on to open a new door for women by being the first woman admitted to practice before the United States circuit and district courts.

First Women to Enter College as Equals to Men: UI

As early as 1839, several years before statehood, Iowa's public school system was coeducational, a fact not true in schools in other parts of America.

Eight years later the General Assembly of the new state of Iowa created the State University. As a natural outgrowth of equality in the public school system, the new University stipulated that women were to be admitted on an equal basis with men.

In the first UI class that enrolled in 1856–57, 83 young men and 41 young women formed the student body, making it the first state institution of higher learning to admit women on an equal basis with men. In 1870, 10 women constitute 27 percent of the initial medical class of 37 students.

Due to a financial recession in 1858, the trustees decided to close the University and reopen only to men, but a wail of protest quickly caused them to scrap that wild idea and continue equal admission rights for women. By the 1860s, even the physical education classes were integrated.

The pioneer Iowa equal rights plan must have been correct, for, since the beginning of the University, 58 percent of all Phi Beta Kappa keys for scholastic excellence have been awarded to women.

For some odd reason, penmanship classes were the last classes to be integrated.

First Women's Army Corps
Training Center: Des Moines

When the thunderclaps of World War II first shook the earth's foundations, President Franklin D. Roosevelt not only drafted men to serve their country but called on women to volunteer service in a military force.

The Women's Auxiliary Army Corps (WAACs) was established by Congress in May of 1942. In July 1942 recruits began streaming into Des Moines at the rate of 150 students each two weeks for the four-week course, which included military customs and courtesies, organization of the Army, map reading, first aid, and supply.

The women saw duty as clerks, typists, drivers, and cooks. This was disappointing because these duties ignored their civilian skills in such areas as accounting, communications, dental hygiene, drafting, linguistics, library science, and teaching.

In 1943 General George C. Marshall asked Congress for regular military status for the WAAC. In February 1943, Congress approved the new status, dropping the *Auxiliary* name from the title, to become the WAC.

At last women assumed the same grades and ranks as military men along with the same benefits, pay and privileges. Now the WACs exercised their skills in a better-suited range of military duties.

President Franklin D. Roosevelt had set a goal of 25,000 women for the first full year of war; however, this goal was met during the first six months. The ceiling was promptly raised to 150,000 women and more training centers were opened.

CONCLUSION

The Level Prairies of Iowa

Like a person who fails to see a water tower because they don't look up, I missed it. Repeated clues in bio-sketches hinted at it over and again. It was always there, waiting to be noticed. Then one day, plodding for the barn like an old plug horse, the concept crept up on me, not unlike baseball ghosts walked out from rows of corn in Kinsella's *Field of Dreams.*

An optical illusion, once defined, is forever simple to see. Same thing here. Once I found it, page after page of *Iowa Pride* confirmed its truth.

That morning I had read and corrected the final draft, hunting typos and scratching my head for answers to my editor's green-penciled questions. By lunch a gnawing hunch had begun to form. In the afternoon I re-read the book in page proofs. When I had finished the second reading, the idea was full-blown, full-grown.

I paged back through the manuscript, taking notes and processing words until there was no escaping the conclusion. I offer now the support for my finding. Tell me if you see what I see. Without fear of misreading the evidence, I report that: *Iowa is the seedbed of gender equality!*

Here is the basis for that belief. These facts are gleaned from the pages of *Iowa Pride,* all depicting events and actions that took place between our muddy shores. Often an occurrence that was the nation's first also became a world first.

257

Conclusion _____

Here are the events that show that gender parity began in Iowa 157 years ago. The date was seven years before the vote for Iowa statehood squeaked by the electorate, beginning with:

1839: Iowa public schools offer coeducation. In those days, almost no public school in the United States admitted female children. American men then clearly believed that "a woman's place is in the home." Iowa men disagreed with that attitude and Iowa women agreed.

1856: Forty-three Iowa women join 81 Iowa men to form the first freshman class at UI. This co-educational admission policy sets a historical first: for the first time women enter a public college on an equal basis with men. Alliance College in Ohio, a private (Methodist) college was the first institution of higher education to break this barrier.

Late-1850s: Amelia Jenks Bloomer of Council Bluffs champions dress reform as part of her suffragist activities and an item of apparel—pantaloons—takes her name as "bloomers."

1864: Annie Wittenmyer of Keokuk creates the first diet kitchen for Civil War hospitals. President Lincoln then appoints her to oversee the managers of 200 Union hospitals.

1864: Lucy Hobbs Taylor of McGregor graduates with a Doctor of Dental Surgery (D.D.S.) degree and becomes the nation's first woman dentist.

1866: Emily Calkins Stebbins of New Hampton accepts appointment as the first woman notary public.

1869: Arabella Mansfield of Henry County reads law in her father's office, passes the bar exam and becomes the first woman attorney in the United States.

1869: Annie Wittenmyer co-founds the Woman's Christian Temperance Union.

258

1870: Ten women constitute 27 percent of the initial UI medical class of 37 students, giving more gender balance than in any medical school in history.

1874: Phebe Sudlow of Davenport accepts a position as first woman superintendent of schools.

1875: Mary Humphrey Haddock becomes the first woman admitted to practice law before U.S. circuit and district courts.

1876: Mary Beaumont Welch of ISU creates the nation's first experimental kitchen in a college.

1894: Elmina Wilson of Harper graduates from ISU to become one of, if not the nation's, first woman engineering graduate.

Late-1800s: Iowa is the first state to allow women to serve on Boards and Commissions.

1898: Elmina Wilson accepts a teaching position at ISU to become one of, if not the nation's first woman teacher of engineering.

Late-1800s: Iowa is the first state to allow women to record deeds.

1902: Mabel Lee of Centerville forms one of, if not the nation's first women's basketball team.

1910: Jesse Field Shambaugh of Shenandoah founds 4-H, which allows girls to compete on a basis skill for the first time.

1913: Ethel R. Outland of Mahaska County, teaching at Coe College, becomes the first woman professor of journalism.

1917: Cora Bussey Hillis founds the first Child Welfare Research Station at UI.

Conclusion ────────────────

1918-1919: Mabel Lee is said to have been the nation's first woman professor of physical education, having been the first women's physical education director at Coe in 1910, then becoming a full professor of physical education in Oregon.

1920: Carrie Lane Chapman Catt leads the ratification fight for adoption of the Nineteenth Amendment, to give the nation's first woman's franchise, i.e., the right to vote.

1921: Carrie Lane Chapman Catt founds the League of Women Voters.

1924: Gertrude Durden Rush, an African-American lawyer, along with four male lawyers from Des Moines, creates the National Bar Association.

1929: Lou Henry Hoover of Waterloo becomes the first First Lady from Iowa as wife of newly elected President Herbert Hoover.

1931: Mabel Lee becomes the first women president of the American Physical Education Association, name later changed to The American Alliance for Health, Physical Education and Recreation.

1935: Viola Babcock Miller of Mt. Pleasant founds one of, if not the first state highway patrols.

1940: Mabel Lee becomes the first woman president of the American Academy of Physical Education.

1942: The first U.S. women in the military, the WAACs (the acronym later changed to WACs) encamp for basic training in Fort Des Moines.

1950s onward: Esther ("Ask Ann") and Pauline ("Dear Abby") Friedman of Sioux City become the world's most-read women.

1953: Mamie Doud Eisenhower of Boone also becomes the nation's First Lady as wife of President Ike Eisenhower.

1955: Beulah Gundling of Cedar Rapids founds the swimming sport of aquatic art.

1956: Dorothy Deemer Houghton of Red Oak is elected the first woman president of the Electoral College Board.

1969: Aerobics pioneer Judi Sheppard Missett, raised in Red Oak, invents the first fun dance-fitness program, Jazzercise.

1974: Mary Louise Smith of Des Moines accepts the position as first woman chair of the Republican Party.

1976: Mary Louise Smith calls the Republican convention to order, becoming the first woman to convene this party.

1983: Judi Sheppard Missett franchises her Jazzercise dance-fitness concept.

1986: The Iowa legislature enacts the nation's first Gender Balance Law for All State Boards and Commissions.

1991: Spearheaded by State Representative Minnette Doderer, Iowa becomes the first state in the nation to endorse the United Nations' Convention on the Elimination of All Forms of Discrimination Against Women.

The prairies of Iowa may have been rolling, but our Iowa ancestors were first to declare these plains must be forever gender-level. The United States has followed suit, and, for this heritage, all Iowans can claim justifiable **Iowa Pride.**

REFERENCES

For those Iowans whose sphere of performance was largely Iowa-based

Noel M. Anderson: *Des Moines Register* article. Personal correspondence.

David A. Armbruster: Newspaper clipping, *Iowa City Press-Citizen,* August 7, 1985. Family Communication.

John Vincent Atanasoff: Mollenhoff, Clark R., *Atanasoff: Forgotten Father of the Computer,* 275 pp., Iowa State University Press, 1988. Personal correspondence with Mrs. Alice Crosby Atanasoff. *" ... from one John V. Atanasoff,"* film of the discovery of the digital computer, produced by Media Production Unit, Iowa State University.

Clifford Berry: Mollenhoff, Clark R., *Atanasoff: Forgotten Father of the Computer,* 275 pp., Iowa State University Press, 1988. Personal correspondence with Mrs. Alice Crosby Atanasoff. *" ... from one John V. Atanasoff,"* film of the discovery of the digital computer, produced by Media Production Unit, Iowa State University.

William P. Bettendorf: *The Davenport Democrat and Leader,* June 5, 1910.

Samuel O. Blanc: Corporate correspondence.

Amelia Jenks Bloomer: Beam, Patrice K., *Iowa Woman,* Waterloo, Iowa, Winter, 1991. Iowa Department of Human Rights, Des Moines, Iowa.

Roy Carver: Family correspondence with Roy Carver, Jr.

Carrie Lane Chapman Catt: ISU, Department of Special Collections.

Arthur A. Collins: Braband, Ken C., *The First 50 Years. A History of Collins Radio Company & The Collins Division of Rockwell International,* Communications Dept., Avionics Group, Rockwell International, Cedar Rapids, 1983. Ewoldt, Harold F., *Cedar Rapids, The Magnificent Century,* Windsor Publications, Inc., Northridge, California, 1988. Rockwell International Corporation, Collins Avionics and Communications Division, private communications.

Marvin Cone: *The Coe Cosmos,* Coe College, Cedar Rapids, Iowa, May 20, 1965; *Cedar Rapids Gazette,* Cedar Rapids, Iowa, March 31, 1988; October 18, 1991.

Jay Norwood "Ding" Darling: Lendt, David L., *Ding: The Life of Jay Norwood Darling,* Iowa State University Press, Ames, Iowa, 1989, pp. 204.

Paul Engle: UI Archives.

William Fisher: Personal correspondence with Thomas Shide.

John Froelich: Froelich Foundation, private correspondence. Broehl, Wayne G., *John Deere's Company: A History of Deere and Company and Its Times,*

References ─────────────────────────────────

Doubleday & Company, Inc., New York, 1954. Deere and Company, Communication Services, private correspondence. Newsletter no. 3, *Two-Cylinder Club*, Agricultural History Productions, Waterloo, Iowa, 1986.

Dan Gable: UI, Sports Information Dept. Personal communication.

George Gallup: Family correspondence with George Gallup, Jr.

Burt Gray: Madison County Historical Society.

Beulah Gundling: *Dancing in the Water*, Linn Litho, Marion, Iowa, 1976. Personal correspondence.

Jesse Hiatt: Miller, Henry C., *The Delicious Apple, Since 1872*, Madison County Historical Society, Winterset, Iowa. *The Stark Story*, Missouri Historical Society, St. Louis, September 1966.

Cora Bussey Hillis: Beam, Patrice K., *Iowa Woman*, Waterloo, Iowa, Summer, 1993.

Arthur L. Hubbard: Personal communications.

W.A. Jennings: Personal communications with A.L. Jennings, CEO and President of EFCO, the Economy Forms Company.

MacKinlay Kantor: Kendall Young Library Archives, Webster City, Iowa. Maxson, Max, *The Daily Freeman-Journal*, Webster City, Iowa, obituary, October 12, 1977. Fadool, Cynthia R., *Contemporary Authors*, Gale Research Company, Detroit, Michigan, 1976.

Karl L. King: Fort Dodge Historical Society.

Nile Kinnick: *A Hero Perished*, edited by Paul Baender, University of Iowa Press, Iowa City, Iowa, 1991.

Mauricio Lasansky: *The Nazi Drawings*, with an essay describing them by Guggenheim Fellow Edwin Honig, University of Iowa Press, Iowa City, 1976. Thein, John and Lasansky, Phillip, under the direction of Mauricio Lasansky, *Lasansky: Printmaker*, with a foreword by art critic Carl Zigrosser, a critical discussion of Lasansky's esthetic development by Alan Fern, chief of the prints and photographs division of the Library of Congress, and a detailed essay on the prints by Stephen Rhodes, director of the Blanden Art Gallery in Fort Dodge, Iowa. Personal correspondence.

Dave Lennox: Corporate correspondence.

Luigi Ligutti: *The Palimpsest*, v. 58 no. 5, 1977. *Des Moines Register*, December 28, 1983.

E.F. Lindquist, "The Iowa Testing Programs—A Retrospective View," *Education*, September-October, 1970, Vol. 91, no. 1. Data from the Iowa Testing Program, UI.

Lester Martin: Donnelley Marketing Inc. corporate correspondence.

Fred L. Maytag: Orville R. Butler, Ph.D., Maytag Archivist. Corporate communications.

James A. McPherson: The University of Iowa Arts Center Relations, The University of Iowa Writers' Workshop.

E.T. Meredith: Corporate correspondence.

Viola "Ola" Babcock Miller: Beam, Patrice K., *Iowa Woman*, Waterloo, Iowa, Summer, 1992.

Clark Mollenhoff: Kendall Young Library archives, Webster City, Iowa. Stevens, Walter B., *Fort Dodge Messenger,* March 3, 1991, article. Raffensberger & Katayama, *Des Moines Sunday Register,* March 3, 1991, article. Steenson, Bob, *The Daily Freeman-Journal,* Webster City, Iowa, article, March, 1991. Metzger, Linda, *Contemporary Authors,* New Revision Series, Volume 13, Gale Research Company, Detroit, Michigan, 1984.

Thomas D. Murphy: Resource documents, Red Oak Library.

John L. Naughton: Personal correspondence.

Christian K. Nelson: Dickson, Paul, *The Great American Ice Cream Book,* Kingsport Press, Inc., Kingsport, Tennessee, 1972. *The Onawa Democrat Advertiser,* selected clippings.

David C. Nicholas: Personal communication. Article from *Des Moines Register,* October 2, 1992.

George P. Nissen: Personal communication. Selected news clippings.

Austin N. Palmer: *The Cedar Rapids Gazette,* Cedar Rapids, Iowa, newspaper clippings. Genealogical Society of Linn County, Iowa.

D.D. Palmer: Gielow, Vern, *Old Dad Chiro,* Bawden Bros., Davenport, Iowa, 1981. Gibbons, Russell W., "Chiropractic History: Turbulence and Triumph, the Survival of a Profession," 1976. Private communications, the Palmer College of Chiropractic.

William D. "Shorty" Paul: Family communication. *Iowa Alumni Quarterly,* Autumn 1993.

Carl Emil Seashore: Moeller, Dorothy; *Speech Pathology & Audiology: Iowa Origins of a Discipline,* 1976, University of Iowa Press, 225 pp.

Jessie Field Shambaugh: Whitmore, Faye; Cheshire, Manila, *The Very Beginnings,* World Publishing, Shenandoah, Iowa, 1963. Friedel, Janice Nahra, "The Mother of 4-H," article in *The Palimpsest,* Vol. 62, Number 4, July/August '81.

Walter A. Sheaffer: Peterson, William J., *Palimpsest,* September, 1952. Corporate correspondence.

Jane Smiley: Gibson, Debra, "Critics' Choice," *Visions,* Spring 1990; ISU Alumni magazine; McMillen, Liz, "Moo U Follies"; *The Chronicle of Higher Education,* May 12, 1995; *A Thousand Acres,* Random House, 1992; *Moo,* Alfred A. Knopf, Inc., 1995.

Cloid H. Smith: The American Pop Corn Company, corporate correspondence. Smith, Wrede, *A History of Pop Corn and the American Pop Corn Company,* 1989, 48 pages.

Frank H. Spedding: Ames Laboratory, Frank H. Spedding papers.

Phil Stong: Paluka, Frank, *Iowa Authors, A Bio-Bibliography of Sixty Native Writers,* Friends of the University of Iowa Library, 1967.

Orland R. Sweeney: ISU Archives.

William P. Switzer: ISU Information Service. Personal communication.

John J. Tokheim: Family correspondence.

Ray Townsend: Personal communication.

James Van Allen: UI archivist, Earl M. Rogers.

References ────────────────────────

Gary J. Vermeer: Personal correspondence.

Henry A. Wallace: Crabb, Richard A., *The Hybrid Corn Makers,* Rutgers University Press, 1947. Corporate correspondence, Pioneer Hi-Bred International, Inc.

Harley A. Wilhelm: Ames Laboratory, Institute for Physical Research and Technology. Private correspondence.

Annie Wittenmyer: Leonard, Elizabeth D., *Yankee Women: Gender Battles in the Civil War,* W.W. Norton & Co., Inc., New York, 1944, pp. 50-103. Archives from the Annie Wittenmyer Home, Davenport, Iowa. *Palimpsest,* Vol. 48, No. 6, pp. 249-255.

F.A. Wittern: Personal correspondence.

Grant Wood: Wood, Grant, "Revolt Against the City," an essay first published in *Grant Wood: A Study in American Art,* circa 1940. Block, Maxine, *Current Biography,* "Who's News and Why," The H.W. Wilson Company, New York, 1940.

Those Iowans who accomplished outside Iowa

Bess Streeter Aldrich: Beam, Patrice K., *Iowa Woman,* Waterloo, Iowa, Autumn, 1993. Iowa Department of Human Rights, Des Moines, Iowa.

Bix Beiderbecke: Sudhalter, Richard M. & Evans, Philip R., *BIX, Man & Legend,* Arlington House Publishers, New Rochelle, New York, 1974.

Mildred Wirt Benson: University of Iowa correspondence. *Cedar Rapids Gazette,* Cedar Rapids, Iowa, April 16, 1993.

Norman Borlaug: Chapman, Mike, *Iowans of Impact,* Enterprise Publishing Company, Waterloo, Iowa, 1984, 152 pp.

Johnny Carson: Biographical sketch from Carson Productions, Burbank, California.

George Washington Carver: Private Correspondence, Iowa State University. Block, Maxine, *Current Biography,* "Who's News and Why," The H.W. Wilson Company, New York, 1940, 1942. McMurray, Linda O., *George Washington Carver: Scientist & Symbol,* Oxford University Press, New York, 1981.

William F. Cody: William F. Cody, autobiography, *The Life of Hon. William F. Cody known as Buffalo Bill, the Famous Hunter, Scout and Guide, An Autobiography,* University of Nebraska Press, reprinted 1978, 365 pp.

Lee deForest: Block, Maxine, *Current Biography,* "Who's News and Why," The H.W. Wilson Company, New York, 1940, 1942. Carneal, Georgette, *A Conqueror of Space: an Authorized Autobiography of the Life and Work of Lee deForest,* Horace Liverwright, New York, 1930, 296 pp.

Wyatt Earp: Lake, Stuart N., *Wyatt Earp, Frontier Marshal,* Houghton Mifflin, 1931, 392 pp.

Mamie Doud Eisenhower: Hanft, Ethel W.; Manley, Paula J., *Outstanding Iowa Women Past and Present,* River Bend Publishing, Muscatine, Iowa, 1980.

266

Kimball, D.L., *I Remember Mamie,* Trends and Events, Inc., Fayette, Iowa, 1981.

Simon Estes: Moritz, Charles and Others, *Current Biography Yearbook 1986,* The H.W. Wilson Company, New York, 1986. Ploski, Harry A. and Williams, James, *The Negro Almanac: A Reference Work on the African American,* Gale Research Inc., 1989, Detroit, Michigan. Private correspondence.

Bob Feller: Chapman, Mike, *Iowans of Impact,* Enterprise Publishing Company, Waterloo, Iowa, 1984, 152 pp.

Esther P. and Pauline E. Friedman: Personal correspondence.

Hamlin Garland: *Twentieth Century Authors,* H.W. Wilson Company, New York, 1942, p. 516.

President Herbert Hoover: Dwight M. Miller, senior archivist, Herbert Hoover Presidential Library, West Branch, Iowa. Clinton, Susan, *Encyclopedia of Presidents: Herbert Hoover,* Children's Press, Chicago, Illinois, 1988. Hilton, Suzanne, *The World of Young Herbert Hoover,* Walker and Company, New York, 1987. Chuck Olin and Associates, "Herbert Hoover: An American Adventure," 23-minute video, Herbert Hoover Presidential Library.

Laurence C. Jones: University of Iowa Archives.

Cloris Leachman: Correspondence with Sutton Saltzman Public Relations, Los Angeles, California. Moritz, Charles & Others, *Current Biography Yearbook,* The H. W. Wilson Company, New York, 1975.

John L. Lewis: Alinsky, Saul, *John L. Lewis, an unauthorized biography,* G.P. Putnam's Sons, New York, 1949, 387 pp. Dubofsky, Melvyn, Van Tine, and Warren, *John L. Lewis: A Biography,* Quadrangle, The New York Times Book Co., 1976, 619 pp.

Glenn Miller: Nodaway Valley Historical Museum, Clarinda, Iowa. Block, Maxine, *Current Biography,* "Who's News and Why," The H.W. Wilson Company, New York, 1940, 1942. Simon, George T., *Glenn Miller & His Orchestra,* Da Capo Press, New York, 1974.

John R. Mott: Postville Historical Society brochure. Rother, Anna, *Current Biography* "Who's News and Why," The H.W. Wilson Company, New York, 1947, pp. 453-456.

Robert N. Noyce: *The Des Moines Register,* article, June 10, 1990.

Donna Reed: Corporate correspondence with the Donna Reed Foundation for the Performing Arts, Denison, Iowa.

Beardsley Ruml: *Cedar Rapids Gazette,* selected clippings. *Des Moines Register,* selected clippings.

William L. Shirer: His autobiographical books: *The Rise and Fall of the Third Reich, The Collapse of the Third Republic, Berlin Diary.* Bennett, James, *International Who's Who, 1993-1994,* Europa Publications Limited, London, England, 1993.

Mona VanDuyn: Correspondence from University of Iowa.

John Wayne: Moritz, Charles & Others, *Current Biography Yearbook,* The H.W. Wilson Company, New York, 1940, 1941, 1943, 1972, 1986. Scar, Ethel

References

C., *The Great American: A John Wayne Biography,* John Wayne Birthplace Society, Winterset, Iowa, undated. Kieskalt, Charles John, *The Official John Wayne Reference Book,* A Citadel Press Book, Secaucus, New York, 1985.

Meredith Willson: Family communications.

BIBLIOGRAPHY

Alinsky, Saul, *John L. Lewis, an unauthorized biography,* G.P. Putnam's Sons, New York, 1949, 387 pp.

American Association of Women Dentists, vol. 117 no. 3, September 1988.

Aossey, Yaha, Jr., *Fifty Years of Islam in Iowa 1925–1975,* Islamic Center and Mosque, Cedar Rapids, Iowa.

Badawi, Jamal, *Muhammed in the Bible,* Islamic Information Foundation, Halifax, Nova Scotia.

Baender, Paul, editor, *A Hero Perished,* University of Iowa Press, Iowa City, Iowa, 1991.

Block, Maxine, *Current Biography,* "Who's News and Why," The H.W. Wilson Company, New York, 1940, 1942 (Grant Wood, Alton Glenn Miller, Lee deForest, George Washington Carver).

Braband, Ken C., *The First 50 Years. A History of Collins Radio Company & The Collins Division of Rockwell International,* Communications Dept., Avionics Group, Rockwell International, Cedar Rapids, Iowa, 1983.

Broehl, Wayne G., *John Deere's Company: A History of Deere and Company and Its Times,* Doubleday & Company, Inc., New York, 1954.

Caney, Steven, *Invention Book of 35 Great Invention Stories,* Workman Publishing Company, Inc., New York, 1985.

Carneal, Georgette, *A Conqueror of Space: An Authorized Autobiography of the Life and Work of Lee deForest,* Horace Liverwright, New York, 1930, 296 pp.

Chapman, Mike, *Iowans of Impact,* Enterprise Publishing Company, Waterloo, Iowa, 1984, 152 pp.

Clinton, Susan, *Encyclopedia of Presidents: Herbert Hoover,* Children's Press, Chicago, Illinois, 1988.

Cody, William F., *The Life of Hon. William F. Cody known as Buffalo Bill, the Famous Hunter, Scout and Guide: An Autobiography,* University of Nebraska Press, Lincoln, Nebraska, reprinted 1978, 365 pp.

Collins Division of Rockwell International Commemorative 50th Anniversary tabloid, Cedar Rapids.

Cooper, Tom C., Executive Editor, *Iowa's Natural Heritage,* Iowa Natural Heritage Foundation and the Iowa Academy of Science, Des Moines, Iowa, 1982.

Crabb, Richard A., *The Hybrid Corn Makers,* Rutgers University Press, New Brunswick, New Jersey, 1947.

Bibliography

Dickson, Paul, *The Great American Ice Cream Book,* Kingsport Press, Inc., Kingsport, Tennessee, 1972, 1973.

Dilts, Harold E., *From Ackley to Zwingle,* Iowa State University Press, Ames, Iowa, 1975, 235 pp.

Dubofsky, Melvyn, and Warren, Van Tine, *John L. Lewis: A Biography,* Quadrangle, The New York Times Book Co., New York, 1976, 619 pp.

Dzierwa, Richard, "Dependably Maytag," *Appliance* magazine, June, 1990.

The EFCO Decades, EFCO video services, Des Moines, Iowa, 9/11/90, 60:00 minutes.

Ewoldt, Harold F., *Cedar Rapids, The Magnificent Century,* Windsor Publications, Inc., Northridge, California, 1988.

Fadool, Cynthia R., *Contemporary Authors,* Gale Research Co., Detroit, Michigan, 1976.

Friedel, Janice Nahra, "The Mother of 4-H," article in *The Palimpsest,* Vol. 62, no. 4, July/August 1981.

Frimrite, Ron, "Nile Kinnick," *Sports Illustrated,* August 31, 1987, issue.

Garland, Hamlin; *A Daughter of the Middle Border,* The Macmillan Company, New York, 1929.

Gerber, John C., Carolyn B. Brown, James Kauffmann, James B. Lindberg, Jr., *A Pictorial History of the University of Iowa,* University of Iowa Press, Iowa City, 1988, 273 pp.

Gibbons, Russell W., "Chiropractic History: Turbulence and Triumph, the Survival of a Profession," *Who's Who in Chiropractic,* 1980.

Gielow, Vern, *Old Dad Chiro,* Bawden Bros., Davenport, Iowa, 1981.

Gundling, Beulah, *Dancing in the Water,* Linn Litho, Marion, Iowa, 1976.

Hake, Herb, *Iowa Inside Out,* Iowa State University Press, Ames, Iowa, 1968, 213 pp.

Hanft, Ethel W.; Paula J. Manley, *Outstanding Iowa Women Past and Present,* River Bend Publishing, Muscatine, Iowa, 1980.

Hilton, Suzanne, *The World of Young Herbert Hoover,* Walker and Company, New York, 1987.

Introducing Islam, Brochure Series No. 1, The Institute of Islamic Information and Education, Chicago, Illinois.

Iowa Journal of History and Politics, Vol. 45, Published Quarterly by the State Historical Society of Iowa, Iowa City, Iowa, 1947.

Iowa State Medical and Chirugical Society, *One Hundred Years of Iowa Medicine,* 1950.

Iowa State University, " *... from one John V. Atanasoff,"* film of the discovery of the digital computer, produced by Media Production Unit.

John Deere Dealer Bulletin No. A-1151-58-12, Des Moines, Iowa.

John Deere, Historical Highlights, Over 150 Years of John Deere Contributions to Agriculture, Corporate Publication.

Kendall, Edward C., *John Deere's Steel Plow,* Paper 2, United States National Museum, Bulletin 218, Smithsonian Institution, Washington, D.C., 1959.

Kieskalt, Charles John, *The Official John Wayne Reference Book*, A Citadel Press Book, Secaucus, New York, 1985.

Kimball, D.L., *I Remember Mamie*, Trends and Events, Inc., Fayette, Iowa, 1981.

Lake, Stuart N., *Wyatt Earp, Frontier Marshal*, Houghton Mifflin, Boston, 1931, 392 pp.

Lendt, David L., *Ding: The Life of Jay Norwood Darling*, Iowa State University Press, Ames, Iowa, 1989, pp. 204.

Leonard, Elizabeth D., *Yankee Women: Gender Battles in the Civil War*, W.W. Norton & Co., Inc., New York, 1944, pp. 50–103.

Lewis, Tom, *Empire of the Air: the Men Who Made Radio*, Edward Burlingame Books, New York, 1991, 421 pp.

Lindquist, E. F., "The Iowa Testing Programs—A Retrospective View," *Education*, September–October, 1970, Vol. 91, no. 1.

McKenzie, Betty, *The People's Art: 1889–1989, One Hundred Years of Calendars from the Thos. D. Murphy Company of Red Oak, Iowa*, An Exhibit Organized by the Montgomery County Historical Society, 1991.

McMurray, Linda O., *George Washington Carver: Scientist & Symbol*, Oxford University Press, New York, 1981.

The Making of an American Classic: The life and times of the Maytag Washer from its birth in 1907, Form No. 755L-ADV., The Maytag Company, Newton, Iowa.

Marquette, Arthur F., *Brands, Trademarks & Goodwill: the Story of the Quaker Oats Company*, McGraw-Hill Book Co., New York, 1967, 274 pp.

Miller, Henry C., *The Delicious Apple, Since 1872*, Madison County Historical Society, Winterset, Iowa.

Moeller, Dorothy, *Speech Pathology & Audiology: Iowa Origins of a Discipline*, University of Iowa Press, Iowa City, Iowa, 1976.

Mollenhoff, Clark R., *Atanasoff: Forgotten Father of the Computer*, 275 pp., Iowa State University Press, Ames, Iowa, 1988.

Moritz, Charles et al., *Current Biography Yearbook*, The H.W. Wilson Company, New York, 1940, 1941, 1943, 1972, 1986.

Murphy, Thos. D., *The Art Calendar Industry, The Story of the Early Struggles of the Founders With a Short History of the Thos. D. Murphy Co.*, Papers Read at the 1920 Salesman's Convention, Press of the Thos. D. Murphy Co., 1921.

The Nazi Drawings, with an essay describing them by Guggenheim Fellow Edwin Honig, University of Iowa Press, Iowa City, 1976.

Newsletter No. 3, 1986, *Two-Cylinder Club*, P.O. Box 2275, Waterloo, Iowa.

Noun, Louise R., *Strong-Minded Women*, Iowa State University Press, Ames, Iowa, 1969, 362 pp.

Offenberger, Chuck, *Ah, You Iowans!*, Iowa State University Press, Ames, Iowa, 1992, 301 pp.

Olin, Chuck and Associates, Chicago, Illinois, "Herbert Hoover: An American Adventure," 23-minute video, Herbert Hoover Presidential Library.

Bibliography

Penner, James, *Goliath: The Life of Robert Schuller,* New Hope Publishing Co., Anaheim, California, 1992.

Ploski, Harry A. and Williams, James, *The Negro Almanac: A Reference Work on the African American,* Gale Research Inc., 1989, Detroit, Michigan.

Plowden, Gene, *Those Amazing Ringlings and Their Circus,* Caxton Printers, Ltd., Caldwell, Idaho, 1967.

Purcell, L. Edward, "Art and Advertising: The Thos. D. Murphy Co. of Red Oak," *The Palimpsest,* Vol. 57, no. 6, Nov./Dec., 1976.

Rasmussen, Chris, Princeton University, Doctorate thesis on the Iowa State Fair, selected portions pp. 289–296.

Rockwell News, vol. 5, no. 9, Sept. 1983, Rockwell International, Cedar Rapids, Iowa.

Rother, Anna, *Current Biography,* "Who's News and Why," The H.W. Wilson Company, New York, 1947.

Sage, Leland L., *A History of Iowa,* Iowa State University Press, Ames, Iowa, 1974, 376 pp.

Scar, Ethel C., *The Great American: A John Wayne Biography,* John Wayne Birthplace Society, Winterset, Iowa, undated.

Schwieder, Dorothy; Thomas Morain, Lynn Nielsen, *Iowa Past to Present: The People and the Prairie,* Iowa State University Press, Ames, Iowa, 1989.

Scott County, Iowa, *Biographical History & Portrait Gallery,* American Biographical Publishing Co., H.C. Cooper, Jr. & Co., Proprietors, 1895: reprinted, 1989, Selby Publishing, Kokomo, Indiana.

Sheaffer, Walter A., *The Life Story of Walter Sheaffer,* Cattermole Library, Fort Madison, Iowa, 71 pp., 1950.

Shirer, William A., *Berlin Diary: The Journal of a Foreign Correspondent 1934–1941,* Little, Brown & Co., Boston, 1941.

Shirer, William, *The Rise and Fall of the Third Reich,* Fawcett Crest, New York, 1950, 1599 pp.

Shirer, William A., *20th Century Journey: A Memoir of a Life and the Times,* Bantam Books, New York, 1984.

Shirer, William A., *An August to Remember,* subtitled *A Historian Remembers the Last Days of World War II and the End of the World That Was,* Thornwillow Press, New York, 1986.

Simon, George T., *Glenn Miller and His Orchestra,* Da Capo Press, New York, 1974.

Smith, Wrede H., Jr., *A History of Pop Corn and the American Pop Corn Company,* 48 pp., 1989, Sioux City, Iowa.

Southern Medical Journal, Vol. 77, Sept. 1984.

The Stark Story, Missouri Historical Society, St. Louis, Sept. 1966.

Sudhalter, Richard M. and Evans, Philip R., *BIX, Man & Legend,* Arlington House Publishers, New Rochelle, New York, 1974.

Tawil, Imam Taha, *Islam in Iowa: the Islamic Center of Cedar Rapids, Iowa, U.S.A.,* published by the Cedar Rapids Islamic Center, 1986.

Tawil, Imam Taha, *Renovation & Restoration of the Mother Mosque of America,* Islamic Council of Iowa, Cedar Rapids, Iowa, 1991.

Thein, John, and Phillip Lasansky, under the direction of Mauricio Lasansky, *Lasansky: Printmaker,* with a foreword by art critic Carl Zigrosser, a critical discussion of Lasansky's esthetic development by Alan Fern, chief of the prints and photographs division of the Library of Congress, and a detailed essay on the prints by Stephen Rhodes, director of the Blanden Art Gallery in Fort Dodge, Iowa, UI Press, 1975.

Van Allen, James A., "What is a Space Scientist? An Autobiographical Example," *Annual Review, Earth Planet, Science* 1990. 18:1–26, Annual Reviews, Inc.

Van Vechten, Carl; *The Tattooed Countess,* A.A. Knopf, New York, 1924, pp. 286.

Whitmore, Faye, Manila Cheshire, *The Very Beginnings,* World Publishing, Shenandoah, Iowa, 1963.

Who Are the Arabs, The League of Arab States, Arab Information Center, New York, undated.

Williamson, Ellen, *When We Went First Class,* Iowa State University Press, Ames, Iowa, 1977, 250 pp.

Wood, Grant, "Revolt Against the City," an essay first published in *Grant Wood: A Study in American Art,* Clio Press, Iowa City, 1935.

Zielinski, John M., with an Introduction by Paul Engle, *Portrait of Iowa,* Adams Press, Minneapolis, Minnesota, 1951, 175 pp.

Selected clippings were reviewed from the following periodicals:

American Penman, Cedar Rapids Gazette, Daily Freeman-Journal, Webster City; *Davenport Democrat and Leader, The Des Moines Register, The Iowan, Iowa City Press-Citizen, Iowa Stater, Iowa Woman, New York Times, New York Herald Tribune, Onawa Democrat Advertiser, Palimpsest, Pella Chronicle, Quad-City Times, Register & Leader,* Des Moines.

ACKNOWLEDGMENTS

Thank You

Accuracy and history sometimes make strange bedfellows. While I'm not a historian, a great deal of history shows up on these pages. The appropriate pains—what a great term for the writing process—were taken to be sure that what you read is true. But, because the stories of celebrated people are often seen through biased eyes, it's sometimes difficult to separate the corn from the cobs, in the Iowa idiom.

Mark Twain said it well when he observed that, "History is written in the ink of lies."

To find kernels of truth, every story in this book has been verified by the subject, a relative, archivist, museum curator, or historian. Profound thanks go to the wonderfully helpful reference librarians at the Cedar Rapids public library.

As we Iowans expect, other Iowans generously produced photos, dates, scrapbook data, and peeks into forbidden files. Thanks, neighbors. I'm proud to live next door.

Profound thanks also to Iowan Loren Horton, past Senior Historian for the State Historical Society of Iowa, who gently pointed me in proper directions and made remarkable contributions to the sense of this book. Thank you, Loren, for your kind comments that got this wagon rollin' across the Iowa prairie.

Special thanks to the super team at Iowa State University Press for making the book-producing process so enjoyable and for impressing their considerable talents into these pages.

I am particularly indebted to Director Linda Speth, Acquisitions Editor Laura Moran, Managing Editor Carla Tollefson, Editor Jane Zaring, Senior Designer Bob Campbell, Cover Designer Kathy Walker and Sales Manager Sally Clayton. Thanks also go to LeaAnn Randall, Designer for the *Iowa Alumni Quarterly* (UI) for additional cover drawings.

Three university presses in the world are not subsidized by tax money. Wouldn't you know that Iowa State University Press is one of them? It's one more reason for us to swell with Iowa pride.

Thank you, Laura Browne, friend, historian, and unparalleled prose polisher, for the fun of working with such a swift mind and genuinely nice Iowan. Thanks to Jon Anderson, feature writer for the *Chicago Tribune,* for writing counsel of inestimable value during the Iowa Writers' Workshop 8th Annual Iowa Summer Writing Festival. Special thanks to my tireless research assistant,

Acknowledgments

Jean Corey of Cedar Rapids, for faithfully slogging out answers to hundreds of questions. Thanks also to Heather Miller, Keystone, for the summer of 1992 background work.

Loving thanks to my wife, Dianne, who offered badly needed balance, perspective, and encouragement. And Papa thanks his ever-loving daughters, Cyd and Catherine, who acted as both sounding boards and contributing editors.

I must thank my Chump Brother Terence Goodman, long-time friend and Iowa-rooted actor, who inspired the idea for this book. Terry, here are your braggin' rights for your Thespian friends who think you hail from Ohio City, Idaho, rather than Fort Dodge, Iowa.

And many thanks to these generous informants:

Marianne Abel, Waterloo (Iowa women)
Keith Altemeyer, Fort Dodge (Karl King)
John Anderson, Ames (ISU)
Mary Vermeer Andringa, Pella (Gary Vermeer)
Betty Ankeny, curator, Nodaway Valley Museum, Clarinda
William Maheaba Aossey, Cedar Rapids (The Mother Mosque)
Merlin Armbruster, Lompoc, California (David Armbruster)
Alice Crosby Atanasoff (John Vincent Atanasoff)
Winston Barclay, UI Arts Center Public Relations
Ruth Bartels, State Historical Society of Iowa, Des Moines (William Bettendorf)
Carolyn Beal, Nevada (Lester Martin)
Harold M. Becker, Cedar Rapids (Pabst® canned beer)
Robert A. Beeston, Des Moines (Iowa Corn Song)
David Berner, Cedar Rapids (Arthur Collins)
Dianne Borgen, Ames (Harley Wilhelm)
Stefanie Breslin, Cedar Rapids (general research)
Douglas R. Bruster, Marshalltown (Dave Lennox)
Evelyn Burke, Indian Harbor Beach, Florida (Chris Nelson)
Orville R. Butler, Maytag archivist (Fred Maytag)
Roy Carver, Jr., Muscatine (Roy Carver)
Elaine Christiensen, Clarinda Historical Association
James Christy, Nevada (Lester Martin)
David C. Clark, Richmond, Virginia (Eskimo Pie®)
Mike Deupree, *The Cedar Rapids Gazette,* Cedar Rapids
Barbara Dicksen, curator, Froelich, Iowa, Museum
Donna Doyle, Des Moines (E. T. Meredith)
Shirley Eden, Monticello (William Hoag)
Barbara Ehlers, Davenport (Annie Wittenmyer)
Tom Elesen, Sioux City (Cloid H. Smith)
Betty Erickson, Ames (Orland Sweeney)
Simon Estes, Zurich, Switzerland

Sandy Everett, Audubon Chamber of Commerce (Albert the Bull)
Dr. Leonard Feldt, Iowa City (E.F. Lindquist)
Thomas Frantz, Fort Madison (Walter Sheaffer)
John N. Froelich, Tomah, Wisconsin (John Froelich)
Joyce Fuchs, Spillville (Antonín Dvořák, Bily Brothers)
Dan Gable, Iowa City
Grant Gale, Grinnell (Robert Noyce)
George Gallup, Jr., Princeton, New Jersey (George Gallup)
Gerald Gray, Union, Missouri (Jesse Hiatt)
Beulah Gundling, Ft. Lauderdale, Florida
The Honorable Albert Habhab, Fort Dodge (The Mother Mosque)
Hassen Habhab, Fort Dodge (The Mother Mosque)
Daniel K. Hayes, Davenport (The Electronic Newsroom)
Vern Hintze, Des Moines (Iowa Corn Song)
Blackie Hubbard, Ankeny
Ann Humbert, Amana (Amana Refrigeration Radarange®)
Patricia Ipsen, New Hampton (Emily Calkins Stebbins)
Glenn Janus, Cedar Rapids (William Shirer)
A.L. Jennings, Des Moines (W.A. Jennings)
Dorothy Johnson, Cedar Rapids (John J. Tokheim)
Becky Jordan, archivist ISU (George Washington Carver)
Carl Kane, Pompano Beach, Florida (A.N. Palmer)
Mary Jo Keating, Johnston (Henry A. Wallace)
Bonnie Kitterman, Webster City (MacKinlay Kantor, Clark Mollenhoff)
Nellie W. Kremenak, Iowa City (B.F. Philbrook; Lucy Hobbs)
Gloria Lake, Arcadia, Indiana (Burt Gray)
Phillip Lasansky, Iowa City (Mauricio Lasansky)
Arlene Leonard, Clarinda Historical Society (Burt Gray)
Walter Logan, Louisiana, Missouri (Jesse Hiatt)
Edward Lueders, Salt Lake City, Utah (Carl Van Vechten)
Tom McCall, Nevada (Lester Martin)
Glenda McIntire, Ames (John Atanasoff, Clifford Berry)
Scott Mahoney, Webster City (MacKinlay Kantor)
Tim Martin, West Des Moines (Henry A. Wallace)
Fritz Maytag, San Francisco, California
Al Miller, Cedar Rapids (Arthur Collins)
Dwight Miller, archivist, West Branch, Presidential Library and Museum
    (Herbert Hoover)
Chub Montgomery, Nevada (Lester Martin)
Rachel Narsh, Carlsbad, California (Judi Sheppard Misset)
Jetta Nash, Davenport (D. D. Palmer)
Mary Delores Naughton, Des Moines (John Naughton)
Marjorie Neil, Washington, D.C. (GOP)
Douglas Neumann, Cedar Rapids, *The Cedar Rapids Gazette*

Acknowledgments

David C. Nicholas, Cedar Rapids
George Nissen, Cedar Rapids
Michael O'Donnell, Cedar Rapids (Maid-Rite®)
Agnes Orslund, Marshalltown (John Tokheim)
Tom Osborn, Cedar Rapids (Maid-Rite®)
Tom Pau, Ames (David C. Nicholas)
Stephanie Pratt, Des Moines, Iowa Department of Human Rights–Division on Status of Women
LeaAnn Randall, Coralville, cover drawings
Chris Rasmussen, Princeton, New Jersey (The Iowa Idea)
Eileen Richardson, Dunnellon, Florida (Austin N. Palmer)
Suzanne Robbins, Burlington Convention Bureau (Snake Alley)
Hall Roberts, Postville (John R. Mott)
Kaye Roberts, Des Moines (F.A. Wittern)
Earl M. Rogers, university archivist, Iowa City (UI)
Mel Schettler, Des Moines (Roto-Rooter®)
Ellen and Dwain Schmidt, Rodney (Christian Nelson)
Thomas Shive, San Diego, California (Bill Fisher)
Michael Smith, State Historical Society of Iowa, Des Moines
Emil Soukup, Cedar Rapids (Arthur Collins)
Tim Spindler, archivist, Circus World Museum, Baraboo, Wisconsin (John Ringling)
Les Stegh, archivist, Deere & Co., Moline, Illinois
John Steiner, Milwaukee, Wisconsin, archivist, Pabst® Brewing Company (Canned Beer)
Gail Stilwill, Des Moines (E.T. Meredith)
Kathie Swift, Des Moines (Iowa State Fair)
William P. Switzer, Cambridge
Imam Taha Tawil, Cedar Rapids (The Mother Mosque)
Dagmar Tomlinson, Los Angeles, California (Meredith Willson)
Ray Townsend, Des Moines
Ted Townsend, Des Moines (Ray Townsend)
Thomas A. Tufo, Hebron, Illinois (The final educational director for A. N. Palmer)
Vernon Tyler, Des Moines (State Historical Society of Iowa)
Julia Wakehouse, Onawa (Chris Nelson)
Glenda Wiese, Davenport (D.D. Palmer)
Harley Wilhelm, Ames
Rosemary Willson, Los Angeles, California (Meredith Willson)
Ariel Wonder, librarian, Onawa
Frances J. Woodworth, Red Oak (Thos. D. Murphy Co.)